Ron's Road to Wealth

Ron's Road to Wealth

Insights for the Curious Investor

Ron Muhlenkamp

Edited by
Wendy Muhlenkamp Miller

John Wiley & Sons, Inc.

Published by John Wiley & Sons, Inc., Hoboken, New Jersey.
Published simultaneously in Canada.

Wiley Bicentennial Logo: Richard J. Pacifico

For general information on our other products and services or for technical support, please
contact our Customer Care Department within the United States at (800) 762-2974,
outside the United States at (317) 572-3993 or fax (317) 572-4002.

Wiley also publishes its books in a variety of electronic formats. Some content that appears
in print may not be available in electronic formats. For more information about Wiley
products, visit our Web site at www.wiley.com.

Library of Congress Cataloging-in-Publication Data:

Muhlenkamp, Ron (Ronald H.)
    Ron's road to wealth : insights for the curious investor / by Ron Muhlenkamp.
        p.   cm.
    Includes bibliographical references and index.
    ISBN 978-0-470-13752-9 (cloth)
        1. Investments—United States.   2. Stocks—United States.   3. Bonds—United
States. 4. Finance, Personal—United States.   I. Title.   II. Title: Road to wealth.
    HG4910.M84 2008
    332.6—dc22

                                                                    2007032151

Printed in the United States of America.

10 9 8 7 6 5 4 3 2 1

To Connie

With special thanks to:
Wendy Miller
Celeste Zingarelli
Jack Kunkle

Contents

Foreword

Ron Muhlenkamp began investing in the stock market in 1968, just as the bull market of the 1960s was about to run head-long into the bear market of 1973–1974 and the stagflation of the 1970s. Decades worth of investment knowledge and conventional wisdom came crashing down, and everything that people thought they knew about stocks and investing quit working.

So Ron began his career by starting from scratch. He studied academic theory and conventional wisdom, but also started asking some fundamental questions. How do you figure out what a company is worth, and how do you know what to pay for it in the stock market? When it comes to investing in stocks and bonds, what works and why?

The book you are holding is the result of 40 years of figuring out the answers to those questions. This is the bedrock, where an investor can plant his or her feet and make rational decisions based on fundamental principles instead of making emotional decisions based on the daily news and on the hype and hope that accompany it—the most expensive four-letter words we know.

In this book Ron identifies fundamental principles that govern intelligent investing. Principles like:

- Stock and bond markets are rational in the long term, and it often takes only three years for the rational long term to override the often irrational short term.
- Investment risk should not just be measured by price volatility, but is better measured long-term by the loss of purchasing power due to falling securities prices, taxes, and inflation.
- You can turn a good company into a bad investment if you pay too much for it, and there is no company so good that it doesn't matter what you pay to get it.
- Retirees don't need income from their principal; they need spending money from their assets.
- Stocks make you more money than bonds over the long term—not because they are riskier, but because company managers work for the people who own it and against the people who lend it money.
- Prosperity has to be produced for it to be consumed.

But he doesn't just identify these principles. He explains the process so you can test his conclusions against your own experience and your own knowledge. He shares the lessons and shows you how to apply those lessons to investing in the stock and bond markets. He shows you where to plant your feet and how to apply the same principles that he does.

Standing on solid bedrock is essential when floodwaters threaten to wash you and all your belongings away. Using solid investment principles when the stock and bond markets are roiled by hype, hope, fear, and confusion is also essential. The following essays provide the principles needed to invest wisely and well. We hope you find them useful.

Anthony Muhlenkamp
2007

Introduction

Why I Want to Publish This Book and for Whom

I've learned some interesting things about economics and investing over the past 40 years. From what I've learned, I've concluded:

- Investment results are closely tied to economic results, not a random crapshoot.
- To invest successfully, you need not forecast the future, but merely be aware of the economic factors operating on the present.

In this book, I want to share with you what I've learned so that you can reach your own conclusions. The best way I've found to do that is to explain what's happened over the past 40 years. Frankly, I find that many of the things we see today are similar to what we've seen before. For instance, the government budget deficits today look much like the deficits of the 1980s. And concerns about China today are similar to concerns we had about Japan in the 1970s. I can't tell you *when* the circumstances of the past will repeat, but I do believe they will. So by understanding the past, you can know what to watch for in the future.

I am often asked how long or how far I expect the price of a stock or the market to rise or fall. The request is often for a date and a number. But that's like asking a gardener to name the date and the size at which she expects to pick her tomatoes. Any gardener would consider that a foolish question. The only intelligent response to "When do you pick your tomatoes?" is "When they're ripe." Determining when a tomato is ripe is a lot easier than predicting ahead of time when that will be.

I can't tell you how to predict the market, but I will show you what to watch for. The market is much like the weather. There are daily changes, there are seasonal changes, and there are climate changes. The challenge is to expect changes in the market, to recognize them when they occur, and to understand their implications.

Many of the essays in this book were written in response to changes in the markets that I perceived but the investing public had not yet recognized. Because I expect these changes to occur again, the essays remain relevant. I've included the essays as they were originally written and added timelines so that you know the context in which these changes occurred. Remember, our goal is to be able to recognize changes as they happen. So if we are to benefit from understanding the changes of the past, we must understand the context in which they occurred.

Other essays in this book were written in response to misconceptions that I found prevalent in the investing industry. I found these misconceptions were leading people to make poor investments, so I wrote the essays to debunk them. These essays are included here because the misconceptions still abound. My hope is to show you why they are false. Then you can recognize for yourself what not to listen to and, therefore, make better investment decisions.

The rest of the essays in this book cover a large range of topics, including personal finance, investment choices, economics, and even politics. This is because the stock and bond markets do not exist in a vacuum. They are driven by economics, and economics is driven by people. People are the consumers, the workers, the business owners, the voters, the taxpayers, the borrowers, and the lenders. The economy (and the market) is just the aggregate result of everyone's economic decisions. These decisions can be emotional in the short term because people can be emotional and the public can get caught up in emotional swings. But in the long term, economic principles drive the markets.

If you want to learn how to invest more successfully, if you are curious about why the markets behave as they do, and if you are willing to invest some thought and effort into finding the answers to these questions, then I'm publishing this book for you.

Ron Muhlenkamp
2007

Part One

THE BASICS OF
INVESTING

The information presented in Part One is what we refer to as the basics of investing. It is a brief overview of the fundamentals of intelligent investment management—an attempt to answer the following questions: What works? What makes sense? What doesn't? And why?

The facts shown in the tables and charts are nothing new. But, hopefully, our interpretation of these facts will give you something new to think about. You may find it gives you a new perspective on investing which shows that the market can be rational. It may even let you see that much of what the media is telling you about the market is simply sensational hype. And knowing this may let you, the investor, sleep better at night.

The first step in understanding investing is to understand money. So in Chapter 1 we talk about money, inflation, and how inflation drives the investing climate. Then we show you how recognizing the investing climate can make you money.

In Chapter 2, we review the three classes of securities: short-term debt, long-term debt, and equities. How do they work? What drives their returns? Where should the intelligent investor put his money?

"The Basics of Investing" is the survivor's guide to investing. Understanding the basics can help make sense of all the changing, and often conflicting, investing information that surrounds us. I find that if you don't get too far from the basics, you won't get tagged too far off base.

Chapter 1

Understanding Money

Adapted from a presentation delivered at the Muhlenkamp & Company Seminar in December 2002. Supporting exhibits are updated through 2006.

I n order to understand investing, you must first understand money. In order to understand today's investing markets, you must first understand the past 50 years, which set the background for today's market. The primary driver of major market changes (what we call *climate* changes) during that time has been inflation and what it has done to our money.

Exhibit 1.1 shows three postage stamps from the years 1968, 1978, and 2007; their prices are 6 cents, 13 cents, and 41 cents, respectively. Each stamp has the same value—each represents the cost of mailing a first-class, one-ounce letter in the United States. Each stamp has a different price and a different date. What changed between 1968 and 2007 was not the value of the stamp but the value of the dollar.

1968   1978   2007

Exhibit 1.1   Inflation and The Value of Money

Between 1968 and 1978, the dollar lost half its value. So to get the same value, you had to double the price of the stamp. From 1978 to 2007 the dollar lost more than two-thirds of its value, so the price of a first-class stamp tripled.

Our federal government has standards as to what constitutes a gallon, so no one can cheat you on a gallon of gas. There are standards on the bushel, there are standards on the ton, and there are standards on the yard and the foot, but there are no standards on the value of our money. We run into trouble when we think of the value of the dollar as being fixed, like our other measures. To illustrate my point, imagine what would happen if there was no standard on one of our other measures.

My wife Connie is a seamstress. She buys fabric by the yard. Suppose the fabric store where she buys fabric manages to shrink their yardstick by a quarter-inch each month. A quarter-inch a month, three inches per year, comes to 8 percent per year. (Between 1968 and 1978, inflation was about 8 percent a year.) So my wife starts getting short on fabric. She remeasures the fabric with her own yardstick and concludes that the store is cheating her.

But what if they also manage to shrink *her* yardstick by a quarter-inch per month? Now she swears that I'm growing taller! Using this analogy, by 1968 dollars I'm 39 feet tall! If our yardsticks had shrunk at the same rate as our money, I'd be 39 feet tall in today's measure. The effects of inflation can easily be overlooked because inflation shrinks everyone's yardstick. Over time, the effect of inflation on our money can be tremendous. We can't afford to overlook it.

Exhibit 1.2 plots the Consumer Price Index (CPI), which is the standard measure of inflation, since 1952. Most people, as consumers,

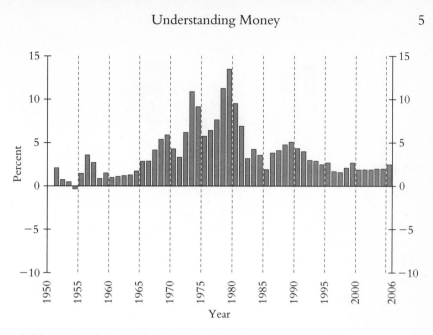

Exhibit 1.2   Inflation, 1952–2006
SOURCE: Bureau of Labor Statistics.

think of inflation as prices moving up—and they've moved up by these amounts, year by year, over that 54-year period. As investors, we think of inflation not as prices moving up but as the value of money shrinking, which is shown in Exhibit 1.3. Same information—different perspective.

Your money, whether income or assets, lost value by this rate each year for the past 54 years. Over that period of time, the value of what used to be a dollar shrank to about 15 cents. This is the rate at which our yardstick has been shrinking. If you are talking about investing, everything is measured in dollars, which means it's measured by this yardstick. The first thing you have to do with those dollars is to adjust them for the shrinking yardstick. Since most people have more experience with real estate (especially homes and mortgages) than with stocks and bonds, let's talk about real estate assets, and particularly mortgages, to explain what has happened to the value of your money over the past 54 years.

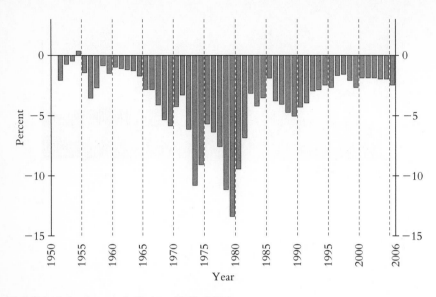

Exhibit 1.3   Inverse Inflation, 1952–2006

Inflation and Mortgage Rates—Understanding Climate Change

Exhibit 1.4 plots the nominal mortgage rate from 1952 to 2006. This is the rate that would have been quoted to you by a bank or a savings and loan organization. In 1951 my father bought a farm and had a 4.5 percent mortgage. All the neighbors said, "Izzy, you'll go broke in the next depression." There had been a depression after World War I, and everybody expected another one after World War II. Even though he put 40 percent down and financed the other 60 percent at 4.5 percent, he didn't eat or sleep for two days because this debt scared him to death. Incidentally, his interest cost him less than it cost to rent a house at that time.

In 1971, my wife Connie and I bought a house with a 7.5 percent mortgage. Dad said, "Ron, that's awful high." I said, "All I know is that on an after-tax basis, this mortgage is costing me no more than the apartment we live in." On a month-to-month basis, after taxes, the cost was the same. That's all I knew. Fortunately, that's all I needed to know.

In 1981 my brother Rod bought a house with a 14 percent mortgage. I said, "Rod, that's high." He said, "Don't worry about it. Inflation

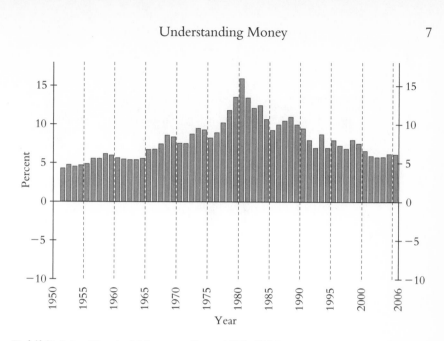

Exhibit 1.4   Nominal Mortgage Rate, 1952–2006
SOURCE: Federal Reserve Bank of St. Louis.

will go up and take care of me. The price of the house will go up. I'm
not worried about it." Think about that. My father feared a 4.5 percent
mortgage. My brother did not fear a 14 percent mortgage. This is a complete reversal of attitude because of a change in the economic climate.

Exhibit 1.5 is simply the nominal mortgage rate plotted along with
the inverse of inflation. At first glance these charts look a whole lot alike.
But, in fact, inflation ran up long before mortgage rates. Then, in the
1980s, inflation ran down quickly, and mortgage rates came down
gradually.

All through the 1970s people said, "Yes, inflation is up, but it will
come back down." All through the 1980s people said, "Yes, inflation is
down, but it will go back up." There was a huge lag in perception behind
reality. Some folks like to say that Wall Street anticipates the future, six
months out. And it does, on some things like earnings. But it was a decade late on changes in inflation—changes in the value of money. Perception of inflation, first up and then down, lagged reality by a decade.
Those lags can make you (or cost you) an awful lot of money.

If we net these two charts, we get *real* mortgage rates (nominal rates
minus inflation), as shown in Exhibit 1.6.

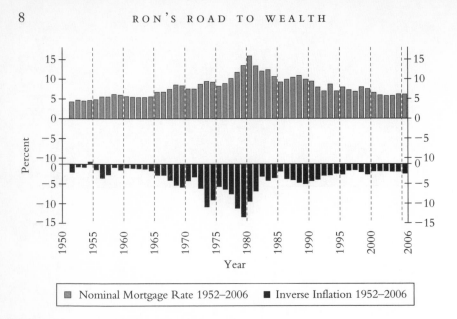

Exhibit 1.5   Nominal Mortgage Rate and Inverse Inflation, 1952–2006

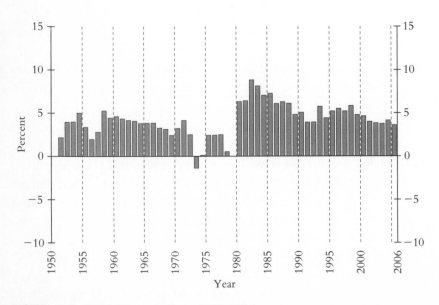

Exhibit 1.6   Real Mortgage Rate, 1952–2006

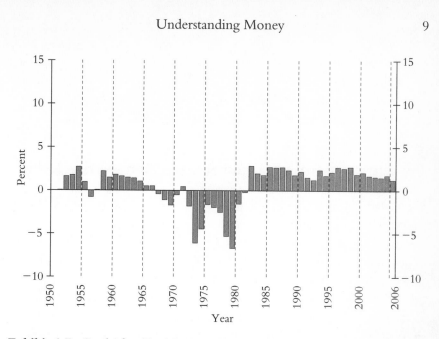

Exhibit 1.7   Real After-Tax Mortgage Rate, 1952–2006

As you know, the interest on mortgages is tax deductible, so if we adjust for taxes, we get Exhibit 1.7.

That looks different, doesn't it? We are seeing three different economic climates:

1. From 1952 to 1967, long-term debt cost you money. My father's 4.5 percent mortgage, after taxes and inflation, was costing 2 percent, so we worked like dogs to pay it off early.

2. From 1968 to 1981, long-term debt actually made you money. Connie and I bought a house in 1971. Within a short period of time, I realized that the last thing I wanted to do was to pay off my mortgage early. My mortgage was making me money! I wish I had bought a bigger house with a bigger mortgage. Remember the phrase, "Trade up on the equity"? From 1968 to 1981, the economic climate made borrowing a winning proposition. Trading up on the equity worked. But the climate changed again.

3. By 1982, borrowing money was once again a liability. My brother's 14 percent mortgage was costing him money. Within a couple of years, he'd rolled it down to 11 percent, still costing him money.

All through the 1980s he was willing to pay 11 percent because he assumed that inflation was going back up. He made this assumption because he thought what he saw in the 1970s was normal. He didn't realize that the economic climate had changed.

When the Climate Changes, It Changes the Rules

Understanding the climate changes illustrated in Exhibit 1.7 is critical to understanding many of the successes and pitfalls of investing for the past 50 years. It is that important. It illustrates why a strategy that works at one time, suddenly doesn't in another. In other words, when the climate changes, it changes the rules. The best thing you and I could do in the 1970s was to borrow money. For most of us, the way to borrow money was to buy real estate. My farmer cousins who bought farmland in the 1970s are millionaires today. Those who started buying farmland in the 1980s went bankrupt.

When the climate changes, when the value of the money changes, it changes everything—certainly everything valued in money. You don't have to predict this, but you do have to recognize it when it happens.

Chapter 2

The Investing Choices

Adapted from a presentation delivered at the Muhlenkamp & Company Seminar in December 2002. Supporting exhibits are updated through 2006.

N ow it's time to turn to the question on every investor's mind—how to increase wealth through investing. There are really only three classes of securities: short-term debt, long-term debt, and equities. We review all three, then show you how to make sense of your choices.

In every investment transaction there are two parties: the lender and the borrower, or the buyer and the seller. When an individual, corporation, or government needs more money, it can take out a loan, issue bonds, or issue stock, but this will only provide money if someone else is willing to issue the loan, buy the bond, or buy the stock. The needs of both parties must be met or the transaction will not take place. So in looking at securities, we must keep both parties in mind.

Investing Choice 1: Short-Term Debt

Short-term debt securities include such things as passbook savings accounts, CDs, and Treasury bills. These investments are considered safe because the principal is often guaranteed by the federal government (i.e., the American taxpayer) through the Federal Deposit Insurance Corporation (FDIC). The interest rates on short-term debt are set by the market but are heavily influenced by the Federal Reserve Board.

Exhibit 2.1 shows the nominal rates on Treasury bills since 1952. Treasury bills (T-bills) are perfectly safe, right? But remember, we need to adjust for inflation. Adjusted for inflation, T-bill rates look like Exhibit 2.2.

Now T-bills don't look quite as good. When the Treasury bill rate is lower than the rate of inflation, the investor is losing *purchasing power*. The Treasury bill principal may be guaranteed in nominal (dollar) terms, but your purchasing power is not. When short-term interest rates are lower than the rate of inflation, the borrower is actually making money simply by borrowing. The lender is losing money. So in 2002, when

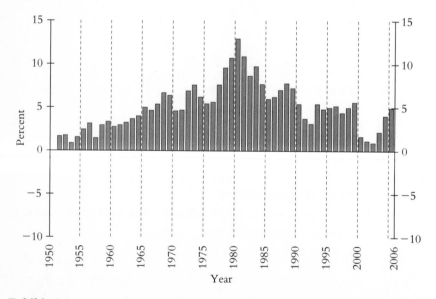

Exhibit 2.1 Nominal Treasury Bill Rate, 1952–2006
SOURCE: Federal Reserve System Board of Governors

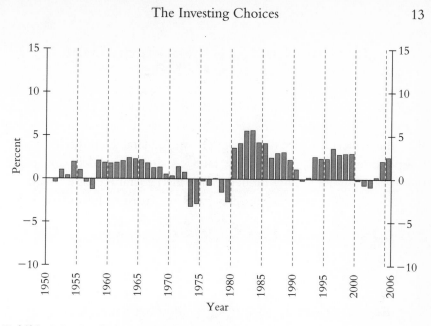

Exhibit 2.2   Real Treasury Bill Rate, 1952–2006

people feared that the Fed was going to raise interest rates, be aware that it *should* have raised interest rates. Interest rates needed to move up to get the inflation-adjusted Treasury bill rates back to a positive real return. As of year-end 2005, the Fed had done it.

If you're a taxpayer, we also need to adjust for taxes, which make T-bills look like Exhibit 2.3.

Notice that this chart shows the same three economic climates we saw in Exhibit 1.7 from Chapter 1:

1. From 1952 to 1965, when inflation was relatively steady and it cost to borrow money.
2. From 1965 to 1982, when inflation skyrocketed and it paid to borrow money (but not to lend it).
3. From 1982 to the present, when inflation was back under control and it again cost to borrow money.

In the 1970s, you and I could borrow money at 7.5 percent on a mortgage. After taxes, it was costing us less than 5 percent, even though inflation was 10 percent, because our mothers and our grandmothers were getting 5.25 percent on their savings. The money you and I were

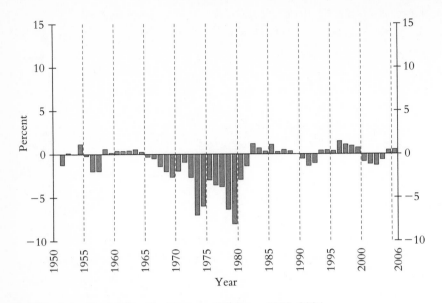

Exhibit 2.3   Real After-Tax Treasury Bill Rate, 1952–2006

making on our mortgages, Grandma was losing on her savings account. After a decade of that, Grandma got tired of losing money, so three things happened:

1. Partly to stop inflation, President Carter named Paul Volcker to be chairman of the Fed.
2. Partly to stop inflation, we put a new man in the White House named Ronald Reagan.
3. All our mothers and grandmothers took their money out of passbook savings and put it into 13 percent money market funds and bankrupted the S&L industry.

I believe that as long as Grandma feared a depression more than she feared inflation, she was willing to keep her money in a guaranteed passbook savings account, even though she was losing money doing it. After a decade of losing money, she came to fear inflation more than depression and changed where she kept her savings. The first time she moved her money was traumatic. Now, Grandma will go across the street for a nickel or a dime—that is, a tenth of a percent. But it took a long time—and it took the fear of inflation becoming greater than the fear of depression—for her to do that. After all, in a depression you don't care about the return *on* your money, you care about the return *of* your money!

The financial pain of the 1970s, depicted in Exhibit 2.3, finally drove Mom and Grandma to respond to inflation. But at the same time, we responded to the fear of inflation and we licked it. Inflation went from 13 percent to 4 percent in three years. These two actions reversed the climate.

Investing Choice 2: Long-Term Debt

Long-term debt includes such things as Treasury bonds, corporate bonds, municipal bonds, and mortgage-backed securities. These investments are guaranteed by the borrower. The rates on long-term debt are driven by the market. We consider here Treasury bond rates because they are the benchmark for the rates of other long-term debt securities as well.

Exhibit 2.4 plots the nominal long-term Treasury bond rate for the past 54 years. It looks a whole lot like mortgages.

When you adjust for inflation, Treasury bonds look like Exhibit 2.5.

You'll notice on Exhibit 2.5 we've drawn a line at 3 percent. Historically, Treasury bonds have yielded 2.5 to 3 percent over the rate of inflation. When interest rates are 3 percent above inflation, bonds are fairly priced and you get the coupon.

From 1974 to 1981, interest rates were unusually low relative to inflation because Grandma feared depression and was willing to lend her money cheaply for a "guarantee." From 1982 to 1989, interest rates were unusually high because my brother, the borrower, was willing to pay 14 percent on his mortgage. This meant that Mom, the lender, could get 11 percent on her money market fund. (The bank maintains a spread of about 3 percent regardless of rate.)

Exhibit 2.5 shows all you've had to know to make money, or avoid losing money, in bonds for the past 54 years.

In October 1993, based on this chart, we said, "Folks, the time to own bonds has just come to an end." Remember when Orange County went bankrupt in 1994? Interest rates jumped about 2 percent. At the end of 1994, we said that there was a 20 percent off-sale in the bond

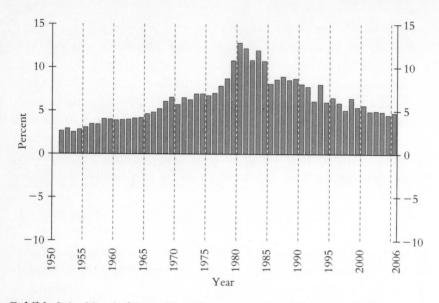

Exhibit 2.4 Nominal Long-Term Government Bond Rate, 1952–2006
SOURCE: U.S. Treasury.
The 30-year Treasury constant maturity series was discontinued on February 18, 2002, and reintroduced on February 9, 2006. From February 18, 2002, to February 9, 2006, the U.S. Treasury published a factor for adjusting the daily nominal 20-year constant maturity in order to estimate a 30-year nominal rate. The historical adjustment factor can be found at www.treas.gov/offices/domestic-finance/debt-management/interest-rate/ltcompositeindex_historical.shtml.

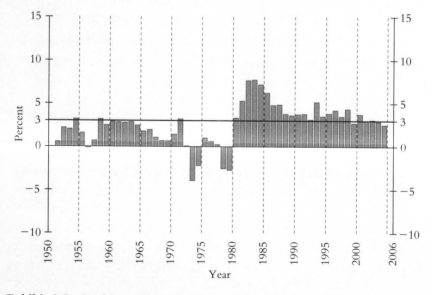

Exhibit 2.5 Real Long-Term Government Bond Rate, 1952–2006

market and in the stock market. At the time of this writing, interest rates on Treasury bonds are about where they should be, which for long-term bonds is roughly 3 percent above inflation.

The period from 1965 to 1993 was dominated by a change in inflation and a lagging perception by bond owners. It probably won't happen again in our lifetime. After all, Mom will now move her money for a dime, and there is no way you are going to get people who now have 7 percent mortgages to refinance to 11 percent mortgages. In the 1970s, people had mortgages at 7 percent and went out and bought bigger houses at higher mortgage rates because they assumed inflation would continue and that the value of the house would increase regardless of interest rate.

Remember the phrase, "Trade up on the equity"? It worked in the 1970s. People still believed it in the 1980s. But from 1990 to 1993, not only did people refinance their mortgages from 11 percent to 8 percent (driving Mom's CD from 8 percent to 5 percent), but a third of those refinancing went from a 30-year mortgage to a 15-year mortgage. That's the opposite of "Trade up on the equity." That's "Prepay the mortgage." They're now paying twice as much principal every month as they used to!

My mental picture of this is Scrooge McDuck in his counting room—his money is coming in at twice the rate that it used to and it's piling up! We said in 1990 and 1991 that within a year banks would be flush because they're getting all this money in. And since 1992–1993, every month you get a chance to open more credit card accounts. Banks have been flush since 1993 because people are prepaying the mortgage.

Changes in public opinion, or changes in public action, tend to happen in a recession. All through the 1980s while there was no recession, people were happy (or at least willing) to pay 11 percent on a mortgage. In 1990–1991, we had a recession, and people took a hard look at their finances; that's when they refinanced their fixed-rate mortgages down from 11 percent to 8 percent. Because they are fixed-rate mortgages, they can refinance them down again (as they have done in 2002–2005), but the bank can't refinance them back up. Adjustable rate mortgages (ARMs) add another wrinkle to this, as we discuss in the essay "Why Interest Rates Won't Go Back Up Any Time Soon" (see Chapter 5).

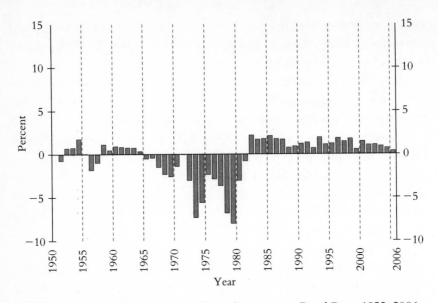

Exhibit 2.6   Real After-Tax Long-Term Government Bond Rate, 1952–2006

What we saw from 1990 to 1993 was a change in action by the American public—one-third of 60 million homeowners choosing to pay down the mortgage instead of trading up on the equity. That's important. That was a major change. It drove interest rates back to normal levels in 1993.

Inflation, and people's response to it, was the major driver of the stock and bond prices for the past 40 years. That period is now over, but you've got to understand what happened then in order to understand what's happening now.

The majority of long-term bonds are held by pension plans, which are tax-free. So the preceding discussion is based on pretax, long-term bond rates (Exhibit 2.5). If you're a taxpayer, of course, Treasury bonds look like Exhibit 2.6.

Investing Choice 3: Equities (Common Stock)

The third class of securities is equities (or common stock). In this case, instead of borrowing money, a company raises money by selling shares of stock in the company. The stockholder is then an *owner* of the company and shares in both the successes of the company (through dividends and capital gains) and its failures (through capital loss). There are no guarantees. Stock prices are set by the market—what someone is willing to pay to own a piece of the company. Over the long term, the price will reflect the true value of the company, but over the short term, the perceived value of the company may not always reflect the company's true value.

Corporate stocks provide higher returns than corporate bonds because the company's management works *for* the stockholder and *against* the bondholder. No management will borrow money (i.e., issue bonds) unless it expects to profit from the investment of those funds in its business. Thus, the return on stockholders' equity must be higher than corporate interest rates. Otherwise, management will cease to borrow, driving interest rates down. Similarly, every corporate treasurer has the same incentive you and I have—to save money. They call their high-rate bonds and reissue low-rate bonds just as we refinance our high-rate mortgages when lower-rate mortgages become available.

In this section, we look at common stock performance over the past 50-plus years. We also look at several misconceptions about stocks. Then we move on to compare our three investment choices.

Exhibit 2.7 depicts the Dow Jones Industrial Average (DJIA) from 1952 to 2006. The year 1952 is particularly interesting to me because Dad bought our farm in 1951. From 1952 to 1965, he'd much rather have owned stocks because they quadrupled. From 1965 to 1982, you'd rather have owned farmland. Stock prices did nothing—you only got the dividend, which was about 3 percent. From 1982 to today, you would rather own stocks; they are up about 12 times.

What's interesting is to place the DJIA chart alongside the real, long-term government bond rate chart, as we've done in Exhibit 2.8. We said in Part One that when the climate changes, it changes everything. Well, Exhibit 2.8 shows several climate changes:

- From 1952 to 1965, you could make 3 percent on bonds and you could quadruple your money in stocks, so you wanted to own stocks.
- From 1965 to 1982, you didn't want to own stocks or bonds; you wanted to borrow money.
- From 1982 to 1993, you could make good money in bonds or stocks. In fact, stocks continued strong until 2000.

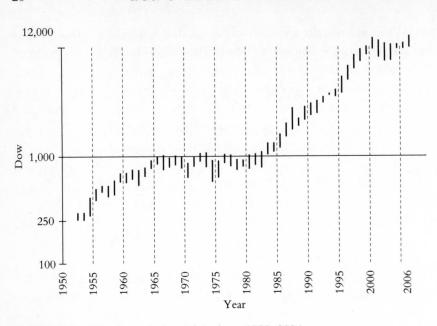

Exhibit 2.7   Dow Jones Industrial Average, 1952–2006

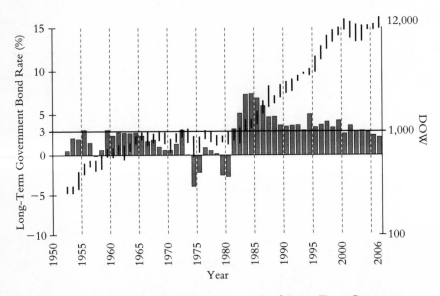

Exhibit 2.8   Dow Jones Industrial Average vs. Real Long-Term Government
Bond Rate, 1952–2006

When the climate changes, it changes everything. When the value of the money changes, it changes everything valued in money.

Aren't Stocks Risky?

This is a common concern we hear about stocks. But to address this concern, we must ask a question of our own: What is your definition of risk? I suspect for most of you it's the possibility of losing money. My definition of risk is the *probability of losing purchasing power*. To me, inflation is a risk because I'm losing purchasing power.

What's Wall Street's definition of risk? Wall Street's definition of risk is *volatility*. Wall Street tells you that the wavy line A in Exhibit 2.9 is riskier than the top line B. I'll buy that. Wall Street also tells you that the wavy line A is riskier than the middle line C, and you might be able to squeeze that by me. Wall Street further claims that the wavy line A is riskier than the bottom line D, and I won't buy that at all. What Wall Street *won't* tell you is that D is available to you, C is available to you, A is available, but B is not. So now which line do you want?

Beware when you are told that stocks are risky. You need to know what definition is being used. Stocks can be volatile (like the wavy line), but let's look at what happens to that volatility over time.

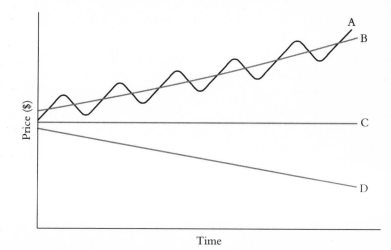

Exhibit 2.9 Volatility versus Risk
SOURCE: Muhlenkamp & Company, Inc.

Volatility and Sampling Frequency

What you see on the top plot of Exhibit 2.10 is the total return for the S&P 500 for each of the past 54 years. In those 54 years there have been 13 down years. Well, to an old farmer, the pattern of returns looks like spring, summer, fall, winter . . . spring, summer, fall, winter. . . . In fact, we used to invest on a four-year cycle. The economic cycle was roughly three to five years and the market ran on a four-year cycle whether the economy did or not.

If you look at this plot as an old farmer, you conclude that maybe one year isn't the proper period of time to measure what's going on. So I took the same data, and did a three-year trailing average, which is the lower plot. A lot of the volatility goes away. The only down periods are around 1975 and 2002.

In the investment industry, when people talk about volatility of a stock, they talk about its *beta*. But what is beta? In the early 1970s when I worked for an insurance company, people from a major brokerage firm came to see us. They had bought a computer that was programmed for linear regressions. So they plugged in "A + Bx" (actually, they got sexy and said "alpha + beta[x]," which is where beta came from), and they looked at prices relative to the S&P 500 or a similar index.

I asked them for their formula, they gave it to me, and I sat down with five years of history for a mutual fund that we ran. First I ran monthly data through their formula, and then I used quarterly data. So I was using the same set of data—just two different sampling frequencies. I got two different betas.

I called up the brokerage people and said, "This is what I did. I got two different betas. Does that make sense?" They said, "Yes, that's what will happen." I said, "But I've got two different betas. Which one should I use?" They said, "We like the higher number because it's more dramatic." I've been skeptical of beta numbers ever since.

The bottom line is that if you price your portfolio every day, you are going to get huge volatility. If you price it once a week, you'll get less. If you price it once a quarter, you'll get less. If you price it once a year, you'll get something like the top plot on Exhibit 2.10. If you price it once every three years, you'll get the bottom plot on Exhibit 2.10, and much of the volatility goes away. So the easiest way to lower the volatility of your portfolio is *don't price it so often*.

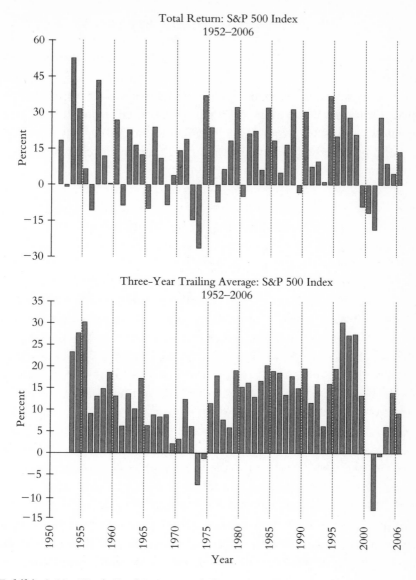

Exhibit 2.10 Yearly Total Return and Three-Year Trailing Average: S&P 500 Index, 1952–2006

Let's look at volatility one more way. How often do you price your house—every 10 years or so? The implicit assumption is that during those 10 years, the price moved in a straight line. But really, the price of your house jumps around a lot more than the price of stocks. Anybody try to sell a house in October 2001? There were no bids. Nobody was interested. In stocks there is always somebody like me with a lowball bid. If you've got your house up for sale and there are no bids, does that mean it's worthless? Or does it simply mean that *today* you got no bid?

People are willing to wait six or nine months to get a good price for their house, but if their stocks drop they panic, as if the price meant something. All it means is that somebody is giving you a lowball bid.

The point is that risk is a matter of definition. Volatility is just one definition, and it changes with the sampling frequency.

Volatility and the Media

We'll have a lot of volatility in stocks as long as people watch the market on a daily basis. I've been on the TV shows. How much time do we spend talking about Treasury bills? Thirty seconds a day? What can you say about Treasury bills? "The yield is 4.2 percent." That's all you can say. What can you say about CDs? "They're guaranteed. The yield is 4.3 percent." That's all you can say. What can you say about bonds? "The yield is 4.8 percent. We think rates are going up," or "We think rates are going down." We can talk about that for two or three minutes. Now we've got eight hours to kill.

What can you say about stocks? You can talk endlessly about stocks. So they do—and that adds to volatility. The reason that people talk about stocks is that you can make money in stocks! The volatility is greater because the returns are greater, and it gives us something to talk about. But you can only talk about it prospectively.

Every year there are two weeks before the Super Bowl when there's all kinds of speculation about who's going to win and what the point spread will be. Five minutes after the game is over, does anybody speculate about the Super Bowl? No. Now you know! So you can't speculate about it anymore.

The reason stocks are so volatile is that we speculate about them so much, and we have so many people who have nothing to do but speculate about them. I've been on the shows. You've got to be entertaining. TV people are in the entertainment business, and they've got hours of air time to fill, so they speculate about stocks.

During a commercial break I once commented to the show's host that I've put out a quarterly newsletter. The reason that I write a newsletter once a quarter is that if I can say something useful four times a year, I'm doing pretty well. Half of my newsletters say, basically, "See last quarter." I mentioned that, and the host said, "Well, we say something useful about four times a year too, but, of course, we're on the air every day." They are in the *entertainment business*. We call that the game of the stock market.

Risk as Frequency of Down Years

So are stocks risky? The top plot of Exhibit 2.11 shows the yearly total return for long-term government bonds from 1952 to 2006. This is nominal, pretax and pre-inflation. There have been 17 down years on bonds. The top plot in Exhibit 2.10 shows that there have been 13 down years in stocks over the same period of time. So if your definition of risk is the frequency of down years, then bonds are riskier than stocks.

I'm not sure one year is the proper period of time, so we did a three-year trailing average for the bottom plots on Exhibits 2.10 and 2.11. Bonds change to eight down years, stocks to four down years. There are still more down periods in bonds than in stocks. If your definition of risk is the frequency of down years, then bonds are riskier than stocks.

When it comes to risk, make sure that the definition that people are using makes sense to you. Wall Street defines risk as volatility. If you think risk is something else (like the frequency of down years or the loss of purchasing power), then stocks are not so risky. Their prices are just more volatile in the short term than other investing vehicles.

Aren't Stocks Overpriced?

This is another popular concern of investors. But, again, we need to look at how Wall Street determines what is "overpriced." Nearly anybody who has done rigorous work with investments over any period of time assesses the values of common stocks based on current interest rates. They use a dividend discount model or something similar to it.

One outfit that has been doing such research for over 30 years is Ford Equity Research. They started with 2,000 stocks, and today it's

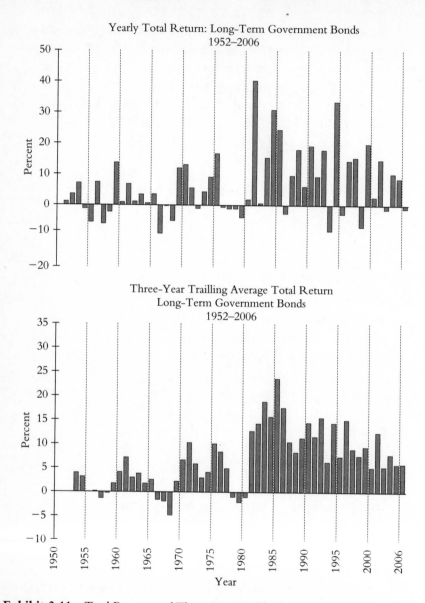

Exhibit 2.11   Total Return and Three-Year Trailing Average: Long-Term Government Bonds, 1952–2006

over 4,000, so their research is statistically significant. Every month they calculate the value of over 4,000 stocks, compare them to current prices and long-term interest rates, and determine a price-to-value ratio for each of those stocks. Then they average it over the 4,000 stocks. The resulting price-to-value ratio (PVA) is pictured in Exhibit 2.12.

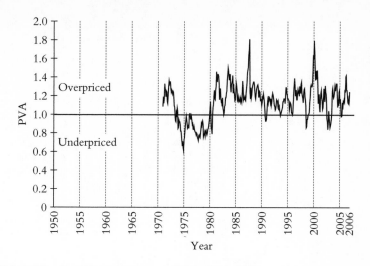

Exhibit 2.12   Ford Equity Research PVA, 1970–2006
Source: Ford Equity Research. Used with permission.

When the PVA is greater than 1.0, they say the stocks are overpriced. When the PVA is less than 1.0, they say the stocks are underpriced.

The only problem is that in 1971–1972, when they said stocks were overpriced, stocks went up (see Exhibit 2.13). During the period of 1972–1982, when they said stocks were underpriced, stocks did nothing. Since 1982, except for a short period during the Gulf War and again when Long-Term Capital Management (LTCM) hit the fan, and the period in 2002–2003 when people dumped their tech stocks and feared the second Gulf War, the model said stocks were overpriced nearly all the time—and stocks went up by a factor of 12! In my opinion, they've been dead wrong for over 20 years and haven't bothered to change the formula.

Remember, they're saying that stocks are underpriced or overpriced *based on current interest rates* (i.e., relative to bonds). So let's look at the PVA and interest rates (see Exhibit 2.14). From 1972 to 1982 when interest rates were unusually low, the folks at Ford Equity Research said that stocks were underpriced—*relative to bonds*. From 1982 to 1990, when interest rates were unusually high, they said that stocks were overpriced—*relative to bonds*. Their assumption is that bonds are always fairly priced—that there's no hope nor fear in the bond market . . . as if

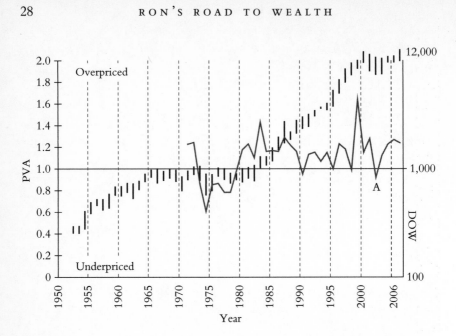

Exhibit 2.13   The Dow Jones Industrial Average versus Ford Equity Research PVA, 1952–2006

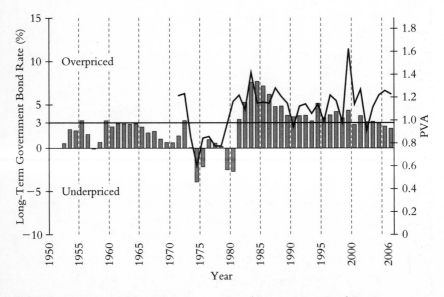

Exhibit 2.14   Long-Term Government Bond Rates versus Ford Equity Research PVA, 1952–2006

my father didn't fear a depression, nor my brother assume inflation. As we've seen, that's nonsense.

We asked them to make one change in their calculations. Instead of using a current interest rate, we asked them to use inflation plus 3 percent as their discount rate. (In Exhibit 2.14, this would be depicted as using the horizontal line at 3 percent *real* interest rates instead of the actual rate each year as depicted in the bar chart.)

When they did that, they got line B in Exhibit 2.15. *It reversed their conclusions!* In 1972–1982, when line A had said stocks were underpriced, line B says they were overpriced. In the early 1980s, when line A had said that stocks were 20 to 30 percent overpriced, line B says they were 50 percent underpriced.

If we compare the revised PVA to the DJIA to see what stocks actually did (Exhibit 2.16), we see that using inflation plus 3 percent is a much more useful tool when deciding whether stocks are overpriced or underpriced.

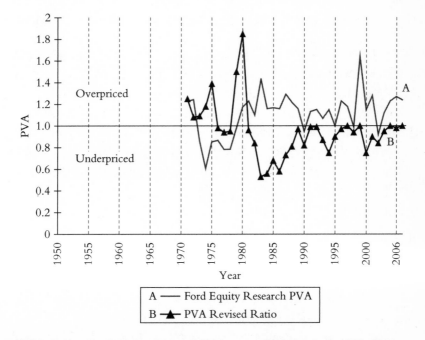

Exhibit 2.15   Ford Equity Research PVA versus PVA Revised, 1970–2006

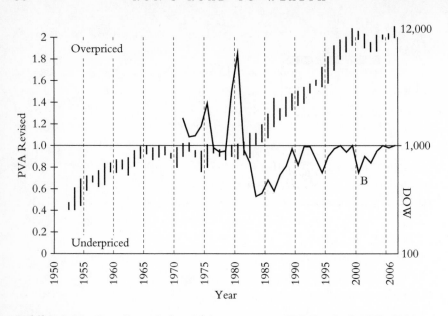

Exhibit 2.16   Dow Jones Industrial Average versus PVA Revised, 1952–2006

Remember, whenever people say stocks are underpriced or over-priced, they need to finish the sentence. They're really saying stocks are over- or underpriced *relative to bonds*. But in stocks, just as in bonds, you have to account for the value of money. Everything measured in dollars is measured by the inflation yardstick (see Chapter 1). You have to take inflation into account when evaluating both stocks and bonds.

One more point: The PVA is an assessment of the average stock. When stocks, on average, are fairly priced, there can be a huge disparity in individual stocks between those that are overpriced and those that are underpriced. This is a stock picker's dream. This is where the good stock picker can make good money.

Making Sense of the Choices

Exhibit 2.17 lets us compare stocks, bonds, bills, and inflation since 1926. Since 1926 we've had several wars, we've had a depression, we've had inflation—we've had most of the troubles that hit mankind.

This chart says that inflation has averaged 3 percent. (Today, 2007, we are at 2 percent.) It says that Treasury bills have averaged 3.7 percent,

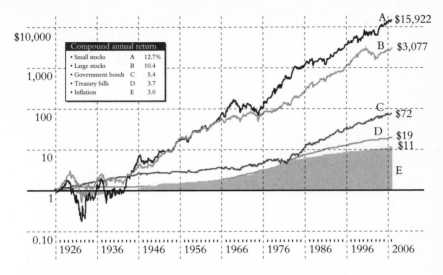

Exhibit 2.17 Stocks, Bonds, Bills, and Inflation, 1926–2006

Past performance is no guarantee of future results. Hypothetical value of $1 invested at the beginning of 1926, with taxes paid monthly. No capital gains taxes are assumed for municipal bonds. Assumes reinvestment of income and no transaction costs. This is for illustrative purposes only and not indicative of any investment. An investment cannot be made directly in an index. © 2007 Morningstar, Inc. All rights reserved. March 1, 2007. Used with permission.

resulting in a real 0.7 percent. Government bonds averaged about 5.4 percent, for a real 2.4 percent. We're back to that. Large-company stocks returned 10.4 percent, and small-company stocks did a little better. It's a beautiful chart, right? But it's totally useless! You can't spend that money—it's pretax and preinflation.

Exhibit 2.18 is the same data, but adjusted for taxes and inflation. Does this chart look a little different? This chart shows what has happened to your investment dollar since 1926.

So let's start with Treasury bills. You can't lose money in Treasury bills, right? They are perfectly safe, guaranteed by the federal government. But if in 1926 you put your money in T-bills, paid your taxes, and never spent a dime, by 2006 the purchasing power of your dollar went to 55 cents—*guaranteed.*

If you owned government bonds, paid your taxes, and never spent a dime—never spent any of the income from your bonds—your dollar went to $1.39. It did 0.4 percent per year. If you owned municipal bonds, it did just a shade better than that.

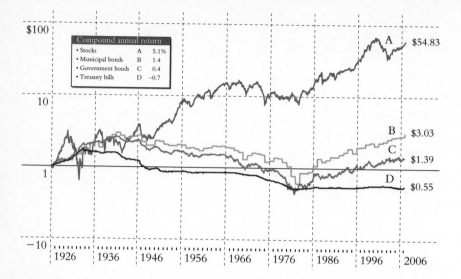

Exhibit 2.18   Stocks, Bonds, and Bills after Taxes and Inflation, 1926–2006
Past performance is no guarantee of future results. Hypothetical value of $1 invested at the beginning of
1926, with taxes paid monthly. No capital gains taxes are assumed for municipal bonds. Assumes
reinvestment of income and no transaction costs. This is for illustrative purposes only and not
indicative of any investment. An investment cannot be made directly in an index. © 2007 Morningstar,
Inc. All rights reserved. May 1, 2007. Used with permission.

If you owned stocks, your dollar went to $54.83—which is a 5.1
percent annual rate.

This chart says to me that if it's guaranteed, most of the time, it's
guaranteed to lose you money. There have been two periods of time
during this 80-year period when you could make money in bonds. One
was in the Depression. If you think that we're in a depression, don't own
anything but Treasury bonds.

The other period of time was from 1982 to 2002, when interest
rates went from 13 percent to 5 percent and you could make money on
bonds. They are now at 4.8 percent and they might go to 4.5 percent.
The game in bonds is pretty much over.

Stocks have been kind of choppy, but over the past 80 years they
have averaged 5.1 percent.

So we need to look at the economic climate to make sense of
the choices. In a depression, government bonds look good. But I have
concluded that we're not in a depression. I hope that the period from
1940 to 1945, World War II, was unusual. If you are experiencing the

kind of inflation and low interest rates that we saw in the 1970s, you want to borrow money. But at this point we fear inflation and would risk recession before we would allow that sort of inflation again.

If you had to draw a parallel to today—a period of time when inflation was relatively low and fairly stable, interest rates were fair and fairly stable, and stock prices were fair—take a look at the early 1960s. Back in the 1960s, you had your choice of making money in stocks, in a jagged fashion, or losing money—consistently—in bonds.

What's Available Today?

It all comes down to this: What are the real returns that are available to an investor today (2007)? Let's take a look at Exhibit 2.19.

On short-term debt you can get something like 4.5 percent per year. If you are in the 35 percent tax bracket you get to keep 65 percent, so your yield comes out to 2.9 percent. If inflation is at 2 percent, then you net 0.9 percent. If you buy Treasury bills today and you pay your taxes, you will make a bit less than 1 percent.

With long-term debt, rates are at about 5 percent. If you pay taxes at 35 percent, you get to keep 65 percent of it; that takes you to 3.2 percent, minus 2 percent for inflation, and you get to keep 1.2 percent. That's a little above the historic rate. If you buy municipal bonds, which aren't shown in this table, the nominal rate is 4 percent and the after-tax rate is 4 percent, so for the real rate, you take 2 percent off of that and you get 2 percent. For most taxpayers, those in the 35 percent tax bracket, municipal bonds (*munis*) look a little better than corporates, and corporates look better than cash.

Exhibit 2.19 Available Annual Returns (Percent)

	Nominal	After-Tax	Real After-Tax
Short-term debt	4.5	2.9	0.9
Long-term debt	5	3.2	1.2
Equity	8	6.8	4.8

SOURCE: Muhlenkamp & Company, Inc.

Stocks are priced to return about 8 percent. If you choose equity investments that provide returns that are taxed at 15 percent, of the 8 percent, you can keep 6.8 percent. Subtract 2 percent for inflation, and you get to keep 4.8 percent.

Your choices today are short-term debt, long-term debt, and equities. These numbers are pretty close to what they have averaged over the past 80 years. The difference, of course, is that equity gains come in spurts. We conclude that there is some value in bonds—not a lot, but they are better than cash. For most people munis are a little better than corporates. But I like the returns of 4.8 percent from stocks a whole lot better than 1.2 percent on bonds, or 0.9 percent on cash.

What Have We Learned?

In Chapter 1 we learned that to understand anything measured in money, you have to understand inflation, because inflation changes the value of your money yardstick. We learned that for the past 40 years, inflation has been the primary driver of major market changes. So to understand today's investment markets, we need to understand today's economic climate. To understand today's climate, we need to understand the climate changes of the past 50 years. If you can understand the economic climate, the investment markets make a lot more sense.

In Chapter 2 we learned that every investment is a transaction between two parties. There are three types of securities: short-term debt, long-term debt, and equities (stocks). Over the past 50 years, changes in economic climate have made the different choices among these three more or less profitable.

We learned that although short- and long-term debt are often marketed as "safe," when you take inflation and taxes into account, there have been many times in the past 50 years where you have lost money in bonds and bills. We learned that stocks, on average, have shown better gains over the past 50 years than bills and bonds. We have learned that stock *risk* is a matter of definition and that stock *volatility* is a function of sampling frequency (how often you price your stocks).

We have learned that many of the models that evaluate stock prices do not explicitly take inflation into account. They assume that interest rates (and therefore bond prices) accurately reflect inflation. In short, they assume that interest rates and bond prices are always fair, which was demonstrably not true in the 1970s and the 1980s.

So when you're told that something is risky, volatile, or overpriced, ask questions. The media are in the entertainment business. You want to be in the investment business—the business of growing your wealth.

Part Two

THE ESSAYS

In Part One, we presented a brief overview of the fundamentals of intelligent investment management. In Part Two, we build on that foundation with a collection of Ron Muhlenkamp's writings from 1979 to 2007. These particular essays were chosen because they illustrate why the market behaves as it does and how the intelligent investor can decide where to invest his money. The essays cover a broad range of topics including personal finance and estate planning, the effects of taxation and government spending, the benefits of free trade and free-market economies, and more. This broad view allows the investor to see more clearly how the economy drives the market and how to leverage that relationship to one's advantage.

The essays are presented in chronological order and grouped by economic climate. Each economic climate is introduced by a time line for historical perspective. Though the essays begin in 1979, the time lines begin in 1965, because the economic climate from 1965 to 1978 influenced the markets for many years thereafter. Therefore, we start in 1965 so we can understand what followed. Also, when reading the time lines, consider the mood of the American public at that time. What did we hope for, fear, and assume? People drive the economy, and the economy drives the stock market. You cannot separate the human experience from the marketplace.

In addition to the time lines, we have added an introduction to each essay to explain when the essay was written and why. On some essays we've also added updates and editorial comments when we felt that hindsight reveals something of interest. The essays themselves are essentially unchanged from when they were first written. This allows you to see what Ron said *at the time,* and then you can determine whether he was right. More importantly, it preserves the context in which the essays were written. Remember, to invest successfully you must be able to recognize economic climate changes as they happen. The best way to do this is to understand the changes of the past and then translate that understanding to the present. To do that, you need to understand the context in which those changes occurred.

In investing, you don't need to predict the future, but you do need to understand the present and recognize changes as they happen. Our hope is that these essays will help you do just that.

Chapter 3

1965–1978: The U.S. Economy Experiences Accelerating Inflation

T he year 1965 serves as a valuable benchmark for our discussion because it was the last normal year before rising inflation changed the rules for interest rates, price-to-earnings (P/E) ratios, and the standards for investing. Let's take a look at it.

In 1965 the American economy was in good shape. Inflation, which had run up in World War II and the Korean War, was at less than 2 percent and had averaged less than 2 percent since 1952. Interest rates on long bonds and mortgages were at 4.5 to 5 percent, which was considered normal. The economy was growing, after experiencing recessions in 1957–1958 and in 1960–1961.

The dominant economic fear was a depression. Having suffered the Great Depression after World War I, many expected and feared a repeat after World War II. Hence, the focus in economics and politics was on preventing recession. The prevailing economic theory proposed printing money to avoid recession. So the Federal Reserve printed money, and the early results were good. The U.S. economic expansion of the 1960s stretched to nine years, the longest economic expansion in U.S. history to that date. Economists were so impressed with their success that at one prominent university, the economics department cancelled its course on the business cycle. They thought they had found a way to beat the business cycle, so students no longer needed to study it.

The federal government was so focused on avoiding recession/depression that during the Nixon administration (1969–1974), when the chairman of the Federal Reserve wanted to tighten the monetary conditions to counter accelerating inflation, the administration said that would be okay as long as unemployment never exceeded 4.5 percent. It's important to note that this stipulation reflected the public (and therefore political) priorities of the time. So, throughout the 1970s, fearing another depression, the Federal Reserve accommodated the politicians and the markets by printing money.

At the same time, our grandmothers (the savers of the world) were putting their savings in passbook accounts, accepting low interest rates in favor of a guaranteed return. (As noted in Chapter 2, during the Depression they had learned that the return *of* their money was far more important than the return *on* their money.)

1965

- Inflation is stable, averaging 1.5 percent for 14 years; long-term Treasury bonds yield 4.5 percent, stable for 10 years; and average price-to-earnings ratios (PEs) for equities are at 17, stable for 7 years.
- President Lyndon B. Johnson outlines initiatives for a "Great Society," including war on poverty, greater enforcement of civil rights laws, immigration law reform, and increased support for education.
- The Voting Rights Act of 1965 outlaws the literacy test for voting eligibility in the South.
- President Johnson authorizes the use of ground troops in combat operations in Vietnam.

1966

- In his State of the Union address, President Johnson says that the United States should stay in South Vietnam until Communist aggression is ended; 215,000 soldiers are there.
- The Soviet Union lands Luna 13, an unmanned spacecraft, on the moon.
- By law, all U.S. cigarette packs carry the warning "Caution! Cigarette smoking may be hazardous to your health."
- U.S. Medicare federal insurance goes into effect.

1967

- President Johnson announces plans to establish a draft lottery.
- Hundreds of thousands of Americans protest involvement in the Vietnam War.
- Race riots sweep across America's largest cities.
- Thurgood Marshall becomes the first African American justice to sit on the U.S. Supreme Court.
- In South Africa, Dr. Christiaan Barnard leads surgeons in performing the first human heart transplant.

1968

- The Viet Cong and North Vietnamese launch the Tet Offensive during a New Year's truce, resulting in heavy U.S. casualties.

- Civil rights leader Martin Luther King Jr., 39, is assassinated. Months later, presidential candidate Robert F. Kennedy is shot and mortally wounded.
- Soviet tanks invade Czechoslovakia and crush the "Prague Spring."
- The Motion Picture Association of America adopts its film-rating system, ranging from "G" for general audiences to "X" for adult patrons only.
- Richard M. Nixon is elected the 37th U.S. president.

1969

- Yasser Arafat officially takes over as chairman of the Palestine Liberation Organization.
- Astronaut Neil Armstrong takes his legendary "one small step for man, one giant leap for mankind," becoming the first man ever to walk on the moon.
- Levi Strauss introduces bell-bottom jeans.
- The Woodstock Music and Art Fair opens in upstate New York.

1970

- "Houston, we've got a problem!" A tank containing liquid oxygen bursts, crippling Apollo 13.
- National Guardsmen unleash gunfire during an antiwar protest on the campus of Kent State University, killing four students.
- The first-ever postal strike paralyzes the U.S. Postal Service.
- President Nixon creates the Environmental Protection Agency (EPA).
- The over-the-counter stock market exchange is transformed into the National Association of Securities Dealers Automated Quotation Market (NASDAQ).

1971

- The U.S. Senate approves an amendment to lower the voting age from 21 to 18.
- The U.S. dollar goes off the gold standard and is devalued by 7.9 percent; the 10 percent surcharge on imports is lifted.
- The Anglican Church ordains two women as priests.
- Walt Disney World opens the Magic Kingdom in Orlando, Florida.
- First-class postage rates increase from 6 cents an ounce to 8 cents an ounce.

1972

- President Nixon makes a historic visit to Red China and meets with Mao Zedong. This is the first trip to Communist China by a U.S. president.
- Five men break into the Democratic National Committee office at the Watergate Hotel, marking the beginning of President Nixon's downfall.
- Palestinian terrorists attack the Israeli delegation at the Olympic Games in Munich, killing two athletes and taking hostages.
- The first scientific handheld calculator, the HP35, is introduced at $395.
- U.S. airlines begin mandatory inspection of passengers and baggage.

1973

- The U.S. Supreme Court legalizes abortion in its *Roe v. Wade* decision.
- A nationwide 55-mph speed limit is imposed.
- U.S. Vice President Spiro T. Agnew resigns from office, pleading "no contest" to charges of tax evasion.
- Oil prices increase fourfold resulting from the OPEC oil embargo; President Nixon imposes price controls on oil and gas.

1974

- The Viet Cong propose a new truce with the United States and South Vietnam.
- President Nixon resigns from office, the first president to do so. Gerald R. Ford is sworn in as the 38th U.S. president.
- The World Trade Center, the tallest building in the world at 110 stories, opens in New York City.
- The value of gold hits a record $188 an ounce in Paris.
- First-class postage rates increase from 8 cents an ounce to 10 cents an ounce.

1975

- U.S. forces pull out of Vietnam.
- In orbit, an Apollo spaceship docks with a Soviet Soyuz spacecraft—the first superpower linkup of its kind.
- The Khmer Rouge of Cambodia executes hundreds of thousands of Cambodians and condemns more than a million to death by starvation and disease.

- The median price for a new house in the United States is $42,100; average size is 1,645 square feet.
- First-class postage rates increase from 10 cents an ounce to 13 cents an ounce.
- President Ford escapes two assassination attempts in 17 days.

1976

- The U.S. Supreme Court allows states to resume capital punishment.
- American wines from Napa Valley take top honors in a tasting competition in Paris.
- Cadillac rolls out the world's largest front-wheel-drive automobile.
- Legionnaires' disease kills 29 in Philadelphia.

1977

- Jimmy Carter is sworn in as the 39th U.S. president and urges Americans to adopt 65°F as the maximum heat in their homes in order to ease the energy crisis.
- Leonid Brezhnev is named president of the USSR.
- Steven Jobs and Steve Wozniak found the Apple Computer Company.
- The ban on women attending West Point is lifted.
- The Concorde makes its first landing in New York City.

1978

- NASA names 35 candidates to fly on the space shuttle, including Sally Ride, the first woman in space, and Guion Bluford Jr., the first African American in space.
- The first test-tube baby is born in England.
- California voters overwhelmingly approve Proposition 13, calling for nearly a 60 percent slash in property taxes.
- Jim Jones leads over 900 religious followers to mass suicide in Jonestown, Guyana.
- Lee Iacocca is fired as president of Ford Motor Company.
- First-class postage rates increase from 13 cents an ounce to 15 cents an ounce.

Chapter 4

1979–1981: Transition from Inflation to Disinflation

The problems of inflation in the United States became evident, resulting in a decline in the dollar internationally, and the fear of inflation became more powerful than fear of a depression domestically. So while Paul Volcker and Ronald Reagan reined in inflation (it went from 13 percent to 4 percent in three years), our grandmothers moved their money out of passbook savings accounts and into money market funds to get a higher interest rate. These two actions reversed the economic climate. Notice that it took 40 years and a decade of inflation for the fear of depression to fade into the background of our collective economic psyche.

1979

- The United States and China hold celebrations to mark the establishment of diplomatic relations.
- Followers of Ayatollah Khomeini seize power in Iran, nine days after the religious leader returned to his home country following 15 years of exile.
- America's worst commercial nuclear accident occurs at Three Mile Island; no one dies.
- President Carter delivers his "malaise" speech in which he laments a "crisis of confidence" in America and appoints Paul Volcker as chairman of the Federal Reserve.
- Saddam Hussein becomes president of Iraq.

1980

- President Carter deregulates the banking industry.
- Honda announces that it will build Japan's first U.S. passenger-car assembly plant in Ohio.
- In a stunning upset, the U.S. hockey team defeats the Soviets in the Olympic Games at Lake Placid. The U.S. team goes on to win the gold medal.
- Ted Turner's Cable News Network (CNN) makes its debut as television's first all-news channel.
- Poland's Solidarity movement, founded by Lech Walesa, wins recognition as the first trade union of the Soviet bloc.

1981

- Inflation is 10 percent; short-term interest rates hit 13 percent; long-term interest rates are 13 percent; average price-to-earnings ratios (P/Es) for equities are 8; and U.S. national debt hits $1 trillion.
- Ronald Reagan is sworn in as the 40th U.S. president as 52 American hostages board a plane in Tehran and head toward freedom.
- In March, first-class postage rates increase from 15 cents an ounce to 18 cents an ounce. In November, first-class postage rates increase from 18 cents an ounce to 20 cents anounce.
- President Reagan and Pope John Paul II survive assassination attempts.
- The IBM personal computer is introduced, using software from a company called Microsoft.

Why the Market Went Down

This essay was written in 1979 for Ron's peers in the investment industry. Price-to-earnings (P/E) ratios on stocks had declined from 17 to 7 in just seven years, and no one seemed to understand why.

Nearly five years after the bear market of 1973–1974, the specter of that market continues to haunt investors—individual, corporate, and professional alike. Most investment decisions are prefaced by the fear of another bear market with the implication that the 1973–1974 decline was divorced from, or unwarranted by, the economics of the period.

In this brief paper, I show that the decline was entirely appropriate to the changes in economics and completely consistent with accepted theory for investing capital, whether in business, in bonds, or in equities. The bear market in equities came as a surprise to investors only because they tried to extrapolate the past in its simplest terms, rather than understanding present changes and building on that understanding. It is my belief that a better understanding of why that bear market occurred should help to relieve the fear of its recurrence and allow more rational investment practices.

Before we begin, I would like to propose two assumptions that will simplify our discussion:

1. Taxes will be ignored. Once the argument has been completed, taxes can be taken into account on an item-by-item basis.
2. Barring an unusually lucid crystal ball, the present will be considered a steady state condition, implying that the future will be very similar to the present. Once the present is fully understood (as a steady-state condition), the implication of any changes in the future will be much easier to understand.

I've summarized my argument in Exhibits 4.1 and 4.2. Frequent reference to these tables should prove helpful.

The Argument

It is 1979. Core inflation is running at a rate of 8 to 9 percent. Since the value of the dollar is shrinking at an 8 to 9 percent rate, most investors would like to *at least* offset that rate as a minimum requirement.

Exhibit 4.1 Derivations

	1979	1965	1951
Inflation (%)	8.0	1.5	7.0
Return on 90-day T-bills (%)	9.5	4.0	2.0
Return on 30-year GM bond (%)	9.5	4.5	3.0
Required return on equity (%) *(to be worth book value)*	15.0	8.0	13.0
Actual average return on equity (%)	15.0	12.0	13.0
Actual price/book value (P/B)	1.0	2.0	1.0
Implicit P/E ratio (P/E = P/B ÷ ROE)	6.0	17.0	7.0

Exhibit 4.2 What Happens in the Real World When Inflation Changes

	1965–1979	1951–1965
Required annual return (%)	8.0	13.0
Actual P/B return (+ or −) (%)	−5.0	+5.0
Realized annual return	3.0	18.0

Short-term Treasury bills (T-bills) are liquid and are considered to be risk-free investments. As such, they provide both a measure of the degree to which inflation can be offset on a current basis and a benchmark against which to measure other investments. Currently, short-term T-bills yield about 9.5 percent. Thus, other investments can be measured against both the inflation rate and short-term T-bills.

Long-term AAA corporate bonds are generally liquid but are considered to be a step below T-bills in quality and less certain in their payout, due to the length of time to maturity. For these reasons, most investors require a higher expected return from 30-year General Motors (GM) bonds, relative to T-bills, before they are willing to invest their money. Today, 30-year GM bonds provide an expected return of about 9.5 percent. This implies that investors would not now prefer such bonds to T-bills, unless they expected inflation and T-bill yields to be lower in the future than they are today.

Equity (stock) investment in a company is generally perceived as being riskier than debt (bond) investment in the same company, because stock prices are generally more volatile than bond prices. Although this volatility becomes less important as investors lengthen their time horizons, most stock investors still require some premium return to off-set the greater volatility and perceived risk of stock investment. Today, based on the 9.5 percent returns on T-bills and long-term bonds, many investors tell me that they need to see a 15 percent potential return to be willing to provide equity capital.

This point can also be made from the perspective of the company. If it costs GM 9.5 percent to borrow money, it must earn an additional return on that money to make being in business worthwhile. In short, if GM can't earn a premium, it has no incentive to pay 9.5 percent for use of the funds. A return on the order of 15 percent would seem to be a sufficient premium.

Consequently, I use a required return on equity of 15 percent in today's marketplace. This implies that if a company is actually earning that 15 percent, it should be worth *book value* (book value is defined as shareholder equity). Today, in fact, the average corporate return is roughly 15 percent, and the actual average price-to-book-value is just over one times book value. So, the market would appear to be fairly valued based on the assumptions and the data in the first column of Exhibit 4.1.

Now then, let's step back in time to 1965. In 1965, inflation aver-aged 1.5 percent. Ninety-day Treasury bills provided returns of roughly 4 percent. Long-term corporate bonds provided a return of 4.5 percent. In this environment, many people tell me that they would require returns of 7 to 8 percent to be willing to provide equity money. Again, if you are a corporate treasurer borrowing at 4.5 percent and earning 7 to 8 percent, it is probably worthwhile being in business.

What we have said so far is that because inflation and interest rates climbed from 1965 to 1979, our required return on equity capital dou-bled in the same way that the required return on corporate bonds doubled. The doubling in the required return on corporate bonds drove the price of 4.5 percent bonds or preferred stocks to 50 cents on the dollar, and this surprised no one. Given a fixed coupon rate, we had to halve the price in order to double the return. Yet people were shocked when the prices of their equities were cut in half, even though it was for the same reason.

Corporate returns on equity in the mid-1960s averaged about 12 percent. This 12 percent was enough above the required return of

7 to 8 percent that actual prices averaged two times book value. The only way in which these premium prices of two times book value could have been sustained is if the corporations had been able to sustain the premium returns (of 12 percent vs. the 7 or 8 percent). What has happened since then is that the required return doubled, and the actual return climbed merely from 12 percent to 15 percent, so that the prices shrank from two times book to just book value. Stock prices fell for the same reason that prices fell on existing bonds; it was the only way to increase future returns.

In order to complete the picture, we can go back to 1951. In the period around 1951, inflation rates were averaging about 7 percent. Ninety-day T-bills were only yielding 2 percent, and returns on corporate bonds were only 3 percent, due to the interest rate controls after World War II. Clearly, these interest rates were not economic, given the rate at which money was losing its purchasing power. Interest rates *should* have been around 8 to 9 percent, forcing required returns on equity to roughly 13 percent. In fact, in 1951 corporate returns on equity averaged 13 percent, and stocks were priced just above book value.

At this point several comments should be made. First of all, as we have derived the numbers in the three columns, each column is consistent unto itself. Anyone in 1951 who bought a 3 percent 30-year bond has in fact received his 3 percent. The bond is about to mature in 1981. Whether he is happy with that 3 percent is another question. He got exactly what he expected. Anyone who bought stocks at one times book in 1951 in companies that were earning 13 percent on equity has received that 13 percent. Since earnings are either paid out in dividends or added to equity, the investor received exactly what the companies earned, because the stock price is once again equal to book value. Like the bond investor, the stock investor has received exactly what he expected.

The difficulty comes when you make a transition from one column (i.e., one set of figures and one set of assumptions) to another. We have made that transition twice, and we are back where we started. However, let's look at what happened during those transitions (see Exhibit 4.2).

In the 14-year period from 1951 to 1965, because the *required* return went down, the prices on equities went up from one times book to two times book. The adjustment did not occur in bonds simply because bonds were pegged too low in 1951 to be economic investments.

When you double numbers in a 14-year period, you are adding about 5 percent on average per year.

In 1951 investors required equity returns of 13 percent, and the average company provided an in-house return of that same 13 percent. In the ensuing 14 years, investors' requirements dropped to 8 percent, while companies were able to maintain in-house returns of 12 percent. This caused the ratio of prices to book values to double, adding 5 percent per year in price appreciation to the 13 percent required. And, in fact, the total returns from equity investments for the period 1951 to 1965 averaged 18 percent.

In 1965, investors required equity returns of 8 percent. In the ensuing 14 years, their requirements rose to 15 percent, and companies' in-house returns rose to 15 percent. This caused the ratio of prices to book values to halve, giving back the 5 percent per year in price appreciation that was realized earlier. But this 5 percent was taken from a base of only 8 percent, leaving a net return of only 3 percent. In fact, the total of returns from equity investments, for the period 1965 to 1979, averaged 3 percent.

At this point it should be noted that the investors who bought 30-year bonds in 1965 can expect to get their 4.5 percent return over the 30-year period. To date they have not received it, because the price of the bonds has dropped dramatically in order to get remaining returns (i.e., on a yield-to-maturity basis) up to 9.5 percent. Nevertheless, if these bonds are held to maturity, people will get the 4.5 percent they originally expected. Their frustration will be that in the interim they have changed their required returns, simply because the economics changed.

The Conclusions

The conclusions from this exercise are several. The first conclusion is that the price of stocks is driven by the same economic factors that determine the price of bonds. Stocks are priced, as they must be priced, to provide the investor with a competitive prospective return, just as are bonds.

The second conclusion is that stocks do have an additional variable in their returns. Whereas a bond coupon is fixed for the life of the bond, the underlying return for stocks is the corporate return on equity, which can, of course, change. If a bond is held to maturity, the investor will realize the exact return he bargained for. Similarly, if the stock is held until the capitalization rate—the price-to-book-value—returns to its level at purchase, the shareholder will receive whatever return on corporate equity the company earned on average during his holding period. Thus, there is an additional variable, but the price determinations are still based on what the company earns. A shareholder owns a share of the company and can expect to receive the company's return on equity capital, provided he manages to sell his share for a capitalization rate equal to the one at which he purchased.

The third conclusion is that if in 1951 bonds had been priced to return 9 or 10 percent (in order to make them competitive with the 7 percent inflation rate), bondholders would have been called out of their bonds somewhere between 1951 and 1965. This means that, rather than allowing the prices of the bonds to increase to 1.8 times par, the companies simply would have called them back in and issued 4.5 percent bonds. The point is that anyone buying a 9.5 percent bond today will not get that 9.5 percent unless the bonds are outstanding to maturity. If interest rates should drop, it is the obligation of the corporation to call them back in and reissue new bonds at a lower coupon rate.

The fourth conclusion is that the return on shareholders' equity is in fact return on shareholders' equity. When a company earns money on shareholder equity, that money goes to only two places: It gets paid out in dividends (in which case the shareholder can invest it or spend it as his heart desires) or it gets plowed back into the equity base. If it is plowed back into the equity base, those dollars do accrue to the value of the enterprise. The difficulty in the past 14 years has simply been that the capitalization rate (i.e., the price-to-book ratio) has declined at a rate nearly offsetting this accumulation of corporate equity, so it has not been apparent to shareholders that they were, in fact, benefiting from corporate retained earnings. Looking at the period from 1951 to 1965, shareholders benefited doubly, but there was very little incentive to look closely or to pursue the argument at that time.

The fifth conclusion is that the reason the stocks can be viewed as a hedge against inflation is that corporate management has the task of earning returns on shareholder equity over and above the costs of borrowing money. When inflation and interest rates rose in 1970, the verbal response of investors was to "buy those 7 to 8 percent bonds while you have a chance" because 4.5 percent was viewed as a normal return on debt. Even coupons of 7 percent to 8 percent on bonds did not deter corporate management. They were earning a 12 percent return on shareholder equity. It had decreased their margin, but it was still worthwhile being in business. In 1973 and 1974 when interest rates rose again, investors concluded that 8 percent to 9 percent bonds were here to stay. At the same time, corporate management reached the same conclusion, indicating that a 12 percent return on shareholder equity was only marginal. Thus, they have since upped their required returns to 15 percent.

The realization that we may have entered a new era of inflation and interest rates, hit both investors and corporate managers (who are often the same people), at the same time. But, whereas a corporate executive body requires several years to upgrade the profitability of their company, investors are able to up their prospective returns in a very short period of time. They simply cut prices. This occurred in the equity markets in 1973 and 1974.

Since that time we have had gradually increasing levels of corporate return on equity, so that today returns are competitive, but returns are not at premium levels as they were in 1965. The capital markets have adjusted to this by simply cutting their price-to-book value ratios from two times to one time. Nevertheless, if inflation continues to climb and interest rates continue to climb, corporate executives will continue to up their required returns. If the investor buys into corporations at prices below book value, he will be taken care of simply by the actions of the executives. It's when the investor insists on paying prices substantially above book value that he is relying on corporations to earn premium returns rather than simply competitive returns.

Postscript

I would like to make just two more points. I consider them axioms of investing:

1. Over the long term (e.g., 30 years) the difference in risk between the stock and the bonds of any given company is minuscule. If the company dies, neither is any good. When Penn Central went bankrupt, owning the bonds was little better than owning stock.

2. Return on shareholder equity is exactly that. If the company earns it, it accrues to the value owned by the shareholder, either through dividends or through increased equity value. Over the long term, the shareholder gets what the company earns. A shareholder can get more or less by buying at a discount (to equity value) or at a premium.

Editor's Note

In this essay, Ron offers insight into the dynamics of the market from 1951 to 1979 by considering the perspectives of both the investor and the businessperson. What rate of return is required for an individual to invest? What rate of return must a company be able to make before it will borrow money? The answers to these questions depend on the inflation rate, interest rates, and perceived risk. Thus, when inflation and interest rates change, the required returns change as well.

In 1973–1974, the realization that inflation was here to stay drove stock prices down. (Remember, the investor has a required return. To meet this in an environment of increasing inflation, corporate profitability must increase or purchase price must drop. Profitability takes years to change. Price changes are much quicker.) The bear market of 1973–1974 was a surprise to analysts because investment models did not take inflation into account. (From 1951 to 1965 they didn't need to, because inflation was steady. But from 1965 to 1978, changes in inflation played the major role in the marketplace.)

The lesson to learn: When you are working with money, you must account for the fact that the value of money can change. You must account for inflation.

Do Ron's insights still hold true in 2007? In Exhibit 4.3 we've added two columns, one for 1998 and one for 2007. In 1998, bond yields and stock prices first reflected inflation rates of 2 percent. Note that the parameters come very close to those of 1965. The real-world numbers in Exhibit 4.4 show that the period 1979–1998 looks a lot like 1951–1965. The numbers also demonstrate why, starting in 1998, Ron has been saying that stocks are priced to do 8 to 9 percent per year going forward. (For more information refer to the "Total Return" segment in his essay entitled "How Much Money Are You Willing to Lose for a Theory?" in Chapter 8.)

Looking at the numbers for 2007, we see that they are very close to the numbers for 1998. The real-world numbers demonstrate returns that are still a bit below the required return since 1998.

Exhibit 4.3 Derivations (Updated)

	2007	1998	1979	1965	1951
Inflation (%)	2.0	2.0	8.0	1.5	7.0
Return on 90-day T-bills (%)	4.0	3.0	9.5	4.0	2.0
Return on 30-year GM bond (%)	4.5	5.0	9.5	4.5	3.0
Required return on equity (%) *(to be worth book value)*	8.0	8.0	15.0	8.0	13.0
Actual average return on equity (%)	13.0	13.0	15.0	12.0	13.0
Actual price/book value (P/B)	2.1	2.1	1.0	2.0	1.0
Implicit P/E ratio (P/E = P/B ÷ ROE)	17.0	17.0	6.0	17.0	7.0

Exhibit 4.4 What Happens in the Real World When Inflation Changes (Updated)

	1998–2007	1979–1998	1965–1979	1951–1965
Required annual return (%)	8.0	15.0	8.0	13.0
Actual P/B return (+ or −) (%)	+0.0	+3.0	−5.0	+5.0
Theoretical annual return	8.0	18.0	3.0	18.0
Realized annual return	7.0	18.0	3.0	18.0

References

Federal Reserve Bank of St. Louis, *U.S. Financial Data.*

Federal Reserve System Board of Governors, *Historical Chart Book,* published annually in Washington, D.C.

Standard & Poor's *Analyst's Handbook,* published annually in New York.

Chapter 5

1982–1992: Bonds Do Well; Stocks Do Well

The inflation of the 1970s changed people's perceptions on how to invest their money. In the 1970s, inflation was high and interest rates were not, so it paid to borrow money. "Trade up on equity" became the mantra.

In the 1980s, inflation was curtailed, but the fear and expectation of its return kept interest rates high. However, people kept trading up on equity regardless of the higher interest rates. Because people were borrowing money regardless of rates, you could make money lending it to them (i.e., you could make money in bonds).

It wasn't until the recession of 1990 that people looked more closely at their finances and refinanced their mortgages. They refinanced for lower rates and shorter terms, completing the bond market's response to the economic climate change of a decade earlier.

Notice that it took a recession for people to realize that with inflation under control, and interest rates up, it no longer paid to borrow money. It took a recession to change the perception from "Trade up on equity" to "Prepay the mortgage."

1982

- AT&T settles the Justice Department's antitrust lawsuit and divests itself of 22 Bell System companies.
- Argentine forces surrender to British troops on the disputed Falkland Islands located in the south Atlantic.
- Capsules of Extra-Strength Tylenol laced with cyanide kill seven people in Chicago, bringing about major improvements in safe sealing methods by consumer companies.
- The U.S. capital gains tax is cut from 28 percent to 20 percent.
- Computer games become a hit in America as Nintendo introduces Donkey Kong and a chubby plumber named Mario.
- Permanent artificial heart is implanted for the first time in Dr. Barney Clark.

1983

- President Reagan orders 1,800 U.S. Marines and Rangers to invade Grenada.
- President Reagan proposes the development of technology to intercept enemy missiles—a proposal that becomes known as the Strategic Defense Initiative, or Star Wars.
- Optical fibers begin replacing copper cables for transmitting information.
- In Beirut, the U.S. Embassy, U.S. Marine barracks, French military headquarters, and international airport are targets of suicide terrorists, killing hundreds.

1984

- Chrysler introduces the first minivan; Boeing releases its first 757 airplane.
- A federal bailout of $4.5 billion keeps the Continental Illinois Bank afloat.
- The median price for a new house in the United States is $78,300; average size is 1,780 square feet.

- More than 4,000 people die and 200,000 are injured after a cloud of toxic gas escapes from a Union Carbide pesticide plant in Bhopal, India.
- A baboon heart is transplanted into 15-day old Baby Fae—the first transplant of its kind.
- Ronald Reagan is reelected with 97.6 percent of the electoral college and 58 percent of the popular vote.

1985

- Politburo member Mikhail Gorbachev becomes the general secretary of the Communist Party and the premier of the Soviet Union.
- General Motors starts its Saturn division.
- Karen Ann Quinlan, the comatose patient whose case prompted a historic right-to-die court decision, dies in Morris Plains, New Jersey, at the age of 31.
- AIDS makes the cover of *Time* magazine.
- First-class postage rates increase from 20 cents an ounce to 22 cents an ounce.

1986

- The space shuttle Challenger explodes in midair, killing its crew of seven, including the first teacher in space, Christa McAuliffe.
- An atomic power plant explodes in Chernobyl, Ukraine, releasing radioactivity 200 times the amount released by the bombs dropped on Hiroshima and Nagasaki during WWII.
- U.S. national debt hits $2,000,000,000,000 ($2 trillion).
- There are over 60,000 farm foreclosures in the rural West and Midwest.
- Pope John Paul II meets with the Dalai Lama in India.

1987

- President Reagan nominates Alan Greenspan to succeed Paul Volcker as chairman of the Federal Reserve Board.
- During a visit to the city of Berlin, President Reagan publicly challenges Soviet leader Mikhail Gorbachev to "tear down this wall."
- The FDA announces a two-year reduction in the drug approval process.

- Astronomers sight a new galaxy 12 billion light years away.
- On August 25, the DJIA hits 2722, a record high; the correction known as Black Monday takes place on October 19 when the DJIA plunges 508 points to 1738—the biggest one-day decline ever.

1988
- The Soviet Union withdraws troops from Afghanistan, acknowledging defeat after nine years of fighting; Saudi-born Osama bin Laden founds Al-Qaeda.
- Pan Am Flight 103 is downed over Lockerbie, Scotland, by a Libyan terrorist bomb, killing 270.
- The U.S. Senate steps up the war on drugs by giving the navy the power to stop drug trafficking on the high seas.
- Medical waste and other debris begins washing up on seashores near New York City, closing several popular beaches.
- Major U.S. banks boost their prime lending rates half a percentage point to 10.5 percent.
- First-class postage rates increase from 22 cents an ounce to 25 cents an ounce.

1989
- George H.W. Bush is sworn in as 41st U.S. president, and L. Douglas Wilder of Virginia becomes the first elected African-American governor in the United States.
- Twenty-eight years after the Berlin Wall was erected, it is torn down, allowing citizens to travel freely across the border.
- Thousands die in Tiananmen Square as Chinese army troops crush a pro-democracy demonstration.
- The nation's worst oil spill occurs as the supertanker *Exxon Valdez* leaks 11 million barrels of crude oil in Alaska's Prince William Sound.
- The first versions of HTML launch the World Wide Web; America Online (AOL) makes its debut.

1990
- The U.S. invasion of Panama begins and ends on February 13, ousting General Manuel Noriega.

- Nelson Mandela is released from a South African prison after being detained 27 years for fighting against apartheid.
- Former junk bond financier Michael Milken pleads guilty to six felonies and pays $600 million in penalties to settle the largest securities fraud case in history.
- Four of the so-called Keating Five go before the Senate Ethics Committee, denying any wrongdoing in helping failed savings-and-loan owner Charles H. Keating Jr.
- Ford acquires Jaguar.

1991
- Operation Desert Storm drives Iraqi forces out of Kuwait in 88 days.
- Financially strapped Eastern Airlines shuts down after 62 years in business.
- A Michigan court bars Dr. Jack Kevorkian from assisting terminally ill patients in suicide.
- Worldwide financial scandal erupts as regulators in eight countries shut down the Bank of Credit and Commerce International (BCCI), charging it with fraud, drug money laundering, and illegal infiltration into the U.S. banking system.
- Civil war in Yugoslavia begins when Croatia and Slovenia proclaim independence.
- First-class postage rates increase from 25 cents an ounce to 29 cents an ounce.

1992
- War breaks out in northern Bosnia as local Serbs lay siege to the capital, Sarajevo.
- Deadly rioting erupts in Los Angeles after a jury acquits four police officers in the videotaped beating of motorist Rodney King.
- Trade representatives of the United States, Canada, and Mexico sign the North American Free Trade Agreement (NAFTA).
- After a reign lasting nearly 30 years, Johnny Carson hosts the *Tonight Show* for the last time.
- Bill Clinton is elected the 42nd U.S. president, defeating incumbent George H. W. Bush and independent candidate Ross Perot, who won 19 percent of the vote.

Wake Up, America—Houses Don't Make You Money!

This essay was originally published in Muhlenkamp Memorandum,[1] *Issue 1, July 1987.*

In the 1970s (when inflation rates were higher than mortgage rates), one of the best investment strategies was to borrow money. The easy way for people to borrow money was on real estate. It worked in housing, in farmland, and in commercial real estate (which was also an effective tax shelter). People continued to believe in the strategy through the 1980s, even though the economic climate had reversed in roughly 1981. Ron wrote "Wake Up, America—Houses Don't Make You Money!" to point out that change.

America is slowly awakening from the dream of benefiting financially from owning a house. We all know houses that sold for $40,000 in the mid-1960s that are worth $120,000 today. It is obvious that anyone who owns such a house has made $80,000. It's obvious, but it's also wrong.

Prices throughout the economy have tripled since 1965. Therefore, housing prices had to triple just to maintain their value. Anyone who bought a house for cash in 1965 and sold it today would get just enough money to buy (before commissions and fees) the identical house next door. Some may call that a profit, but the buyer hasn't improved his financial position.

Nevertheless, in the past 20 years, many people have improved their position dramatically through house ownership. But they didn't make money on the house; they made it on the mortgage.

During the decade of the 1970s, interest rates were below the rate of inflation in housing prices. Borrowing at 8 percent tax deductible, to buy a house appreciating at 10 percent, made money for people throughout the 1970s. Today, interest rates are well above the rate of inflation; if you borrow money, it costs you money.

Exhibit 5.1 represents annual mortgage rates for the past 35 years, adjusted for taxes at the (then) maximum rate, and for inflation (at the annual change in the Consumer Price Index). For much of the period 1968 to 1980, after-tax interest rates on mortgages were less than the

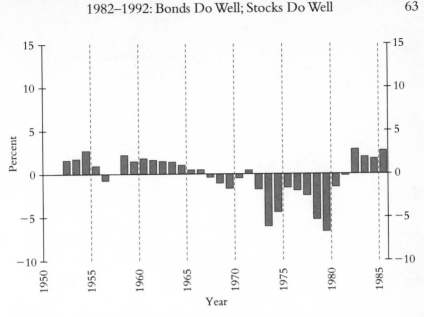

Exhibit 5.1   Real After-Tax Mortgage Rate, 1952–1986

inflation rate. In fact, mortgage rates were 8 percent or less as long as savers were willing to accept 5 percent on their passbook savings. This allowed borrowing at 8 percent to buy houses appreciating at 10 percent. When borrowing money at 8 percent (4 percent after taxes) to finance a house appreciating with inflation at 10 percent, purchasing power increases by a net 6 percent of the amount borrowed. You get paid to borrow money! As the chart shows, from 1968 to 1980, this net gain averaged 4 percent per year, or $4,000 on a $100,000 mortgage. So the key to getting ahead between 1968 and 1980 was to buy a big house with a big mortgage.

The dream ended in 1981, and the awakening is just now occurring. As the chart shows, it now costs money to borrow money (real after-tax mortgage rates have turned positive). By shopping around, savers learned they could do better than a passbook with CDs or money market funds. This caused mortgage rates to rise at the same time inflation in housing prices was coming down.

In 1986, mortgage rates of 10 percent (5 percent after taxes) exceeded the 2 percent inflation rate by 3 percent and led to a $3,000 real cost on that same $100,000, a considerable change from the gain of $4,000 experienced from 1965 to 1980. In addition, the after-tax cost of borrowing is increasing as a result of the new tax bill.

Today, many people continue to buy big houses with big mortgages, stretching and adding incomes to meet the 10 percent or 12 percent interest payment on a house that appreciates only 3 percent or 4 percent per year. They don't realize that the house will not appreciate enough to earn a profit; they will awaken too late to the real cost of borrowing in the 1980s.

2007 Update

Today, 30-year fixed-rate mortgages are a bit above 6 percent. With a top income tax bracket of 35 percent, the after-tax cost of borrowing is 4+ percent. We judge inflation to be 2 percent (house prices have been rising faster, but we find no reason to expect that to continue). So the real (after- inflation) after-tax cost of carrying a mortgage is a bit above 2 percent, which is close to the historic norm.

The interesting thing is that a few years ago, some people were again making money on houses, but this time the reason was different. Normally, house prices track with inflation. For a few years, the growth in house prices well exceeded inflation because, as mortgage interest rates fell, buyers could bid up the purchase price without increasing the monthly payment. (The limit on what you can pay for a house is the amount of the monthly mortgage payment.) When mortgage rates reached normal levels in 2005, I did not expect house prices to continue to rise faster than inflation. In fact, house prices have leveled off, and the game is over.

Worker Capitalism Triumphs

Originally published in Muhlenkamp Memorandum, *Issue 2, October 1987, this essay points out that through pension plans, American workers own a major portion of the business assets of the United States.*

As reflected in literature and the popular media from Dickens and Marx to Studs Terkel and Jesse Jackson, people have always viewed themselves as workers. As workers, they think of themselves as being in direct competition with owners and managers for a share of the wealth created by business enterprise. They see the return for their efforts in the form of a weekly or semimonthly paycheck and often conclude that their pay would be greater if only the owners took less.

People naturally think in terms of net take-home pay, money that is then spent on the day-to-day necessities and luxuries of life. Yet take-home pay is only a part of the benefits received for work. Other items— whether deducted from gross pay, such as taxes, or those not appearing on the pay stub at all, such as medical insurance or pension benefits—are much less tangible and are often taken for granted or ignored by the worker. Yet the least tangible part of the paycheck, the pension benefit, has resulted in American workers owning a major portion of the business assets of the United States. The growth in pension and retirement assets has been so great that Peter Drucker calls wage earners "the only true capitalists in developed countries today."

Workers Are the Owners

Today the workers are the owners; they just don't know it yet. According to *Pensions & Investments,* in late 1986 the 100 largest U.S. pension funds had assets exceeding $845 billion. Of these 100 funds, only 48 were company related. The aggregate market value of the 48 sponsoring companies was $583 billion. Thus, the 100 largest pension funds could easily own all of the shares of the 48 companies. Individually, the pension funds of the employees of 14 of these companies exceeded the total market value of their respective stocks. Thus, the employees of General Motors, through their pension plan, could buy all of the stock of their company. So could the employees of AT&T, USX, Alcoa, Lockheed Martin, Union Carbide, and Delta Air Lines.

Of the 100 largest pension plans not company related, most are plans for public employees. The California Public Employees Retirement System exceeded $37 billion, an amount sufficient to buy all the stock of General Motors and Ford. Similarly, the Pennsylvania State Employees Retirement Plan could have bought out USX. The Pennsylvania School

Employees Retirement Plan, at over $10 billion, could have bought out USX plus Alcoa.

The point is that workers already own a huge chunk of America's capital assets, yet are largely unaware of it. A person retiring from USX with a $20,000-per-year pension and a life expectancy of 15 to 20 years thinks he's poor, but if he receives the same amount in a lump sum, he thinks he's rich. Same data—different perceptions.

Though the workers seem unaware of their ownership status, managers are rapidly becoming more aware. Directors and managers see huge blocks of their stock in the hands of (potentially nonfriendly) pension funds and mutual funds, so they try to maintain their positions of power and influence with various "poison pills" and so-called shareholder rights plans. Managers sometimes literally buy off unfriendly holders through greenmail payments or share repurchase. Some do both. When General Motors paid $700 million in hush money to H. Ross Perot because Perot refused to keep quiet about GM's loss of market share, the firm was besieged by its other larger shareholders, including the comptroller of the New York City Pension Funds. It seems these other shareholders were not happy with H. Ross being the only beneficiary of the firm's largesse, so they made noises about replacing Roger Smith as chairman. GM announced a share repurchase soon thereafter.

Other firms undermine the shareholder's say in management by creating separate classes of stock, one with the great majority of voting power, the other with very little. The trouble with this strategy is that the New York Stock Exchange has something called the "one-share, one-vote" rule, and firms opting for this strategy face delisting of their securities. Opposition to these and other corporate tactics is increasing as institutional shareholders come to recognize their collective power.

1995 Update

We wrote in 1987 that institutional shareholders and pension plans were beginning "to recognize their collective power." Much has been made of the push in recent years for a greater focus on shareholder values, frequently resulting in corporate cutbacks, including large layoffs. But the public is unaware that the major pension plans have been aggressive drivers of this trend.

Specifically, in each of the past several years, California Public Employee Retirement System (CalPERS) has targeted a number of major companies, pushing for greater efficiencies and greater profitability. Its targets have included General Motors, Eastman Kodak, Westinghouse, and so on, and its pressure has resulted in the firings of chief executives and whole tiers of corporate managers—in the name of, and for the benefit of, workers' pensions.

2007 Update

In recent years, many companies have closed their defined benefit plans and shifted to defined contribution plans. We have seen a number of articles discussing the ramifications of such shifts, but none giving the historic causes.

A defined benefit plan is just what it says. The plan defines a benefit, say $200 a month, which is promised to be paid to a retiree beginning on some date.

The plan can be specific to a company, such as General Motors (GM), or a union bargaining group, such as the Pennsylvania Teachers or the Central States Teamsters. Administration of the plan is the responsibility of a board of trustees whose job it is to make sure that the plan and its assets are run for the benefit of the plan members, who are the workers and the retirees. The trustees then hire actuaries to aid in the administration of the plan. The actuaries make assumptions and calculations about life expectancies, inflation rates, wage rates, and so on, in an attempt to make sure that the $200 per month will be available when needed. The fact that the future liability went from $0 to $200 per month on the day the contract was signed adds an additional complication. Most firms are not able to come up with the funds overnight, so the law allows them to fund these obligations over a period of time, often 20 to 40 years.

Okay. So it's 1965, and your plan has been in place for 20 years. Most of the actuarial assumptions have been reasonably close. Life expectancy has increased, but the other assumptions have been close, including wage levels and returns on plan assets. Over the 20-year period, the company made annual contributions and has brought the plan to a fully funded level.

Now, fast-forward to 1980. In the prior 15 years, because of the increase in interest rates and the decline in price/earning ratios, the return on the plan assets have not met expectations, forcing up the company contributions. Meanwhile, the company has lost market share and has had to scale back its workforce just as a lot of people are about to retire. So the company offers early retirement packages, alleviating the problem of cutting back the workforce. But now there is a problem in the retirement plan: It means the number of retirees is climbing rapidly while the number of active workers is declining. In addition, the retirees are pointing out that (as a result of inflation) $200 per month doesn't buy what it did 15 years ago. They're demanding $400 per month in the upcoming wage contract. As a matter of negotiation (and as a matter of equity), the retiree benefit is doubled and the plan becomes underfunded by one-half overnight. Note that this occurred despite the best intentions of all the people involved.

The reason companies are moving to defined contribution plans is that no management can say with assurance that history won't repeat itself. They are unwilling to risk corporate bankruptcy as a result of basic assumptions that didn't hold up in the past and may not hold up in the future. To ask IBM or Microsoft to support a defined benefit plan today is to ask them to risk a future as problematic as that of GM and Ford today. Any management that does so is irresponsible.

Exhibit 5.2 lists some summary data from the largest plans.

The data in Exhibit 5.3 is reprinted with permission from *Pensions & Investments*, January 22, 2007 (Crain Communications, Inc.). Exhibit 5.3 lists the top 200 pension funds and their sponsors in the United States, along with the assets (in millions) in the fund. We have included a column labeled "Market Value" that shows the market value of the respective corporations as of September 30, 2006. When you look at this exhibit, pay particular attention to the company market values with the asterisks. These are the companies whose (funded) pension plans are greater than the market values of the companies themselves. Note that most of the airlines have recently declared bankruptcy and that the auto companies are flirting with similar problems.

Exhibit 5.2   Summary Data from Largest Pension Plans (Assets in $ Billions)

Pension Plans	1986	2002	2006
Top 1000	N/A	4,700	6,487
Top 200	N/A	3,560	4,911
Top 100	845	2,900	4,062
CalPERS	37	143	218
Market value of top 100 companies	583	2,192	4,028
Number of public companies within top 100 plans	48	41	41

Exhibit 5.3   Top 200 Pension Funds/Sponsors and Market Value (Ranked by Total Assets)

Ranked By Total Assets (In Millions as of 9/30/06)

Rank As of 9/30/06	Sponsor	Pension Assets (in Millions)	Market Value
1	California Public Employees	218,214	
2	Federal Retirement Thrift	188,086	
3	California State Teachers	149,008	
4	New York State Common	144,289	
5	Florida State Board	124,450	
6	General Motors	118,992	18,812★
7	New York City Retirement	114,598	
8	Texas Teachers	100,717	
9	New York State Teachers	94,347	
10	Wisconsin Investment Board	80,853	
11	IBM	79,567	124,699
12	General Electric	76,039	364,415
13	New Jersey	75,544	
14	Ohio Public Employees	73,572	
15	Boeing	72,848	62,679★
16	AT&T	71,556	126,468
17	North Carolina	70,016	
18	Ohio State Teachers	67,965	
19	Verizon	62,639	107,630
20	Washington State Board	60,045	
21	Michigan Retirement	59,988	
22	Oregon Public Employees	58,549	
23	Pennsylvania School Employees	58,490	
24	Ford Motor	57,282	15,217★
25	University of California	54,433	

(continued)

Exhibit 5.3   *(continued)*

Rank As of 9/30/06	Sponsor	Pension Assets (in Millions)	Market Value
26	Virginia Retirement	51,340	
27	Georgia Teachers	48,675	
28	Minnesota State Board	48,214	
29	Lucent Technologies	44,825	10,488★
30	Lockheed Martin	44,721	36,478★
31	Massachusetts PRIM	43,535	
32	Colorado Employees	37,868	
33	Illinois Teachers	37,361	
34	Los Angeles County Employees	35,877	
35	Maryland State Retirement	35,430	
36	United Nations Joint Staff	34,419	
37	Northrop Grumman	33,434	23,451★
38	Pennsylvania Employees	31,978	
39	Tennessee Consolidated	30,699	
40	Teamsters, Western Conference	30,158	
41	National Railroad	29,383	
42	Alabama Retirement	29,103	
43	United Technologies	29,032	64,074
44	DaimlerChrysler	28,584	51,074
45	DuPont	27,515	39,490
46	South Carolina Retirement	27,129	
47	Exxon Mobil	26,721	398,907
48	Missouri Public Schools	26,229	
49	Bank of America	25,867	242,451
50	BellSouth	24,972	77,625
51	Arizona State Retirement	24,863	
52	Texas Employees	23,890	
53	Raytheon	23,563	21,543★
54	Connecticut Retirement	23,528	
55	Citigroup	23,494	245,566
56	Utah State Retirement	22,705	
57	Altria	22,045	160,254
58	JPMorgan Chase	21,921	163,018
59	United Parcel Service	21,395	77,768
60	Illinois Municipal	21,143	
61	Honeywell	21,080	33,495
62	Iowa Public Employees	21,027	
63	Mississippi Employees	20,428	

64	Nevada Public Employees	20,334	
65	Teamsters, Central States	19,652	
66	Chevron	18,983	142,561
67	American Airlines	18,641	4,929★
68	FedEx	18,333	33,325
69	Shell Oil	17,010	208,978
70	Dow Chemical	16,920	37,395
71	Procter & Gamble	16,778	196,792
72	Alaska Retirement	16,776	
73	State Farm	16,746	
74	BP America	16,600	216,907
75	San Francisco City & County	16,359	
76	3M	16,155	56,056
77	Wells Fargo	15,883	121,826
78	Hewlett–Packard	15,700	100,492
79	Prudential	15,562	37,134
80	Kentucky Retirement	15,493	
81	Georgia Employees	15,433	
82	Kaiser	15,325	
83	Illinois State Universities	15,106	
84	United Methodist Church	15,096	
85	Indiana Public Employees	15,054	
86	Caterpillar	14,623	43,148
87	Texas County & District	14,524	
88	Delphi	14,444	899★
89	Kentucky Teachers	14,431	
90	Illinois State Board	14,252	
91	Los Angeles Fire & Police	14,111	
92	General Dynamics	13,951	28,912
93	Louisiana Teachers	13,938	
94	Pfizer	13,636	206,786
95	Eastman Kodak	13,440	6,434★
96	Qwest	13,347	16,614
97	Texas Municipal Retirement	13,343	
98	PG&E	13,291	14,497
99	Wachovia	13,269	88,694
100	National Electric	13,258	
101	World Bank	13,122	
102	Johnson & Johnson	12,862	189,951
103	Kansas Public Employees	12,703	
104	Exelon	12,600	40,531

(continued)

Exhibit 5.3 *(continued)*

Rank As of 9/30/06	Sponsor	Pension Assets (in Millions)	Market Value
105	Alcoa	12,380	24,308
106	Deere	12,195	19,400
107	New Mexico Public Employees	12,029	
108	Chicago Public School Teachers	11,649	
109	International Paper	11,405	17,076
110	Merrill Lynch	11,218	69,340
111	Ohio Police & Fire	11,155	
112	ConocoPhillips	10,400	98,094
113	MetLife	10,350	43,042
114	Consolidated Edison	10,330	11,836
115	Federal Reserve Employees	10,298	
116	Ohio School Employees	10,277	
117	Idaho Public Employees	10,267	
118	Hawaii Employees	10,200	
119	Southern Company	10,191	25,579
120	Delta Air Lines	10,122	270★
121	Motorola	10,103	61,251
122	United States Steel	10,068	7,099★
123	Maine State Retirement	10,029	
124	Los Angeles City Employees	9,945	
125	Siemens	9,900	77,614
126	Northwest Airlines	9,831	60★
127	Koch Industries	9,660	
128	Weyerhaeuser	9,555	15,278
129	Wal-Mart Stores	9,461	205,617
130	Arkansas Teachers	9,446	
131	Sears Holdings	9,324	24,352
132	Eli Lilly	9,187	64,433
133	Operating Engineers International	9,116	
134	Abbott Laboratories	8,905	74,190
135	1199 SEIU National	8,895	
136	Episcopal Church	8,875	
137	J.C. Penney	8,851	15,334
138	New York State Deferred Compensation	8,788	
139	Morgan Stanley	8,781	78,157
140	Aetna	8,766	21,662

141	Xerox	8,722	14,415
142	National Rural Electric	8,659	
143	PepsiCo	8,657	107,593
144	Merck	8,592	91,180
145	Southern Baptist Convention	8,590	
146	Tennessee Valley Authority	8,535	
147	New Mexico Educational	8,468	
148	Oklahoma Teachers	8,408	
149	SUPERVALU	8,332	6,275★
150	Intel	8,303	118,648
151	Boilermaker-Blacksmith	8,221	
152	Allstate	8,155	39,489
153	Nebraska Investment Council	8,138	
154	Indiana Teachers	8,073	
155	Duke Energy	8,068	37,841
156	Louisiana State Employees	8,044	
157	I.A.M. National	8,001	
158	Time Warner	7,854	74,141
159	GlaxoSmithKline	7,748	154,109
160	Rhode Island Employees	7,694	
161	San Diego County	7,612	
162	Bristol-Myers Squibb	7,601	49,006
163	Electronic Data Systems	7,596	12,692
164	New York City Deferred Compensation	7,570	
165	Montana Board of Investments	7,516	
166	CBS	7,421	21,994
167	Unisys	7,416	1,946★
168	Presbyterian Church	7,290	
169	Dominion Resources	7,237	26,989
170	Missouri State Employees	7,150	
171	Cook County Employees	7,100	
172	ITT	7,081	9,468
173	American Electric	6,968	
174	Textron	6,964	11,048
175	South Dakota	6,950	
176	Oklahoma Public Employees	6,898	
177	Tyco International	6,871	56,392
178	Los Angeles Water & Power	6,856	
179	FirstEnergy	6,820	18,425
180	Wyeth	6,743	68,413

(continued)

Exhibit 5.3   *(continued)*

Rank As of 9/30/06	Sponsor	Pension Assets (in Millions)	Market Value
181	Electrical Industry, Joint Board	6,716	
182	UMWA Health & Retirement	6,707	
183	Target	6,697	47,443
184	West Virginia Investment	6,596	
185	Delaware Public Employees	6,527	
186	Ohio Deferred Compensation	6,493	
187	Southern California Edison	6,485	
188	Orange County	6,474	
189	Reynolds American	6,458	18,315
190	Chicago Municipal Employees	6,438	
191	Walt Disney	6,421	64,606
192	California Savings Plus	6,295	
193	Arizona Public Safety	6,272	
194	Wyoming Retirement	6,174	
195	American Express	6,060	68,129
196	Federated Department Stores	6,047	23,487
197	Hartford Financial	6,008	26,393
198	Evangelical Lutheran Church	6,001	
199	Sacramento County	5,997	
200	UFCW Industry, Illinois	5,957	

*Denotes pension plan is greater than market value.

Source: Reprinted with permission from *Pensions & Investments,* January 22, 2007 (Crain Communications, Inc.).

Muhlenkamp's Musings on Economics

This essay was originally published in Muhlenkamp Memorandum, *Issue 3, January 1988. More observations were added in October 1996. Themes include free will and the government, the effects of inflation and recession on spending patterns, the effects of investment on the economy, and the effect of income taxes on work incentive.*

Economic Maxims

"There is No Free Lunch." —MILTON FRIEDMAN

Therefore, everything consumed must be produced. Every dollar spent must be earned.

Prices are set by the (potential) buyers.
No person or company can make you buy their product (only government can do that). Unless the product and price attract a buyer, there will be no purchase.

Organizations don't exist; only people exist.
An organization is just a number of individuals who have some common interest(s).

We are all volunteers.
We cannot be effectively coerced into doing what we don't want to do. We can be prevented from doing what we want to do.

Observations

- People are diverse in talent, skills, desires, and interests. No matter how you write the rules, 10 percent of the people will fail. But the rules must be written for the 90 percent. The 10 percent can be treated as exceptions.
- We cannot spend ourselves rich. We can only earn and invest to become rich.
- People have three working speeds:
  1. They work for someone who can't or won't fire them, typically government.
  2. They work for someone who can fire them, typically a business.
  3. They work for themselves.
- People have four spending modes:
  1. Spend their own money (money they've earned) on themselves (private economy).
  2. Spend money they've earned on someone else (private charity).
  3. Spend someone else's money on themselves (see the Senate office building).
  4. Spend someone else's money on someone else (government programs).
- Inflation is much more detrimental to the long-term prosperity of people than is recession. When in a recession, people work harder, spend less, and are more careful about the expenditures they do make. This is a self-correcting mechanism. In inflation, the incentive of people is not to work harder, but to speculate; not to borrow less, but to borrow more; not to spend less, but to spend more.

Farmers in the 1970s perceived it in their best interest not to plant corn but to borrow more money to buy more farmland. People working a 40-hour job found it in their best interest to borrow more money and buy a bigger house. We engendered a belief that you can spend yourself rich and, as long as interest rates were well below inflation, it worked.

This was done at the expense of the savers of the world. As long as people were willing to take 5.25 percent interest on their savings, others were able to borrow at 7.5 percent (pretax) and buy houses that appreciated by 10 percent. This worked fine for borrowers, but it didn't do much for savers.

Then savers got smart and raised interest rates. The tables turned, and they remain turned today. Savers can now earn enough on their savings to offset inflation, pay the taxes, and have a penny or two left over. Today, borrowing a lot of money to buy a big house is a losing proposition. From 1965 to 1980 it was a winning proposition. Yet that fact educated a whole generation in the belief that they could spend themselves rich. You cannot spend yourself rich, individually or nationally.

- The economy is not strengthened by spending; it is strengthened by investment. My grandfather farmed with horses. One hundred years ago, two-thirds of the American public were farmers, and they farmed with horses. We live much better than they did with a lot less effort, not because they spent a lot, or because we spend a lot, but because people invested time and effort (or in lieu of that, they invested savings) in ideas ranging from Ford's car and tractor to McCormick's reaper and Edison's electric power. Today we benefit from these investments. If those people had spent their money (after all, wine, women, and song have always been available), we would not have these items today.

  Mr. Singer, who invented the sewing machine, when asked why, said, "For the money." We are taught today that greed is a negative emotion. In some ways, greed is great. It makes a person very easy to motivate. I am grateful that Mr. Singer was greedy. It allows me to wear much better and cheaper clothing than my great-grandfather did, because he was reliant on my great-grandmother and her fingers and needle and thread for everything he wore.

Further Observation

You can force people to put in their time, but you can't force them to do anything useful. Any nonmarket economy is evidence of this. If you want the ultimate description of how much time can be spent doing little useful work, read Aleksandr Solzhenitsyn's *One Day in the Life of Ivan Denisovich*.

I have an uncle who is a farmer. A few years ago he toured Russia. When he returned, he told me it was no surprise to him that Russia had economic difficulties. He observed 11 people baling hay and, in his words, "doing the work I do with two." I commented that he thought of them as farmers. He said, "Yes, of course." I noted they were working not for themselves, but for the government.

Another Observation

The following excerpt is from an article entitled "When Economics Rises above Politics," by David R. Henderson, published in the *Wall Street Journal,* October 9, 1996:

> The Royal Swedish Academy of Sciences awarded the Nobel prize in economics to . . . William S. Vickrey . . . and James Mirrlees.
>
> Mr. Mirrlees . . . was an adviser to the British Labor Party. In 1971 he published an article in which he took as a given that the government should redistribute income from rich to poor. Making reasonable assumptions about people's skills and earning power, and taking account of tax rates' effect on the incentive to earn, Mr. Mirrlees used some heavy mathematics to calculate the top marginal tax rate the government should impose on high-income people. Any guesses about what he found? Was it 83 percent, the top rate in Britain at the time? Perhaps 70 percent, then the top U.S. rate? Not quite. The top marginal tax rate, concluded Mr. Mirrlees, should be no more than about 20 percent. Moreover, he found that the marginal tax rate should be that same 20 percent for everyone. In short, the optimal tax structure, said this left-wing economist, is what we now call a flat tax.

Mr. Mirrlees was stunned by his own result. "I must confess," he wrote, "that I had expected the rigorous analysis of income taxation in the utilitarian manner to provide arguments for high tax rates. It has not done so."

Mr. Vickrey, in an article in the *Palgrave Dictionary of Economics,* wrote that the marginal tax rate on the highest-skilled person in society should be zero. . . . "There is no point to deterring him from earning the last dollar of income, since if he does not earn it there will be no revenue from it." Arthur Laffer couldn't have said it better. . . . Mr. Vickrey wrote [in 1964]: "There still remains the fact that money income from gainful work is subject to an income tax while imputed income from leisure is not taxed. . . . Accordingly, an income tax tends to make individuals choose leisure in preference to gainful work to an uneconomical extent.

Folks, my conclusions aren't novel or new, but they require politicians to relinquish some of our tax money and therefore some of their power. And politics is all about power.

One Family's Perspective on the U.S. Federal Budget

This essay was originally published in Muhlenkamp Memorandum, *Issue 4, April 1988. It was updated in 1992 and 2002. This essay looks at the federal budget and entitlement programs on a per-person basis, which allows people to review them in terms they understand. It points out that government spending is a concern not just because of debt, but because it removes money from the private sector. Every dollar the government spends, we, the taxpayers, must earn. There is no free lunch.*

When people set out to discuss the federal budget, they often get glassy-eyed after the first few $100 billion. We have all seen graphic examples of the sums involved, such as the stacks of dollar bills rising to the moon and beyond. Designed to help us understand the magnitude of federal finance, these visual aids are often as overwhelming as the raw numbers and don't really help at all.

I find it useful to view the federal budget in terms of cost per person or cost per household. Exhibit 5.4 does just that and allows me to determine what my family or I pay for each category. Note that the numbers in Exhibit 5.4 are for federal budgets only and do not include state and local budgets. In 2002, public education spent an additional $370 billion ($3,500 per family) at the state and local level. In 2006, public education spent an additional $431 billion ($3,767 per family) at the state and local level.

I have also gone one step further. Where possible, I calculated the dollars involved per intended recipient (very approximate). Thus retirees now average over $20,000 per household (1988) from Social Security, Medicare, and federal pensions.

We originally visited this subject in our spring 1988 newsletter where we calculated federal spending on a per-capita and per-household basis. We have updated that data in Exhibit 5.4. The 1992 budget for federal spending was 9 percent greater than in 1988 (after adjusting for inflation). In turn, the 2002 budget is 16 percent greater than the 1992 budget, again adjusted for inflation—and the 2006 budget is 14.5 percent greater than the 2002 budget, after adjusting for inflation.

While many people focus on the federal deficit, we've argued for years that the problem was in the level of government spending. Since every dollar spent by the government is a dollar removed from the free market, a primary source of weakness in the private sector is the increased level of government spending.

Coming to Grips

As you can see from Exhibit 5.4, the major growth segment in the federal budget is entitlements, particularly Social Security and Medicare. We have reached a point where the elderly constitute 15 percent of our population but receive over 60 percent of all federal social spending. Our politicians are well aware of this. Tip O'Neill was well aware of it a decade ago, and Barbara Jordan made a point of it at the Democratic Convention.

Few people realize that people who retired six years prior to 1992 had already received every dime they had ever paid into Social Security, and could expect to receive an additional three multiples of their contribution during their remaining lifetimes. (Yes, all of the numbers are

Exhibit 5.4 Federal Budget Programs, 1988–2002

	1988	1992	2002	$/CAP	$/Household	Number of Recipients (millions)	Dollars per Recipient
				2002	2002	2002	2002
Population (millions)	245	257	288				
Number of households (millions)	90	95	105				
Consumer Price Index (CPI)	355	424	533				
Category (in billions of dollars)	1988	1992	2002	2002	2002	2002	2002
Social Security	219	288	456	$ 1,583	$ 4,343	46.45	$ 9,817
Medicare	79	119	231	$ 802	$ 2,200	40.4	$ 5,718
Federal pensions	47	58	83	$ 288	$ 790	2.65	$ 31,321
Income security★	83	142	230	$ 799	$ 2,190		
Veterans	29	34	51	$ 177	$ 486		
Defense	290	298	349	$ 1,212	$ 3,324		
International affairs	10	16	22	$ 76	$ 210		
Energy	3	5	0	$ —	$ —		
Science	11	16	21	$ 73	$ 200		
Resources and environment	15	20	29	$ 101	$ 276		
Agriculture	17	15	22	$ 76	$ 210	0.8	$ 27,500

Commerce and housing	9	8	0	$ —	$ —
Transportation	27	33	62	$ 215	$ 590
Community	5	7	13	$ 45	$ 124
Education	31	43	71	$ 247	$ 676
Health	44	89	197	$ 684	$ 1,876
Justice	9	14	34	$ 118	$ 324
General government	9	13	17	$ 59	$ 162
Undistributed offsetting	−37	−39	−48	$ (167)	$ (457)
Receipts Net interest	152	199	171	$ 594	$ 1,629
Total outlays★★	**1064**	**1382**	**2011**	**$ 6,983**	**$ 19,152**
Revenues	909	1091	1853		
Deficit ★★	−155	−290	−158		
Total outlays in $ 2002	**1597**	**1737**	**2011**		
Increase from previous year shown		9%	16%		
Total federal outlays as a percentage of GDP	**21.2%**	**22.2%**	**19.5%**		

★Income security includes unemployment compensation, food stamps, Supplemental Security Income (SSI), Temporary Assistance for Needy Families (TANF), and Earned Income Tax Credit (EIC).

★★May not add up due to rounding.

Source: Office of Budget and Management, Historical Tables, Budget of U.S. Government, Fiscal Year 2004.

adjusted for inflation and company contributions. Details are available upon request.) In 1992, $14 billion in Social Security benefits went to people with cash incomes over $100,000 per year. In 2002, the numbers are higher. I've yet to hear an argument why anyone with assets over $1 million or income over $50,000 should receive more from Social Security than they paid into it.

Although I am encouraged by the changes that I see proposed, considered, and discussed in this fascinating political year, I will remain skeptical of the American public's desire to reach a solution to our economic problems until I see them come to grips with the simple arithmetic of the federal budget and Social Security.

2007 Update

(Note: Between 2002 and 2006 the Office of Budget and Management (which is the source of our data) changed its classifications in ways that make it difficult to compare the old numbers with the new numbers. So we've listed the comparison prior to 2002 using the earlier classifications in Exhibit 5.4, and the comparison of 2002 and 2006 using the current classifications in Exhibit 5.5.)

In 2007, very little has changed except that many other departments, from Education to Defense to Agriculture, are now vying with Social Security and Medicare as the fastest-growing segments of federal spending. See Exhibit 5.5.

The Inflation Time Bomb

This essay was originally published in Muhlenkamp Memorandum, *Issue 9, June 1989.*

In 1989, a friend of Ron's was widowed. She went to a well-known financial planner (who was also a friend of Ron's), and the financial planner told her that, as a widow, she shouldn't be taking risks with her money. Therefore, she should invest in a ladder of Treasury bonds. (A ladder means you own bonds of a number of different maturities, so that no matter what interest rates do, some of the bonds are appropriate. Of course, it's also an admission that you have no idea what interest rates will, in fact, do.) The planner ran projections out 15 years, and she looked pretty good.

Exhibit 5.5 United States Government Statements of Net Cost

	2002	2006
Population	288	299
Number of Households (millions)	109	114
Consumer Price Index (CPI)	533	597
Gross Domestic Product (GDP) (billions)	10,470	13,247

Years Ended September 30, 2002 and 2006 (In billions of dollars)	Sep–02 Net Cost	Sep–06 Net Cost	$/Cap 2006	$/Household 2006	$/Recipient 2006
Department of Defense	406.5	633.9	$ 2,120	$ 5,561	
Department of Health & Human Services	472.9	627.4	$ 2,098	$ 5,504	
Social Security Administration	492.6	592.8	$ 1,983	$ 5,200	$ 14,000
Interest on Treasury securities held by the public	175.4	221.5	$ 741	$ 1,943	
Department of Veterans Affairs	215.8	113.8	$ 381	$ 998	$ 28,500
Department of Agriculture	70.9	97.6	$ 326	$ 856	
Department of Education	45.1	92.6	$ 310	$ 812	
Department of the Treasury	62.4	81.4	$ 272	$ 714	
Department of Transportation	63.8	66.0	$ 221	$ 579	
Department of Energy	–7.8	65.8	$ 220	$ 577	
Department of Homeland Security	—	56.6	$ 189	$ 496	
Department of Labor	64.7	48.2	$ 161	$ 423	
Department of Housing and Urban Development	34.1	42.0	$ 140	$ 368	
Department of Justice	27.2	27.6	$ 92	$ 242	
Office of Personnel Management	0.2	19.7	$ 66	$ 173	
National Aeronautics and Space Administration	14.6	19.2	$ 64	$ 168	
Department of the Interior	14.3	17.1	$ 57	$ 150	
Department of State	10	13.8	$ 46	$ 121	
Agency for International Development	8	10.4	$ 35	$ 91	

Exhibit 5.5 (Continued)

Years Ended September 30, 2002 and 2006 (In billions of dollars)	Sep-02 Net Cost	Sep-06 Net Cost	$/Cap 2006	$/Household 2006	$/Recipient 2006
Environmental Protection Agency	7.7	9.6	$ 32	$ 84	
Department of Commerce	6.2	8.2	$ 27	$ 72	
Federal Communications Commission	5.7	7.6	$ 25	$ 67	
Railroad Retirement Board	9.3	7.1	$ 24	$ 62	
National Science Foundation	4.2	5.7	$ 19	$ 50	
Federal Deposit Insurance Corporation	1.1	1.7	$ 6	$ 15	
Small Business Administration	0.8	1.4	$ 5	$ 12	
U.S. Nuclear Regulatory Commission	0.2	0.4	$ 1	$ 4	
General Services Administration	-0.4	0.4	$ 1	$ 4	
National Credit Union Administration	-0.3	0.1	$ 0	$ 1	
Tennessee Valley Authority	1.1	-0.5	$ (2)	$ (4)	
Export-Import Bank of the United States	1.5	-0.2	$ (1)	$ (2)	
Pension Benefit Guaranty Corporation	11.8	-4.3	$ (14)	$ (38)	
U.S. Postal Service	16.7	-12.7	$ (42)	$ (111)	
All other entities	22	30.5	$ 102	$ 268	
Total*	**2260**	**2901**	**$ 9,703**	**$ 25,450**	
Consolidated revenues	1878	2441			
Unmatched transactions and balances	17	11			
Net operating cost (government deficit)	-365	-450			
Total cost in 2006 dollars	**2531**	**2901**			
Increase from previous year shown		14.6%			
Total federal cost as a percentage of GDP	21.6%	21.9%			

*May not add up due to rounding.

SOURCE: Office of Budget and Management, Financial Report of the U.S. Government, Fiscal Years 2002 and 2006.

> *Ron pointed out to the financial planner that this plan would protect the widow against the short-term risk of volatility, but did nothing to protect her against the long-term risk of inflation, which would likely be the greater risk since her financial needs were long-term. (See the essay, "What Is Risk?" later in this chapter.) Not only that, given the interest rates of the time and her level of spending, she would have depleted her assets in less than 25 years. The lady was only 52 years old.*
>
> *The advice the financial planner gave to the widow was not unusual. His advice was firmly rooted in the conventional wisdom of the time. Ron wrote "The Inflation Time Bomb" to point out what he saw as a major weakness of that conventional wisdom.*

The very rules that we were taught to conserve principal have become a trap. Today, people are desperately trying to maintain their incomes by buying investments with high yields, believing that if they "spend only the income—don't touch the principal," the value of their assets and their incomes will remain intact. But it's a trap!

Suppose in 1967 you were a 52-year-old widow attempting to live off your investment income. Your house was paid for, and you had $200,000 in investable assets. At the then-prevailing interest rate of 4.5 percent, these assets generated $9,000 per year. In 1967, the dollar was worth 3.72 times what it is today (in 1989), so you were able to live rather nicely on this income (3.72 × $9,000 = $33,500 in 1989 dollars). See Exhibit 5.6.

Then came inflation, and with it higher interest rates. By 1981 inflation was 10 percent and interest rates were 14 percent. Notice from

Exhibit 5.6 Effect of "Spend the Income—Don't Touch the Principal"

Age	Year	Principal	Interest Rate	Interest "Income"	Inflation	CPI	Value of Dollar*	Purchasing Power of Income*
52	1967	$200,000	4.50%	$9,000	1%	100	3.72	$33,500
66	1981	$200,000	14.00%	$28,000	10%	281	1.32	$37,000
74	1989	$200,000	8.00%	$16,000	5%	372	1.00	$16,000
79	1994a	$200,000	8.00%	$16,000	5%	475	0.78	$12,500
	1994b	$200,000	5.00%	$10,000	1%	390	0.95	$9,500

*Value of dollar and purchasing power of income are stated in 1989 dollars.

Exhibit 5.6 that because interest rates rose slightly more than the consumer price index (CPI) during this period, your income kept pace with the CPI; the purchasing power of your income held up. You were feeling pretty comfortable—and the time bomb was set to go off.

In 1981, we said that one of two things could happen:

1. The time bomb could go off slowly. Inflation could stay at 10 percent and interest rates could stay at 14 percent. Each year, your income would lose 10 percent of its purchasing power, thereby cutting it in half in only seven years.
2. The time bomb could go off quickly. Inflation and interest rates could decline significantly. Income would drop with interest rates. The result would be a rapid loss of the purchasing power of your income.

We all know that the time bomb went off quickly. As inflation fell, so did interest rates.

Fourteen percent CDs are no more. Our widow and her friends living off the income from their assets have seen their incomes and purchasing power shrink since 1981. They search for the highest payouts available, trying to maintain their incomes. Although vigorous and healthy at 75, they find it increasingly difficult to maintain the homes they love and to visit the grandchildren they love even more. But the squeeze is not over yet!

Inflation as a Defining Factor

Today (1989) we are set up to repeat the process. Those assuming that interest rates will stay at 8 percent are implicitly assuming inflation of 5 percent, in which case purchasing power will shrink 27 percent in only five years. If, in fact, we get inflation down to 1 or 2 percent, interest rates of 5 percent are much more likely, and income will be cut rapidly once again. These scenarios are shown in Exhibit 5.6 as 1994a and 1994b. One of them will happen; it's already built in.

In a period of only 27 years, people living on the income from their assets will have lost two-thirds of their purchasing power. They will have done this while following the "spend only the income—don't touch the principal" rule, which was meant to protect their assets from shrinking.

They've been snookered because they think in terms of principal and income, rather than purchasing power.

When inflation was 10 percent, the principal had to grow by 10 percent per year merely to offset inflation. Only the additional 4 percent interest (on the 14 percent CD) was spendable if the purchasing power of the principal was to be maintained. Today (1989), at 5 percent inflation, the principal must grow at 5 percent just to offset inflation. Whether in the form of income or appreciation, only those returns in excess of inflation represent gains in purchasing power.

The crime of inflation is that it depletes the value (purchasing power) of money, both assets and income. Our federal government sets standards for weights and measures so that no merchant can cheat you on a pound of sugar or a gallon of gas. But it sets no standard on the purchasing power of money, allowing itself to cheat you out of the value of your savings. Contrary to popular opinion, only governments can create inflation because only governments can print money.

"Spend only the income—don't touch the principal" is a superb discipline when inflation is zero. But it becomes a trap when inflation soars. People really believed that if they didn't touch their principal, it would stay intact. So they invested only for income. Only now are they discovering that assets must grow with inflation, or the income they receive will be rapidly depleted.

2007 Update

It took a little longer than five years, but the outcome we warned about has come to pass. We have added two lines to the table. (Refer to Exhibit 5.7.) For 1994 we've used an average of interest rates over the 1993–1995 period to smooth out the dramatic swings of the period. For 2006 we've used the current interest rates.

The right-hand column demonstrates the effect of inflation on the conservative rule of "spend only the income—don't touch the principal." As we round-tripped from inflation of 1 percent back to 2 percent over a 39-year period, the purchasing power of the income fell by 81 percent as the value of the dollar fell by 81 percent.

Exhibit 5.7   Effect of "Spend the Income—Don't Touch the Principal" (Updated)

Age	Year	Principal	Interest Rate	Interest "Income"	Inflation	CPI	Value of Dollar*	Purchasing Power of Income*
52	1967	$200,000	4.50%	$9,000	1%	100	3.72	$33,500
66	1981	$200,000	14.00%	$28,000	10%	281	1.32	$37,000
74	1989	$200,000	8.00%	$16,000	5%	372	1.00	$16,000
79	1994a	$200,000	8.00%	$16,000	5%	475	0.78	$12,500
	1994b	$200,000	5.00%	$10,000	1%	390	0.95	$9,500
2006 Update								
79	93–95**	$200,000	6.76%	$13,520	2.8%	449	0.83	$11,222
91	2006	$200,000	5.00%	$10,000	2.0%	571	0.65	$6,500

*Value of Dollar and Purchasing Power of Income are stated in 1989 dollars.
** Numbers are an average for the years 1993 to 1995.

Editor's Note

So what happened to Ron's widow friend? Well, in 1989, she let Ron invest her assets in a diversified portfolio of common stocks instead of the ladder of Treasury bonds that the financial planner recommended. Nearly 20 years later, her assets are greater than they were then, adjusted for inflation, and her spending has exceeded what the bonds would have provided. If she had taken the advice of the financial planner and invested solely in Treasury bonds, she would have had interest income, but she would have had to live on less and would have consumed the principal.

Defusing the Inflation Time Bomb

This essay was originally published in Muhlenkamp Memorandum, *Issue 10, July 1989, in response to questions about "The Inflation Time Bomb." It discusses alternatives an investor faces in trying to maintain purchasing power. (Numbers for 2007 are in parentheses, where appropriate.)*

The intent of "The Inflation Time Bomb" was to point out that long-term investment planning that focuses only on dollars and income, while ignoring purchasing power and assets, can be a trap. Dollars must be adjusted for inflation to get purchasing power, and incomes must be adjusted for the loss of purchasing power. Without these adjustments, assets will be depleted and so will income.

The problems that arise from neglecting to make these adjustments have come to the fore over the past 30 years as inflation created large differences between nominal and real interest rates. They have been exacerbated by the fact that many people now seek to retire and live off the income produced by their assets for 20 or 30 years. If you are planning this same sort of "live off the income" strategy, we cannot emphasize the following point enough: Only those returns in excess of inflation can be spent if purchasing power is to be maintained over long periods of time.

Given the task of maintaining purchasing power versus inflation, an investor faces three natural investment markets: short-term debt, long-term debt, and equities.

Short-Term Debt

From the borrower's perspective, short-term debt finances such items as installment and credit card purchases, corporate inventories, and government working capital. From the saver's perspective, short-term debt includes passbook savings accounts, Treasury bills, certificates of deposit, commercial paper, and money market funds. Anyone who has a 9 percent (4.5 percent in 2007) CD, for example, and is paying 18 percent on a credit card balance is participating on both sides of the short-term debt market, and paying dearly for the privilege.

Historically, rates available to savers on these investments have roughly equaled inflation. That is, with no effort and little risk you've made no real money—*after* inflation. Only since 1981 have these rates consistently exceeded inflation, after being well below inflation during the 1970s. Because returns in the short-term debt markets cannot be expected to beat inflation for long periods of time, there is no reason to believe the current, 1989, premium over inflation will endure.

Long-Term Debt

From a borrower's perspective, long-term debt finances factories, homes, and government spending. From an investor's perspective, long-term debt takes the form of corporate bonds, Fannie Mae and Ginnie Mae mortgage pools, and Treasury and municipal bonds. Differences in interest rates among these securities reflect creditworthiness, time-to-maturity, and taxation (municipals).

Historically, long-term debt of good quality has returned about 2 to 3 percent annually over inflation. In the 1970s, it returned substantially less; in the 1980s, substantially more. (For a look at these same numbers from a borrower's perspective, see our "Wake Up, America—Houses Don't Make You Money!" essay earlier in this chapter.) There is no reason, however, to expect to earn more than 3 percent over inflation for very long. Therefore, if you own long-term bonds and want to maintain purchasing power, spend only about 3 percent of your assets per year. If you think inflation and interest rates will decline and want to lock in current rates, be sure the bonds you buy are noncallable.

Equity

Equity investments represent ownership and are normally long-term. Equity ownership can be real estate, tangible assets, or business enterprise. It can be sole ownership, partnership, or shares in a corporation. Most investors hold real estate through sole ownership of their homes, and corporate enterprise through shares of stock. Corporate shares are usually more liquid than real estate—that is, they can be bought and sold much more readily. This advantage is partly offset by the short-term volatility of share prices.

The key is to focus on the long-term nature of equity investing and not get caught up in short-term price oscillations. Long-term studies of total returns from owning common stocks of corporations demonstrate returns of 5 to 7 percent annually over inflation. Some of this return comes as dividends and some as capital gains. No one disputes that returns from equity investments are higher than those from debt. However, there are a lot of misleading opinions as to why they are higher.

Corporate stocks provide higher returns than corporate bonds because management works for the stockholder and against the bondholder. No management will borrow money (issue bonds) unless it expects to profit from the investment of those funds in its business. Thus, the return on stockholders' equity must be higher than corporate interest rates. Otherwise, management will cease to borrow, driving interest rates down. (In 1981 and 1982, when long-term interest rates exceeded the average corporate return on shareholder equity, this observation convinced us that interest rates had to fall.)

Similarly, every corporate treasurer has the same incentive that you and I have: to save money. They call high-rate bonds and reissue low-rate bonds; we refinance our high-rate mortgages. Looking at it from the lender's perspective, that's why most of the bonds we buy are noncallable. We want to avoid having our high-return investment rolled into one with a lower return.

Wall Street types say stocks provide higher returns than bonds because they are riskier. But Wall Street's definition of *risk* is volatility—that is, how much prices fluctuate on a daily, weekly, or monthly basis. We believe most people's definition of risk is the probability of losing money. These are fundamentally different views.

In 1987, stock market volatility was very high—both up and down. No one complained about the volatility up, only the volatility down. The total return for the 12 months was roughly zero. Any businessman will tell you that to have a disaster and break even for the year isn't bad. The key is to view equity investments as long-term business investments, with a horizon of at least three years. This means that if your planned use for the funds invested is next year's vacation, or college tuition two years from now, don't buy long-term stocks or bonds. But if you'll need the funds for retirement 10, 15, or 20 years down the road, don't worry about price oscillations.

Editor's Note

Notice that even though in 1989 short-term rates exceeded inflation, Ron did not expect it to last. And it didn't. He didn't have a crystal ball. He simply looked at the historical data, understood it, and applied it. Historically, interest rates on short-term debt equal inflation, interest rates on long-term debt are 2 to 3 percent over inflation, and common stocks return 5 to 7 percent over inflation. So for the long-term investor (more than three years), stocks normally perform better than bonds.

What Is Risk?

This essay was originally published in Muhlenkamp Memorandum, *Issue 11, October 1989. It discusses risk in two categories: the risk of volatility and the risk of losing money. It also discusses long-term investing and diversification as preventive measures to these risks. The 2005 update suggests a third, often overlooked risk: paying too much for a stock in the first place. The preventive measure for this is knowing how to value stocks.*

When people seek investment advice, the first response from professionals is usually "How much risk can you take?" The ensuing discussion is then governed by the concept of *risk*. In today's financial world, however, the definition of risk used by professional financial planners and stockbrokers has become completely divorced from the definition that most people use.

We believe most people define risk as the possibility of losing money. At Muhlenkamp & Company, we define risk as the probability of losing purchasing power (i.e., money adjusted for inflation). But Wall Street has come to define risk as the volatility in price. By Wall Street's definition, those securities whose prices move the most (up or down) in a short period of time are considered the riskiest. Those whose prices don't move, like certificates of deposit, are considered the safest. We reject this definition of risk. We call price volatility *volatility*.

In the late 1960s and early 1970s, when Wall Street and academia started using computers to study patterns in stock prices, they, too, spoke of volatility, but few people read their articles. So they began calling volatility *risk,* and more people took notice. Unfortunately, they have gone on to speak of volatility risk as if it were the only risk, and they have built elaborate schemes to limit the volatility of portfolios, often with little or no thought to the underlying assumptions.

Feature articles in the *Wall Street Journal* on September 19 and 20, 1989, stated that many pension funds are currently investing in real estate. Despite poor returns, pension fund managers are doing so because real estate prices (which are set by appraisals) seem to fluctuate less than stock prices (which are priced every day). These people have convinced themselves that real estate is less risky than stocks simply because it is not priced every day.

Expanding Your Horizons

We would like to make several points here. The first consideration in investing is time horizon. Most investors, like most businesspeople, should have a time horizon of at least three years—the minimum time for long-term dynamics to come into play. Pension funds have horizons best measured in decades. For a pension fund to worry about how much the prices of its assets fluctuated in 1987 makes about as much sense as a farmer worrying about how much his crops grew in February or a ski shop owner worrying about his July sales. For both these businessmen, a year is the minimum period of measurement, and since each can expect two or three poor years in a decade, a three- to five-year period is the more appropriate minimum.

The same is true of pension funds. Pension funds should truly be long-term investors. Yet Wall Street's concentration on the "risk" of vola-tility has pension funds focusing on *quarterly* returns. (The longest base we have seen for the measurement of volatility is one year.) The real irony is that these same pension funds are overseen by businesspeople who know that in their business the appropriate time frame for measurement is at least three to five years. We have seen any number of astute businesspeople who manage their companies for long-term real growth in value but manage their pension funds by criteria that are short-term and artificial.

For 20 years, we have watched corporate management invest pension funds in a manner that is the opposite of what they were currently doing in managing their companies. They continue to do so today. To improve their corporate returns, many companies are currently selling real estate and buying back stock. Their pension plans are simultane-ously doing the exact opposite (buying real estate and selling stocks). Obviously, they're using different criteria in evaluating these assets. We fail to understand why.

Many people are impressed with the money they make on their houses. They price their houses once every five or 10 years and are per-fectly willing to wait six months to get a fair price when selling. Warren Buffett has said he wouldn't care if they closed the stock market for two years. Peter Lynch says the market (i.e., daily prices) is irrelevant to investing. Both individuals have great investment records. So the answer seems to be, if you want to get rid of the risk of volatility, don't price your portfolio so often. We don't understand why pension funds are happy with their real estate investments, but not with their company (stock) investments.

A caveat: Volatility is a risk. If you had to sell on October 19, 1987, either for financial or psychological reasons, it was a very important risk. But the solution is to not get into a position where you have to sell in a short period of time. Any businessman, whether a farmer or a ski shop owner, who didn't keep enough working capital to get through the slow season, would be called a fool. Any investor who invests money needed for groceries in the next few months will soon be called needy.

To succeed as an investor, you must adopt the attitude and time perspective of a businessperson, not that of an hourly employee. What we tried to point out in our "Inflation Time Bomb" essay is that the securities whose prices are least volatile in the short term are most likely to cost you purchasing power in the long term. Conversely, those assets that are most likely to enhance your purchasing power long-term are often most volatile in price short-term. Wall Street's focus on the short term and faulty definition of *risk* lead most people to invest in ways that are counter to their long-term financial goals.

Diversifying for Maximum Return

The second parameter in the discussion of risk is the possibility of losing money. Any investment asset has the possibility of losing money, even though the probability of gain is high. That's the reason for diversification. But this does not mean you should diversify into poor investments.

A financial planner might tell you that if you have stocks, bonds, real estate, mortgages, and commercial paper, you are diversified. But he's looking at pieces of paper, not the companies (and people) behind them. We will tell you that if your real estate is under a Sears store, your mortgage is on the Sears store, your stock is in Sears, your bonds are Sears bonds, and your commercial paper is with Sears, you are not diversified! You simply have several pieces of paper with the same name on them. And Sears management is working to minimize your return on four of these five pieces of paper. Why would you want management working against you?

We believe you are much more diversified if you invest in good companies in five different industries. Finally, put the management of these companies to work for you instead of against you; own their common stock.

2005 Update

We've just come through a period when Wall Street's definition of risk proved to be a trap. In 1999 and early 2000, many people were caught up in the Wall Street fad centered on Internet, telecom, and technology stocks. Most of the people who played these stocks knew they were speculating.

As an offset to this speculation, many invested in "quality growth stocks" (or funds), believing that such stocks were safe because of their low volatility, or low beta. So they felt safe investing in Coca-Cola, Disney, General Electric, and Home Depot. But these stocks, partly because of their reputations, were selling well above their values as companies. Each then had its stock decline by more than 50 percent.

The big risk in stock investing is not volatility; it's paying too much for the company or its stock.

2007 Update

Many companies are currently selling bonds and real estate to buy back their stocks. Their pension plans are selling stocks to buy bonds and real estate. Yep, it's 1989 being repeated.

This Is 20/20

This essay was originally published in Muhlenkamp Memorandum, *Issue 12, January 1990. It looks back at the international growth of free-market economies since the 1960s and their effect on America's economic position in 1990. By understanding the past, we can better assess the present and better prepare for the future.*

As a new year and a new decade begin, there is a great human temptation to predict the future. At Muhlenkamp & Company, we don't know how to predict the future, so we don't try. Those who *do* try have proven that they don't know how either, so we don't feel too bad.

We do find it useful to assess the present. An accurate assessment of the present is often the best available predictor of the future. Understanding the past is in turn a key to understanding the present, so while everyone else is telling you how the 1990s will be, we'll review some history to obtain a perspective on where we are today. This risks falling prey to the "Lightning Bug Effect," but we'll take our chances.

The Lightning Bug Effect
(Some call it hindsight.)

The Lightning Bug is a brilliant bug
but its vision is in the past;
It flies through the darkness
with its headlight on its . . . [posterior].
—*Author Unknown*

From 1945 to 1968 the United States exemplified the strength of a free-market economy. Other countries (primarily Western European) also utilized free markets, but most were somewhat less free and less successful. U.S. advantages in climate, raw materials, size, and lack of war damage were often the rationale for the differences.

During much of this time, the Soviet socialist economy was believed to be improving. Intellectual discussion focused on the rivalry between the United States and the Soviet Union, economically as well as militarily. Although the United States was obviously ahead, the Soviet Union appeared to be gaining on us. This apparent rivalry was prolonged by the economic problems of inflation and stagnation that the United States experienced in the 1970s, so that by 1979 few people viewed the United States as an unqualified economic success. Meanwhile, economic experiments on the other side of the globe were coming to fruition. Free-market economies in the Far East, particularly Japan and Hong Kong, achieved undeniable success, with none of the natural advantages of the United States.

By 1979, Japan's economy had grown to be a major player on the world scene, and its currency a potential alternative to the U.S. dollar. A combination of yen strength and dollar weakness forced President Carter to name Paul Volcker as chairman of the U.S. Federal Reserve, with a charter to reduce inflation and strengthen the dollar. Thus a U.S.

domestic economic policy was dictated by international concerns, an unusual occurrence in the postwar period. Shortly thereafter, Jimmy Carter was himself replaced by Ronald Reagan, as the U.S. electorate responded to domestic economic concerns.

Ronald Reagan's success in reviving the U.S. economy demonstrated that the problems of the 1970s were a result of poor policies, and not endemic to free markets. The continued success of free-market economies in the Far East reinforced this point, as did improvements in Great Britain. In France, François Mitterrand was elected in 1981 as a Socialist, but within a year he had to reverse his policies and move toward free markets.

Finally, as 1990 neared, it became apparent that socialist and communist economies were not improving the lot of their citizenry. Even their governments admitted it. The ruble is acknowledged to be so worthless that the Russian government has reportedly offered to pay its farmers incentives in dollars to encourage them to increase output. Can you imagine the U.S. government offering to pay postal workers in yen? Some U.S. congressmen and a few intellectuals may continue to argue whether Reaganomics and free markets work, but the rest of the world has no doubts!

Today, the majority of Americans believe our biggest competitor is Japan. This means that the contest is economic, not military. Japan is the ultimate example of achieving economically that which it could not achieve militarily. And just as we have been challenged by Japan, she is now challenged by Korea, Thailand, and Malaysia. With a little luck, a decade from now these Asian tigers will in turn be challenged by Poland and other countries of Eastern Europe.

To sum up, today it has been shown that:

1. Free economies work. Socialist economies don't. Free markets are ruled by and provide benefits to the consumer, who also happens to be the worker that Marx talked so much about.
2. Free economies work regardless of natural resource advantages or disadvantages.
3. Growth is not inflationary, although some Keynesian economists still believe that it is.
4. Russia appears to be capitulating. We believe a political reaction will come at some point, but it looks like changes in many areas of Eastern Europe are irreversible.

5. If the United States is not willing to lead the free world economically, others (Japan) are willing and able to do so. U.S. domestic economic policy will continue to be constrained by international markets, much as we've constrained other governments since 1945. It will be much harder for our government to inflate its way out of economic difficulties.

6. Our government's current focus is on lowering inflation (the Fed) and taxes (Congress). For the Fed, this continues the task of the past decade. For Congress, it's a new idea. Senator Moynihan doesn't like President Bush's proposal to lower capital gains taxes (for the rich), so he suggested lowering Social Security taxes (for the working man) as part of an overall package to raise income taxes. But the press (and probably the senator's office) is really only talking about the tax cut side of his proposal. The senator is an intelligent individual and a savvy politician, but someone is going to suggest that we cut capital gains taxes and Social Security taxes and skip any increase in income taxes (I think I just suggested it), and Congress will find that this is what people really want.

Those of you who have been with us for 10 years know that in 1980 we said that if Reagan could get inflation under control, we would have a good decade in the stock and bond markets. This has in fact happened. Anyone invested in the stock market for the past 10 years has quadrupled his money. More importantly, his purchasing power is up 2.5 times. But no one is celebrating. A pervasive fear exists that we will give it back. We think it's unlikely. The 1980s were a mirror image of the 1970s, when inflation and interest rates ran up, causing very poor returns in the stock and bond markets. We risk giving back the gains of the 1980s only if we reinflate. Today all the pressures, domestic and international, are against it. So we see inflation continuing below 5 percent. At that rate, current interest rates are fair, and stocks are fairly priced.

Editor's Note

In 1990, inflation was 5 percent, and Ron called the 30-year U.S. Treasury rates fair at 8 percent. He expected we would not reinflate (though many thought we would) because the domestic and international pressures were against it. In 2007, in spite of all the unforeseen international turmoil and market fluctuations we've seen since 1990, inflation is about 2 percent and the 30-year U.S. Treasury rates are 4 to 5 percent. By looking to the past to understand the present, he was able to assess long-term market conditions, because long-term market behavior is driven by economic principles.

Open Letter to My Congressman

This essay was originally published in Muhlenkamp Memorandum, *Issue 16, October 1990. At that time, much discussion in Washington, D.C., revolved around the federal budget deficit, taxes, government spending, and entitlement programs. The letter offers fresh ways of looking at all of these things and their effects on the economy and the American people.*

Dear Doug:

I am disturbed by the current state of affairs in Washington, D.C. You and your colleagues in Congress are addressing issues important to the future of our nation and our economy. Here are my thoughts on these issues.

Congress and the executive branch maintain that our biggest problem today is the budget deficit. The deficit has two parts—taxes and spending. Many would like to shrink the deficit by raising taxes, but we've tried that and it doesn't work. During the 1970s, we allowed inflation to raise effective tax rates to the highest level in our nation's history. People quit working, and the result was 10 percent unemployment and 10 percent inflation.

I'd like to make several points about taxes:

First, the focus seems to be on taxing the wealthy by raising income tax rates. Income is not wealth; wealth is assets. When you tax income, you tax those who are trying to become wealthy, not necessarily those who already are.

Second, a simple definition of wealth versus poverty is that the wealthy have more options. There would be no point in trying to become wealthy, through concentrated time and effort, if it did not increase your options.

Third, in the final analysis, the payment of taxes is voluntary. You can tax my income, but you cannot force me to earn it. Much of the political and economic dialogue of the past decade concerned the maximum tax rate at which people are encouraged to earn the most and, not incidentally, to pay the most taxes. Two of my offspring received their first real paychecks this year, and judging by their reactions to the amount withheld for taxes, we're pushing the limit. I know you're pushing my limit! If you raise my tax rates, I'll do less work. Even a mule will quit if you load him too heavily, and most people are smarter than mules.

If income taxes are too high, the wealthy will simply buy municipal bonds, or they'll buy farmland and get paid not to grow food. Doctors will defer income or play golf. Businesses will be managed to minimize taxes rather than to grow and to create new products and new jobs. This isn't hypothetical; we saw all of the above in the 1970s. They gave us 10 percent inflation and 10 percent unemployment. Do we really wish to return to those circumstances?

Among all income taxes, the most voluntary is capital gains. The truly wealthy, having the most options, can live off their dividends and interest. They have no need to sell appreciated assets.

Ronald Reagan knew that people work harder and produce more if you lighten the tax load. (Maybe it was his experience with horses.) So he lowered tax rates and people went to work, creating over 20 million new jobs. (Politicians don't seem to understand how jobs are created. Jobs are created when one person can benefit or profit from hiring another. If you tax away the profit, you tax away the job.) They also paid more in taxes. By 1990, federal tax receipts exceeded 1980 receipts by more than $240 billion *per year,* adjusted for inflation. In your wildest dreams, you've never imagined a "peace dividend" of $240 billion per year. Yet we have a "growth dividend" of $240 billion per year in tax receipts! Surely that's enough. But no, federal spending has grown even more.

Congress makes noises about cutting spending, but I see no real effort to do so. In the current year, each appropriations bill which went through the House was loaded with pet projects and pork barreling. Not one bill was held to the overall budget limits!

In your recent newsletter, you said you voted to limit spending on a number of provisions in these bills, but you never mentioned whether any actually passed. One was a provision to limit subsidy payments to farmers earning over $100,000 per year, hardly a draconian cut. The provision failed in the House by a two-to-one margin. This says to me that Congress is not interested in cutting subsidies, even to the wealthy.

You said at a recent town meeting that the effect of special interests in Congress is limited because you must get 218 representatives on the same side to pass anything. Yet experience shows that when a congressman adds pork to a bill, it stays in. No congressman has an incentive to delete another's line items, and the president isn't allowed to. The result is an inherent bias toward spending, which I've encouraged you to remedy by supporting a line-item veto.

I've noticed that your town meetings are well attended by people who receive checks from the federal government. Invariably they want more, and certainly not less. My wife characterized the theme of a recent meeting as "gimme." After attending a number of these meetings, I can understand why members of Congress believe they are elected to spend more money. Nevertheless, at election time the taxpayers have sent clear signals for over a decade that they're carrying as big a load as they're willing to carry.

So you're faced with a dilemma: how to keep your promises to the recipients of federal programs without raising taxes. The answer is: You can't! You've promised money you don't have, and you've promised money the taxpayer is unwilling to pay. For a decade we've made up the difference by borrowing, but we've exhausted our credit.

One of the great dangers of the current circumstance is that the dichotomy between taxpayers and recipients has become intergenerational. While taxes are paid by working people, 60 percent of federal outlays go to senior citizens and retirees. And the percentage is still climbing! In a recent debate, a spokesman for a senior group said that "Other than cost of living [adjustments], Social Security benefits to a retired individual haven't been raised since 1972." I don't know why these raises should exceed the cost of living in the first place, but as an individual worker my Social Security taxes have *tripled* in real terms since 1972. I'm 46, and I've already paid more in Social Security taxes than someone who retired five years ago. At the same time, anyone, rich or poor, who has been retired for five years has already received more from Social Security than they ever paid in, again adjusted for inflation. Enough already!

Entitlement programs such as Medicare, farm subsidies, and Social Security are always justified based on the financial need of the poorest participants. But the benefits paid out are not determined by need. As a consequence, the benefits go disproportionately to those who are not needy. The bulk of farm subsidies go to wealthy farmers. Wealthy retirees pay only 25 percent of the cost of their Medicare benefits. Five hundred thousand millionaires will receive Social Security benefits that exceed five times what they paid in. Taxpayers pay the rest—how is this equitable?

Congress is trying to cope with the intergenerational problem, in its own way. At the insistence of a group of senior citizens, Congress passed the Medicare Catastrophic Coverage Act of 1988, and provided that it be paid for by Medicare participants. Once they saw the cost, a larger group of senior citizens immediately got the bill repealed.

Several years ago, Tip O'Neill proposed taxing 85 percent of Social Security benefits. At the time, I wondered how he came to the 85 percent number. He used a study that concluded that the average Social Security recipient would receive benefits roughly seven times what he paid in. Or put another way, of the benefits received, only 15 percent represented personal contributions. Tip proposed taxing the other 85 percent. The proposal went nowhere, but the idea was again floated at the recent budget summit. Taxes would have been progressive, affecting only those retirees earning more than $25,000 per year. But at the first whisper of "tax Social Security," a great hue and cry shot the idea down.

So the summiteers turned to Medicare. I'm embarrassed at how long I thought Medicare was for poor people. Then I learned that Medicaid is for poor people. Medicare is simply for people over 65, rich or poor. Today, these people directly pay 25 percent of the cost of their Medicare. The budget summit proposed raising this to 30 percent through higher deductibles and copayments. Again the great hue and cry! I can sympathize with the complainers. I don't like paying the cost of medical insurance either, but I don't expect you to tax them to subsidize me.

I don't object to subsidizing the needy. But, as currently run, entitlement programs tax me and my children to subsidize people who are better off than we are simply because they've reached a certain age. A senior citizen told me he counted on Social Security and Medicare to provide a cushion to prevent his being a burden to his children. Someone should tell our seniors that the biggest financial burden their children have is paying for Social Security and Medicare!

Sincerely,
Ron Muhlenkamp

Editor's Note

There is no free lunch. Government spending is a response to constituents' demands for more. However, anything the government spends must ultimately come from taxes. And the taxpayers are also America's workers. If we overtax our workers, we risk economic stagnation (as in the 1970s).

Why I Like Long-Term Treasury Bonds Instead of CDs or Money Market Funds

Originally published in Muhlenkamp Memorandum, *Issue 18, October 1990, this essay discusses the "callability" of Treasury bonds, CDs, and money markets and how that influences their value as investment options.*

As we noted in an earlier essay entitled "Defusing the Inflation Time Bomb," it is unlikely in the future that short-term interest rates will stay significantly above inflation rates. Therefore, to get a real return, investors must opt for long-term debt (bonds) or equity (stocks). Each of these has associated risks, some of which are well known. We want to point out some of the risks in long-term bonds that are not well known or understood.

Price volatility is obviously one risk, but so is the risk of the bonds being paid off or "called" early. Just as individuals borrow mortgage money to buy houses, companies borrow bond money to finance expansion. The government also borrows bond money to fund the deficit. Similarly, just as people who took out mortgages at 12 percent or more have since refinanced them at lower rates, companies that issued bonds at 12 percent or more have called those bonds when interest rates fell. The government has not called its bonds, because most U.S. Treasury bonds are noncallable by law.

The reason we recommend long-term Treasury bonds to investors seeking income for three years or more is because we want to lock in current interest rates for a long period of time. We also want the decision of when to cash in these bonds to be ours, not the issuer's. Treasury bonds are quite liquid. They can be bought and sold on any given day. Therefore, buying a 20-year Treasury bond does not lock you in for 20 years. It merely allows you to decide when to sell it. Of course, as interest rates change, the price will fluctuate, but these fluctuations will decrease as time goes on and the time to maturity of the bond shortens.

A list of currently outstanding Treasury bonds appears in the *Wall Street Journal* every day under the heading "Treasury Bonds, Notes and Bills."[2] Items in this listing include:

- Rate: the nominal rate or coupon. The number of dollars paid out in interest per year per $100 of face value.
- Month/year: the maturity date of the bond.
- Bid and ask: currently quoted price.
- Ask/yield: the compounded yield-to-maturity based on the asking price. Note that higher coupons have higher prices so that the yields-to-maturity are similar.

As an example, on Wednesday, April 17, 1991, the 8.75 percent bond maturing in 2008 was priced at 104 to return 8.18 percent compounded to maturity. These bonds can be bought and sold any day through any stockbroker. Many banks, including Mellon and Pittsburgh National, now also have this capability. They charge a fee for this service.

Each quarter the U.S. Treasury also issues new bonds (borrows more money). Bonds of 3-, 10-, and 30-year maturities will be available at auction on May 7, 8, and 9, 1991, respectively. Check with your bank; sometimes they charge a lower fee on new issues.

Editor's Note

So if you choose to invest in bonds, be sure you understand whether and how they are callable. You want to be in control of when to cash them in. Bonds, like all financial products, are simply agreements written on paper. Read them— especially the fine print. Read them again and again, until you are sure you understand them. You want no surprises when it comes to your investments.

The More Things Change, the More They Stay the Same

This essay was originally published in Muhlenkamp Memo-randum, *Issue 19, July 1991. At that time, most economists agreed that the recession of 1990–1991 was over. However, they were concerned with the shape the recovery might take. Some economists feared that any strength in the gross national product (GNP) would result in higher inflation. Others feared that the recovery would be aborted by a combination of high inflation and modest growth in the money supply. The same economists had feared the same things in 1982, and they were wrong. Ron believed they were wrong again. There were no indications that we were headed toward inflation, and though he believed interest rates were still high (relative to inflation) and that might slow the recovery, he felt (contrary to most) that rates were likely to fall. Ron wrote this essay to explain why.*

One major function of recession is to dampen consumer enthusiasm, typically after years of growth. Another function is to make the public reevaluate and reappraise those areas where prices have gotten most out of line with economic reality.

During the 1970s, for example, farmers who sold land for twice its economic price watched their neighbors bid it still higher. In Texas, the assumption that the price of oil could only increase drove other prices up as well, especially real estate. Oil and farmland were subsequently reappraised in the recession of 1980–1982, but the rest of the country ignored the warnings. During the 1980s, the public's perception of ever-rising real estate prices was unshakeable. Eventually it became apparent that the economic realities of both commercial and residential real estate had changed dramatically from the 1970s. In 1987, we wrote an essay entitled "Wake Up, America—Houses Don't Make You Money!" attempting to point out these changes. We received many responses of "Yes, but not in Boston" or "Yes, but not in Washington D.C.," Philadelphia, and so on. Real estate nationwide is now in the process of being reappraised.

Among homeowners we are seeing a shift in attitudes and actions from "trade up on equity" to "prepay the mortgage." Demographers have been saying for years that when the baby boomers turn 40-something, their focus would shift from borrowing for houses to saving for college tuition. We suspect that the traumatic events of 1990 (recession and the Gulf War) may have helped to accelerate this shift. We don't yet know how large the shift will be, and we are not likely to know for some time. But any shift at all will have tremendous effects on the shape of our economy for at least the next decade.

While the 30-something baby boomers have been paying high interest rates without giving it critical thought, their retired parents have been receiving correspondingly high rates on their savings, and assuming it would continue indefinitely. These retirees were taught to "protect principal and spend income," a rule of thumb that works well in a low inflation (0 to 1 percent) environment. But they continued to use this rule when inflation soared to over 10 percent in 1980–1982 and then settled at 2 to 5 percent for a number of years. Such inflation destroyed much of the purchasing power of their principal (see our essay "The Inflation Time Bomb") without their knowledge. They only became aware of the destruction when interest rates (and thus their income) subsequently fell.

During the first leg down in interest rates in the early 1980s, many bought high-yield bond funds or other securities which promised high incomes, only to discover that the promises were empty. Many lost sizable portions of their assets. We are now in the midst of a repeat of that experience. Many retirees have come to depend on interest income yields of 8 to 9 percent. Yet, since last winter, short-term rates have dropped to 5 to 6 percent. Relying on their rule of thumb, many retirees are facing a spending cutback of up to 30 percent. Some are simply hoping for a return to higher rates (very unlikely, in our opinion). Others are moving money to various areas where they are promised (often only implicitly) rates of 8 to 9 percent. Some of the things they are buying will not fulfill that promise.

As investors, our thoughts on solutions to this dilemma have been covered in earlier essays. Our point in this essay is that, in addition to a reappraisal and subsequent lower spending by baby boomers, we are also likely to see a reappraisal and a reduction in spending by retirees as well. Such a reappraisal would reinforce the decline in interest rates we've been warning about.

Editor's Note

When the economic climate changes, there is often a lag in public perception. Recessions and traumatic events often trigger a reassessment by the public, which then gets things caught up to reality.

In the 1970s, prices of real estate and oil got out of line with reality. The recession of 1980–1982 brought back oil and farmland. The recession of 1990 brought back interest rates. In 1999, tech stock prices got out of line with reality. There was a recession in 2001, and the tech stocks gave it all back. Short-term emotions and lags in perception can make the stock market stray from reality. Eventually the perceptions catch up with reality, and the market returns to rational pricing.

Basic Financial Maxims I Want My Kids to Know

This essay was originally published in Muhlenkamp Memorandum, *Issue 19, July 1991. Although addressed to Ron's children, the maxims in this essay are useful no matter who you are. As Ron says, "I often see people in their sixties and seventies making basic financial mistakes, even though they may know better. We all need to be reminded of the basics, even if we already know them." And yes, Ron reviews them periodically himself.*

"There is No Free Lunch." —MILTON FRIEDMAN
There's no free income either.
The essentials of life are cheap. Only the luxuries are expensive.

A bad product is always a bad deal. Don't buy a car or appliance with a poor service record. Don't buy a house with a cracked foundation.

A good product can be a bad deal if the price is wrong. How do you know a good price? Shop around and be willing to walk away from any "bargain."

The purpose of insurance is to protect against financial disaster. Any loss that is nonfinancial cannot be remedied by insurance.

Any loss that is not a disaster does not require insurance.

Financial products are simply agreements written on paper. Although written in English, they are written by lawyers and designed so you won't read them. Read them anyway, and read them again, and again, until you understand them.

The price of borrowing money is interest—and worry. Keep all borrowing below the worry point and don't borrow to buy things that depreciate; you will lose on both ends.

Don't rely on appreciation of the asset. If the price is too high, wait. It's too high for everyone else as well, and they will realize it in due time. The public tends to extrapolate trends long after the financial justification is gone. Read our essay, "Wake Up, America—Houses Don't Make You Money!" earlier in this chapter.

Any agreement has two parties; the other person will be working for himself. Figure out whether he is working for or against you. Always check one level deeper, and follow up.

The assumptions that you make consciously won't hurt you. The assumptions you take for granted (what "everybody knows") will kill you. Always check the assumption behind the assumption you make.

If it's complicated, it is probably a bad deal.

If you don't understand it, it *is* a bad deal. Don't buy any product or service from someone who can't or won't explain it to you in terms you understand.

Don't confuse income and wealth. Income can end with a dismissal notice or a change in interest rates.

Don't confuse wealth with the current price of an asset. People get carried away with prices—up and down.

Don't count on Social Security. The benefits you receive will be a small fraction of what your grandparents now receive.

People think of inflation as prices going up. It's not. It's the value of money going down.

There are no guarantees, there are only guarantors. The phrase "It's guaranteed" requires the response, "By whom?"

Only the Ten Commandments were written in stone. All other laws are at the whim of politicians who will change them in response to current pressures.

When you change the rules a little, you change the game a lot.

Convenience is usually expensive. Ignorance is deadly.

Collectibles are faddish. They come and go. When everyone knows it's a "collectible" the game is over.

You can't spend yourself rich. You've spent a lot of time and effort to make a buck pretax. The money you don't spend is worth more than the money you earn—it's after-tax.

Fund your IRA every year—early if possible. Invest in an equity or total-return mutual fund. Equity returns compounded over long periods can be truly amazing.

Why Interest Rates Won't "Go Back Up" Anytime Soon

This essay was originally published in Muhlenkamp Memorandum, *Issue 20, October 1991. In 1991, whether or not interest rates would "go back up" was a hot topic in economic and investing circles. In June of that year, Ron went to his M.I.T. reunion. He spent half an hour debating interest rates with an old classmate who has a Ph.D. in economics and is the chief economist at a major investment firm. His classmate was certain that interest rates were going to "go back up" because of the federal budget deficit. Upon returning from the reunion, Ron wrote this essay to explain why the shift in the public from "Trade up on equity" to "Prepay the mortgage" would drive rates down.*

In our first newsletter, dated July 1987, we published an essay entitled "Wake Up, America—Houses Don't Make You Money!" In that essay we demonstrated that the long period—1968 to 1980—of house price inflation exceeding after-tax mortgage rates ended dramatically in 1981. Exhibit 5.8 is an updated version of the bar chart that we used to present this information.

Our essay of 1987 and others like it had no impact. The public wasn't ready. Homebuyers continued to hold attitudes and exhibit behavior that made sense only in the 1968–1980 period. Houses continued to be viewed as a good investment. The limit on size was not family need in any real sense, but the amount that could be financed. Conventional wisdom continued to favor trading up on the equity in the belief that an even bigger house (mortgage) was an even better investment.

Yet the chart makes it apparent that the game had changed in 1981. Since that time, after-tax mortgage rates have been well above inflation, making a big mortgage a big financial burden. But as long as people believed that house prices in their local area were outpacing inflation, our warning fell on deaf ears.

A Rude Awakening

Recession and the decline in house prices in many parts of the country are now rudely awakening the American public. People who two years ago fully expected to continue trading up are now prepaying their mortgage. If there wasn't nearly a decade of financial pressure (see Exhibit 5.8) at work here, we could dismiss this trend as an emotional shift, subject to short-term reversal. But with this background, we must view it as a delayed realization, which will last at least as long as fundamental pressures remain. In a recent month, 20 percent of those refinancing their mortgages went to 15- to 20-year fixed-rate contracts, which says to us that homeowners are making long-term commitments

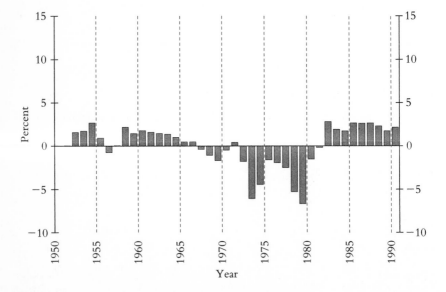

Exhibit 5.8 Real After-Tax Mortgage Rate, 1952–1991

to "prepay their mortgage" (relative to the standard 30-year contract) in ways not easily reversed. We therefore conclude that the American public is reversing its 25-year mind-set. Instead of "trade up on the equity," the new rallying cry of homeowners is "prepay the mortgage." Please reread this paragraph three times; it's that important!

But the second part of the new reality has not yet sunk in. Despite a 10-year decline in interest rates, the mortgage-borrowing public, fearing that rates will go back up, is still insisting on fixed-rate mortgages. Any fixed rate below 10 percent is being locked up in the belief that it's a temporarily low rate. Meanwhile, the borrower's retired parents are *hoping* that rates will go back up. Banks and savings and loans are telling us that despite the big drop in short-term CD rates (to the current 5 percent level), many retirees are shortening maturities to 30 or 90 days until rates "go back up." Due to the broad attitudinal changes that we've just outlined, we believe these people will be disappointed.

Contrary to popular opinion, bankers and other financial intermediaries don't care about the level of interest rates. They work on a 2 percent or 3 percent spread. The savers of the world (our parents) will receive 2 percent or 3 percent less on their deposits than we, the borrowers, are willing to pay. As long as borrowers were willing to pay high rates (because they expected to make money on the asset) they were not active in negotiating lower rates. In the past year, this expectation has reversed. Borrowers are no longer willing to pay 10 percent or 11 percent, so lenders (savers) will no longer receive 8 percent.

But that doesn't stop them from looking for it! Some walk into brokerage offices and buy anything that promises 8 percent. Today the demand for mortgage participation is so great that yields have been driven down to Treasury levels, even though the mortgages are subject to prepayment at the option of the borrower. People who buy Fannie Mae or Ginnie Mae certificates hoping for an 8 percent long-term return are going to be disappointed because, as we have previously noted, mortgage prepayments are increasing. These same people will be back in the marketplace two or three years from now looking for 8 percent again, and it will not be available.

Other people make basically the same mistake by buying current-coupon corporate and municipal bonds or *preferreds*. As interest rates fall, these instruments will be called or redeemed at the earliest profitable opportunity. An October 11, 1991, *Wall Street Journal* headline reported that the U.S. Treasury is purchasing some bonds for early retirement, a move it said "will shock many investors." Folks, all borrowers call or redeem their paper for the same reason you or I refinance our mortgage: lower interest costs. The ability to recognize and (more importantly) make your portfolio reflect this fact comes from asking simple questions: Who is on the other side of the piece of paper? What will he or she do? It takes some thought and effort sometimes to get the answer, but it's worth it.

Here is our final comment: We know what the baby boomers are doing—they are paying down their mortgages—but we don't know what the retirees are going to do. In our 1989 essay "The Inflation Time Bomb," we warned that interest incomes were likely to drop from 8 percent to 5 percent or lower. The facts have now verified this, but the realization has not yet sunk in for most retirees. Most still live by the maxim "Spend the income—don't touch the principal." In the inflationary cycle of the past 20 years, this maxim has become a trap. Now, becoming aware of the trap they are in, retirees' actions so far have merely been stopgap, searching for 8 percent short-term fixed-income returns in a 5 percent world, with little attention paid to whether they are callable. Retirees are faced with the choice of investing in long-term assets, which carry price risk, or accepting a 40 percent cut (maybe more soon) in their interest income.

As is often the case in investing, those who saw the pitfalls early have more and better options available for avoiding them. Those options are rapidly diminishing. You do not have to predict economic climate changes, but you must recognize them when they occur.

2007 Update

Normally, T-bills are priced to yield about 1 percent over inflation.

Normally, 30-year T-bonds are priced to yield 2.5 to 3 percent over inflation.

Normally, 30-year mortgages are priced to yield about 1 percent over 30-year T-bonds.

Normally, adjustable rate mortgages (ARMs) are priced to yield 2.5 to 3 percent over T-bills.

During the period 1998–2004, nominal interest rates on 30-year mortgages fell from 8 percent to 6 percent (see Exhibit 1.4 in Chapter 1) So the cost of borrowing for a mortgage came down dramatically. And, during the 2001–2004 period, T-bill yields were unusually low at a nominal 1 percent (and a real, after-tax rate that was negative; see Exhibits 2.1 and 2.3 in Chapter 2). Given the above-listed spreads, ARMs were available at about 4 percent (and various teaser rates were even lower). So if you refinanced your 8 percent fixed-rate mortgage of 1998 into an ARM in 2003, you could cut your rate in half.

Many people buy houses based on the monthly payment required, so they were able to bid up the price over this period. The game ended in 2005–2006.

As the Fed raised short-term interest rates to levels a bit above historic real rates, ARM rates rose above 30-year fixed rates. As a consequence, people are now refinancing their adjustable rate mortgages into fixed-rate mortgages. The remaining question is to what extent the rise in mortgage rates will exceed the capability of some people to make the payments. As I write this in August 2007, economic commentary and the credit markets have focused on the "repricing" of subprime adjustable rate mortgages (ARMs).

Although long-term Treasury rates and long-term fixed-rate mortgage rates have been stable for the past five to six years, many mortgages were written with adjustable rates based 2.5 to 3 percent above the unusually low short-term interest rates of two to three years ago. These mortgages are now being "adjusted" to correspond to the change in rates. What is unknown (and probably unknowable) is how many homeowners will be unable to pay the higher rates.

Mom—The Squeeze on Your "Income" Will Continue

This essay was originally published in Muhlenkamp Memorandum, *Issue 21, January 1992. Ron wrote it as a letter to his mother because he saw that even though the borrowers in our economy were responding to lower interest rates by paying down their debts and refinancing their mortgages, the lenders (like his mother and her*

friends) were reluctant to accept that the lower rates were here to stay.
This essay reviews why interest rates fell, why this was putting the
squeeze on retirees, and what they could do about it.

Since November 1990, you've seen the interest rate paid on one-year
bank CDs fall from 8 percent to 4 percent. Many of your friends are
waiting (hoping) for these rates to go back up, but it isn't going to happen. To understand why, you really need to look no further than the
actions of your children. Today your children are paying down their
debts and refinancing their mortgages, often for a shorter term.

Most people believe that interest rates are set by banks and savings
and loans, but they're really not. Banks normally operate on a 2.5 to
3 percent point spread, so the interest rates that you receive on your
savings will be 2.5 to 3 percent less than your children are willing to
pay on their borrowings. And the biggest class of borrowing in the
country is home mortgages. As these mortgages are paid down more
rapidly (15-year mortgages instead of 30-year), the downward pressure on interest rates will continue.

The inflation of the 1970s taught the baby boomers (your children)
that a big house with a big mortgage was a good way to make money. It
was true for 15 years, long enough to convince us that it is always true.
We came to believe that houses were moneymakers regardless of the
price we paid for the real estate or the interest rate we paid on the loan.
In essence, we believed that as long as we spent our money on real
estate, we could spend ourselves rich. We didn't call it spending, of
course; we called it investing. And it worked, right up until interest rates
went up and inflation came down in 1981. Soon thereafter, falling farm
prices cured the farmers of the delusion, but the homeowners continued to hold on to the fantasy—until now.

The Public Changes Its Mind

For the past five years, you have heard and read our arguments in "Wake
Up, America—Houses Don't Make You Money!" You have seen our
chart depicting the costs of home mortgages versus house price inflation, which we've been foisting on friends and family alike. What has
changed in the past year is that much of the public now realizes
house prices don't always go up. As long as people believed that a

big house was a good investment (regardless of interest rates) they were willing to pay 10 percent to 11 percent rates on a mortgage. With the help of the recession, that conviction died in the past year.

As recently as November 1990, mortgage rates were still 10.5 percent and CDs were 8 percent. So this realization and the current incentive to refinance is only a few months old. The incentive to refinance is still considered news and receives extensive coverage in your local newspaper. And any mortgage written in the past 10 years is now susceptible to being refinanced at lower rates.

Conversations with banks and savings and loans indicate to us that only about 20 to 30 percent of eligible mortgages have been refinanced to date. Of these, roughly 20 percent have opted for 15- to 20-year mortgages (as Sis has done). If this is truly a trend, it has a long way to go, and it will continue to drive rates even lower. Trend or not, you can monitor its progress by simply talking to your children and to your friends about their children. As long as mortgages are being refinanced for shorter periods, the increased monthly principal payments will keep downward pressure on rates. As long as mortgages are being refinanced at lower rates, these new lower rates will be reinforced. Fixed-rate mortgages are refinanced down, not up, which is why many homeowners are now replacing their adjustable-rate mortgages with fixed-rate mortgages.

When you remember that in the 1950s and 1960s, mortgage rates were 4.5 percent and passbook savings were 2 percent, you get a good idea of where rates may be headed. As recently as 1972, the treasurer of the insurance company where I worked adamantly maintained that normal mortgage rates were 4.5 percent. Each of us who has a mortgage will do our best to drive rates back to those levels.

Meanwhile, on the other side of the ledger, you and your friends have seen CD rates drop from 8 percent to 4 percent. (I almost said "seen CD rates drop through the floor," but the floor is likely to be on the order of 2 percent.) This has been a shock to those who had come to believe that "normal" CD rates were 8 percent (and who relied on such rates for their income). But such high rates were an anomaly of the 1980s. They resulted from the high inflation rates of the 1970s and the baby boomer belief that such inflation rates were normal. I have already argued that inflation and inflationary expectations (in housing at least) have just died. If so, "normal" CD rates may be 2 percent, and other short-term "riskless" instruments may reach similar levels.

Changing Your Mind

Mom, you said last week that you wouldn't change your lifestyle in response to lower interest rates on CDs. You needn't—provided you change your mind about the acceptability of various kinds of investments. For background, please reread our essays from 1989 titled "The Inflation Time Bomb," "Defusing the Inflation Time Bomb," and "What Is Risk?" Be aware that earning good returns on your assets normally requires significant amounts of thought and effort. This is true in farming, and it's true in investing (and in every other endeavor that I can think of). Only in the past 10 years have short-term rates (on no-effort investments) been significantly above inflation, and those days are over.

For over a decade financial planners, advisers, and other experts have maintained that long-term investments (like stocks and long-term bonds) are risky, and that CDs and other short-term debt instruments are risk-free. But their definition of risk looks only at short-term price changes. They have ignored the long-term loss of the purchasing power of your assets, and they've simply assumed, contrary to history, that the high interest rates of the 1980s would continue.

The simple truth is that all investments have risks. There is no free lunch. If you focus too narrowly on short-term risks, you will be vulnerable in the long term. If you focus on the long term (as we do), you will suffer setbacks short-term. My complaint is that many advisers have encouraged you to finance your long-term retirement (for 20-plus years) using only short-term instruments, which were clearly at unsustainably high rates.

These same advisers are now helping your friends buy longer-term investments, which they will be called out of as interest rates continue to drop. The most popular have been mortgage-backed securities, which still promise rates of 7.5 percent. But these rates will hold only until the mortgages are refinanced, at which time people will have to reinvest at lower rates, just as you did a year ago. Others are buying corporate bonds, which are also callable, leading to the same problem.

The only investments that allow you to benefit in a climate of falling inflation and interest rates are common stocks and long-term Treasury bonds. By law, Treasuries are noncallable (unless, of course, Congress changes the law). Most other fixed-income investments are subject to call or redemption. Remember, there is someone on the other side of the piece of paper whose job or incentive is to lower his borrowing costs.

Finally, look carefully at your own investing experience. In 17 years of investing in common stocks, you've had one down year. Your annual returns have averaged 15 percent (9 percent over the average inflation rate of 6 percent). So your assets multiplied 10 times, while the cost of living nearly tripled. Has this been so risky that you'd rather not have participated?

During this same 17 years, your short-term investments (CDs, etc.) have averaged about 8 percent (2 percent over inflation). With inflation, each year your income bought less. In the past year, this income has been cut in half. Has this been riskless investing?

Mom, the recent period of high interest rates on CDs is over. It is over because your children are no longer willing to pay an 11 percent interest rate on their mortgage. So your choices in sustaining yourself through the rest of your retirement have become more difficult. You can still do well, but it will require more thought and effort on your part. You must think for yourself and be skeptical of the conventional wisdom.

Editor's Note

In fact, interest rates continued to fall. As of 2007, fixed-rate mortgages have fallen from 8 percent to 6 percent. With help from the Fed, 5 percent interest rates on CDs fell to 1 percent before rebounding. Ron considers "normal" CD rates to be roughly 1 percent greater than inflation.

Investing and Farming: Know the Climate

This essay was originally published in Muhlenkamp Memorandum, *Issue 22, April 1992. It reviews changes in the investing climate since the 1970s and illustrates them in terms of the farming climate. It also shows how the people, in aggregate, determine the investing climate. Finally, it continues the farming analogy to demonstrate the transitory nature of short-term swings in the market and the need to stay focused on the long-term climate through such swings.*

The longer I manage money, the more it looks like farming. In mid-February, we had 70° weather in Pittsburgh. While looking at the calendar one day, I started to ponder how a farmer without a calendar would know whether it was February, normally a poor time to plant crops, or April, normally a good time to plant. Of course, this very problem resulted in the invention of the calendar in the first place. It then occurred to me that investing in the stock and bond markets isn't much different from farming—but without the benefit of a calendar.

In either endeavor, the first thing you need to know is the climate in which you live. The climate for farming is determined by temperature and rainfall, and changes are very gradual in a given geographic area. So, in any one lifetime, changes in climate are usually associated with changes in locale. When my parents moved from Coldwater, Ohio, to Albuquerque, New Mexico, they built a house and, like other Midwesterners, planted a lawn. Then they learned that unless they watered the lawn every other day, it soon returned to sand. When they built a second house, they landscaped the yard in sand and rocks. In Albuquerque, brown—not green—is beautiful.

The climate for investing is heavily influenced by the levels of inflation and interest rates, and it can change fairly rapidly. In the 1970s, the investing climate in the United States was determined by inflation levels well above interest rates. You could not offset inflation by lending money. Anyone who had a savings account or bought bonds was a sure loser—and most paid taxes for the privilege. Rather than lending money, the climate favored borrowing money—and buying hard assets like gold, oil, and real estate, which held their real value versus the depreciating (deflating) dollar. By the end of the decade, many people believed that prices of these assets could only go up, so they continued to borrow money to buy them. They borrowed money regardless of the rate, and interest rates climbed.

But, while this was happening, inflation was being brought under control. Inflation fell while interest rates climbed. Since 1981, interest rates have been well above inflation, reversing the investment climate of the 1970s. Other influences (like tax laws) have reinforced this change in climate, so it has paid to lend money. Savings accounts, bonds, and stocks have been big moneymakers. Owning gold or oil or mortgaged real estate has been very expensive—sort of like trying to grow cotton in Ohio or grass in New Mexico.

Anticipating Change

The fundamental difference between farming and investing is that, in the aggregate, we the people determine the climate for investing. Inflation is determined by government action in response to our demands. Interest rates are determined directly by the levels that people are willing to pay or receive. Our unwillingness to pay directly for the Vietnam War (through spending cuts or increased taxes) in the mid-1960s led us to print money, setting off an inflationary spiral (and a change in climate) that lasted until inflation became intolerable to the average voter.

Meanwhile, the public's awareness of inflation lagged the reality; throughout the 1970s, the public accepted interest rates well below inflation. This came to a head in 1979–1980, when the voting public insisted on lower inflation (by voting Ronald Reagan into the presidency) and higher interest rates (by moving their money from passbook savings to money market funds)—and changed the economic climate. People who bought gold, oil, or farmland in the late 1970s soon learned that the climate had changed. Those who did so with borrowed money lost on both sides. Their interest costs went up while the market and collateral values went down, and many lost their assets.

Changes in tax laws and the regulatory rules for banks and savings and loans enabled professional lenders to deny the change in climate for a while, building increasingly expensive commercial buildings. By 1986, the excesses became apparent, even to our politicians. Once again they changed the rules—just in time to compound the retrenchment in commercial real estate.

The remaining vestige of the 1970s inflationary climate was the popular belief that a highly mortgaged single-family home would make you money. We've been discussing the fallacy of this belief in our newsletter (*Muhlenkamp Memorandum*) since 1987. In the past year (as of 1992), the belief seems to have died. We cite as proof the public's focus on paying down their mortgages, which reflects the current climate and is the direct opposite of trading up on the equity, which was appropriate to the climate of the 1970s.

This focus on paying down the mortgage, along with the Fed's successful slowing of the economy, has also resulted in short-term interest rates falling from their unusually high levels of the past decade. Since

1989, we have argued that high short-term rates were an anomaly that could only be temporary. These rates have now fallen, and are forcing the savers in this country to face a broader choice of options in an effort to reach their goals.

As investors review these options, they will find the investment climate in the United States remains positive for stocks and bonds.★

Weathering the Storms

Even within a given climate, the seasonal and daily weather patterns have great variability. In Ohio, planting that is done in April is less likely to suffer frost than that done in February, but a late frost cannot be ruled out. The hot, humid weather of July and August, which is ideal for growing a corn crop, also creates ideal conditions for hailstorms.

Seasonally speaking, the U.S. economy is now (1992) coming out of a recession, albeit following a couple of false starts. For the past couple of years, our choices of cyclical stocks have focused on those with strong balance sheets. We waited to be sure that the companies we invested in would survive and thrive even if the economic recovery was delayed and some of their competitors failed. Just as any farmer who doesn't allow for a late frost or a hailstorm will soon be wiped out, we expected that the weaker companies in a number of cyclical industries might face extinction. As we see the economy strengthen, we may loosen these balance sheet standards.★★

The emotional swings of the investing public, which affect the daily prices of securities, are at least as variable as the daily weather. These swings are part and parcel of all investing climates. The key is not to confuse the daily changes with seasonal changes or the climate!

I've often compared the October 1987 stock market crash, which dropped prices 25 percent in two days, to a hailstorm that wiped out one year's crop. But the storm (crash) changed neither the climate nor the

---

★The positive climate for bonds ended in late 1993 when long-term interest rates returned to inflation plus 3 percent. Except for brief periods, bonds have been a poor investment since 1993. Stocks reached fair value in 1998. Since then we've had a split market. In 1999, a fad group of stocks skyrocketed while the majority of NYSE stocks went down. After March 2000 these trends reversed.

★★Reading this paragraph in 2007 is déjà vu.

fertility of the soil (the strength of the real economy). So the appropriate response was to plant a new crop, and 1988 produced a bumper crop.

The year 1990 was a poor year. The Middle East problem became a war and resulted in both scaring the public (bad weather in our analogy) and postponing the end of the recession (a delayed spring). But it also set the stage for a bumper crop in the following year. We don't expect such a bumper crop this year (1992), but we do expect an average year because the climate remains favorable and spring is here.

2002 Update

(Note: This update was written at a time when current events were overriding the normal business cycle. The severity and number of these events made it hard for most people to see that the business cycle was still intact. Therefore, Ron wrote this update to point out that the upswing of the market was only delayed, not dead. The year 2002 is also an interesting time to consider because it is the same point in the economic cycle as 1992—when the above essay was originally written.)

In 2002 we are once again recovering from a recession, implying springtime in our analogy. But this economic springtime is complicated by an unusually large number of factors with major psychological impact: the hangover from the fad stocks of 1999; the impact of the terrorist attacks of September 11, 2001; the threat of war with Iraq; corporate malfeasance; the drought in the U.S. farm belt; the dock strike; and so on. The combined effect has been to drive stock prices lower and to delay the expected springtime in the market. In fact, 2002 has been the first time in the 10 recessions since 1945 that the stock market hasn't done well as the economy recovered from recession.

Our best description of the current market is a drought. Just as the two-day drop in 1987 was similar to a hailstorm (short and quick but destroying the year's crop), the decline in 2002 is similar to a drought—a long, drawn-out combination of adverse weather (psychology) that destroys the crop.

As farmers and investors, you and I know that droughts are part of the business—and we're likely to face one sometime in our lifetime. But it's very hard to predict when. Our only recourse is to allow for drought and to make sure we survive it when it comes, but it doesn't change the climate or the seasons. So the proper response is to plant a new crop. The previously listed psychological factors appear to have peaked, and we believe that the combination of economic recovery and current stock prices now favor planting that crop.

Editor's Note

Springtime did in fact come to the stock market. The S&P 500 was up 25 percent in 2003 and 11 percent in 2004. Ron believes that after the transition year of 2006, when the Fed successfully engineered a slowdown but no recession ("soft landing"), we are once again in springtime, a good time to plant investment crops.

How We Benefit from Free Trade

In 1992, Ron was invited to address the Ohio Valley Chapter of the National Management Association at the Wheeling Pittsburgh Steel Corporation on the advantages of free trade. At the time, there was much debate as to whether the United States should sign the North American Free Trade Agreement (NAFTA). There was concern that such a large free-trade zone would hurt the U.S. economy. Unions feared jobs going to Mexico and Canada. Companies feared their prices would be undercut and they would lose business.

Ron's first reactions to the invitation were:

1. *"I'm not sure I'm qualified, but then not many other people are qualified either."*
2. *"This is a chance to explain what I believe to people like my father, who worked in a foundry (and was a member of the United Steelworkers Union) for 20 years to pay for the farm."*
3. *"Wheeling is far enough away that the audience won't chase me all the way home if they don't like what I have to say."*

And so Ron presented this address on the benefits of a large free-trade zone.

When your father was your age, did he work as hard as you do? When your grandfather was your age, did he work as hard as you do? When your father was your age, did he live as well as you do? When your grandfather was your age, did he live as well as you do?

My grandfather was a farmer, which means that at my age, he farmed with horses. At my age, my father farmed with a tractor and worked in a foundry making farm equipment. Me? I sit and I think.

During my short lifetime (and you'll believe me when I say that the longer it gets, the shorter it seems), I've been very lucky. I've never had to farm with horses, but I had a neighbor who did, and I worked with him just enough to be grateful that I didn't have to. Dad bought our farm when I was seven years old. Unlike the previous farmhouse, this house had indoor plumbing, central heating, and a propane cookstove—three absolutely marvelous inventions (and except for the cookstove, all used more iron and steel than their predecessors)—but my sisters and I lost our jobs of carrying water and kindling for the cookstove. We no longer took hot bricks to bed to keep our feet warm, and the outhouse became a backup system to handle the overflow generated by seven children and one bathroom. The barn was equipped with a vacuum pump for milking cows, and we lost that job also. Folks, your schoolbooks lie. Cows don't give milk; you have to take it from them.

The following year, when I was eight, we planted 14 acres of corn. Beginning in mid-October, each day after school I would go out and shuck corn. My mother and sisters would do the milking, and my father would join me in the field after getting off work at the foundry; we'd shuck corn until dark. It took us six weeks to shuck 14 acres. Since then, I've seen a number of boring assembly lines, but every one of them looked absolutely thrilling compared to six weeks shucking 14 acres of corn. The following year, Dad hired a neighbor with a corn picker.

But we still burned wood for heat, and we cut the wood with a cross-cut saw. Dad was six-foot-four, and I was eight years old. I couldn't get into his rhythm, and he couldn't seem to understand why not. I came to love a one-man tool called the ax and let Mom have the other end of the saw. She managed both the saw and my father much better than I ever did!

The following year, he bought a buzz saw for the tractor and cut the crosscut work by about 80 percent. The year after that, my cousin bought a chain saw and we teamed up with him and got serious about cutting wood. It was still hard work and required every third or fourth Saturday all winter, but those metal tools removed much of the drudgery and frustration. Today, of course, I heat with gas; and believe me, it's cheap!

By now you may be starting to understand why I like machinery. A boy on a tractor is a happy boy, but this boy also loved the hay elevator because he lost a job throwing bales of hay up into a haymow. He loved the self-unloading wagon because he lost a job shoveling corn. But his all-time favorite machine, hands down—bar none—was the manure loader. Folks, my first true love was a tractor, but that tractor wasn't complete until Dad put a manure loader on it.

You may wonder why I am telling you all this. I'm telling you this partly because I'm grateful. I spent 11 years losing jobs to metal machines. I'm grateful to the people who produced that metal and those machines. As for the jobs, I don't miss a damn one of them!

But I'm also telling you this for two other reasons. The first is because it didn't have to happen, and it certainly didn't have to happen to me or in my lifetime. In parts of Eastern Europe today, my distant cousins farm with horses much as my grandfather did. In much of the rest of the world, the people don't yet even use horses. It's not that they don't have the desire for modern machinery. It's that the machinery is not available or they don't have the means by which to obtain it.

Why did I get so lucky? I've thought about this a good bit and concluded that it boils down to two reasons:

1. We live in a (relatively) free economy.
2. We live in a large free-trade zone.

Let me explain my reasoning. A free economy is a volunteer economy. In a free economy, the consumer is king. As a consumer, no person or company can make you buy their product.

They can advertise, pitch, cajole, promise, sweet-talk, bribe, and seduce, but they can't make you buy their product. Unless the producer makes a product you want and offers it at a price you're willing to pay, you keep your money in your pocket. Over time, most companies learn that their best sales gimmick is to provide a quality product at a cheaper price. Years ago, I was taught that there are natural monopolies, but I no longer believe that. The only monopolies I can find are government sanctioned.

The corollary to a consumer-driven free economy is that it allows a person with a good idea, a talent, or a lot of energy to profit from it. Whether you're Henry Ford, Sam Walton, Bill Cosby, or Michael Jordan, if you provide a product or service that the public is willing to pay for, you can get rich. If Steve Jobs thinks he can build a computer in his garage and call it an "Apple," no one will stop him. If I think I can serve people better on my own than by working for another company, I need only convince enough people to hire me to allow me to feed my family.

In 1899, Charles H. Duell, director of the U.S. Patent Office, suggested that the office be shut down because, in his words, "Everything that can be invented has already been invented." I'm quite sure that he was an intelligent, educated man, but I am grateful that he didn't have the power to implement his suggestion or I'd be farming with a horse.

My wife Connie and I have a son, Jeff, who is serving with the U.S. Army in Germany. We recently took 10 days to visit him and his wife. We borrowed his car and took a trip around the country. At the Polish border at 7 P.M. on a Thursday evening, we saw a line of trucks three and a half miles long waiting to pass through a toll gate that was closed for the night. We saw a similar thing at the Czechoslovakian border. Somebody in those countries is deciding what goods and materials should be available to their people and doesn't mind wasting the time of a lot of truck drivers for their own convenience. Would you want someone telling you what you can or cannot buy?

My point is this: Free economies are driven by the consumer. Command economies tend to focus on production and be driven by the producers. At one time, Henry Ford built most of the cars in this country. He would have been happy to continue making Model Ts, all of them black. Had he been able to get a government-sanctioned monopoly on the manufacture of automobiles, he'd have had no reason to change or improve his cars.

In Czechoslovakia today, most of the cars are Wartburgs and Trabants. These cars are about the size of a VW Rabbit and have a two-cycle engine of about 20 horsepower, and they also have the quality of junk. But because the people were not allowed to buy imports, the manufacturer had no reason to improve them. Someone in charge decided what the consumer should want. The consumers themselves had no vote. Therefore, there was no incentive to improve the product.

Today it seems popular to judge people by their motivation rather than by their competence and to disparage those who are deemed to be merely "greedy" in the production of goods. Personally, as a consumer, I don't care about the motivation. I don't care whether Ford built cars and tractors for money, fame, or the good of mankind; I'm just grateful that he allowed me to farm with a tractor. The point is that in a free economy, the consumer is king and the producer must serve the consumer.

But the second reason that Ford, Walton, Cosby, and Jordan have done so well is that they benefit from a large free-trade area. If Ford's market had been confined to Detroit, he wouldn't have sold so many cars or tractors, and living in Ohio, I'd have had to farm with a horse. If Cosby had been born 50 years earlier, before television, he'd be a comic in Philadelphia. If Michael Jordan had been born 30 years earlier, he'd be paid like Bill Russell was paid. Michael Jordan receives $3 million per year playing basketball and $15 million from endorsements. How much of that would he make if television weren't able to bring his talents into 80 million American homes and millions outside the United States as well?

If Sam Walton had to pay a tariff on all goods shipped across state lines, you and I would pay a lot more for the goods we buy. For that matter, if General Motors had to pay a 20 percent tariff for all out-of-state materials, how big do you think the steel business in West Virginia would be? How well would West Virginians live if your state government decided that you should be self-sufficient? How well would you live if all out-of-state goods had a 20 percent tariff? West Virginia is rich in coal and in good people. But so is Albania. And Albania is destitute.

I've been asked, "Who in the United States benefited from all of the Japanese cars we've purchased over the past 20 years, with the attendant loss of auto and steel jobs to Japan?" Well, it seems to me, the first beneficiaries were the people who bought the cars. They received better value for their money, or at least they thought so. The second beneficiaries were the people who bought American cars who got better deals because there was effective competition. The third beneficiaries are people who buy American cars today. In the United States, we now make good quality cars. If I were to buy a new car today, I'd buy American. But there isn't an American car built between 1973 and 1984 that I'd want to own, and I owned a couple of them.

But the benefits didn't stop there. The dollars we sent to Japan for cars all came back here. After all, dollars are no more useful in Japan than yen are in the United States. These dollars came back in a number of ways. Some bought airplanes: Most of the aircraft being used in Japan has been built by Boeing. Some bought computer software. Some bought U.S. Treasury bonds, allowing you and me to borrow money at lower rates. Seventy-six billion dollars bought U.S. commercial real estate, right at the peak of the market. Remember the uproar in the news over the purchase by Japanese investors of Los Angeles office buildings, the Pebble Beach Golf Course, and Rockefeller Center? I saw the prospectus on Rockefeller Center; it looked to me like they paid three times what it was worth. Since then, the public price of the shares has fallen by half.

A recent article in *Pension & Investments,* dated October 26, 1992, cites an estimate by Kenneth Leventhal & Co., an L.A. accounting firm, that Japanese investors lost at least 30 percent of their investment, or $22 billion in U.S. real estate, from 1986 through 1991. So we bought their Toyotas and we sold them airplanes and we sold them empty office buildings at inflated prices. It seems to me that we got the better deal!

The flip side of a consumer-driven free economy is that no one can guarantee your job unless you provide a product that the consumer wants and at a price he or she is willing to pay. Unless you deliver the goods, you and your company will be out of work.

The third reason I tell you all this is because when I look at the steel industry, I see patterns similar to what I've seen in farming. From 1860 to 1960, we took much of the heavy labor out of farming. With the help of machinery, each of my farmer cousins tills three to six times the acreage their fathers and our grandfather did. But since we haven't found five more continents, there is only room on this one for one-fifth the farmers (in number) that we used to have. In 1860 two-thirds or 67 percent of American workers were farmers. It's less than 3 percent today.

If anyone had predicted this change in 1860, some congressman would have predicted a resulting unemployment rate of 64 percent and introduced a bill to outlaw all machinery. Actually, he may have been right. My grandfather was never unemployed, and I doubt whether there's unemployment among the Amish. Frankly, I've always been amazed when steel workers complained about losing jobs to machines. Without machines, there wouldn't have been a steel industry in the first place.

Similarly, since World War II, we've taken much of the heavy labor out of basic industry. In the United States, we now produce the same tonnage of steel that we did in 1950, but we do it with one-fourth the man-hours. (Partly because of this, the hourly wage has nearly tripled from $10 per hour, adjusted for inflation, to $27 per hour.) But unlike farm products, which are consumed (literally) at a stable rate and have few substitutes, many steel products have long lifetimes and numerous substitutes. In many products, iron and steel have been replaced; in others, we're using fewer tons of higher-strength steel.

Alcoa's annual report of 1985 documents many of the great successes of aluminum. Remember when it was macho to crunch a tinplate beer can in your hand? Now, 97 percent of beverage cans are made of aluminum. In 1976, the average U.S. automobile had 81 pounds of aluminum. Today it has 160 pounds. In 1985, new coal hopper cars were 85 percent aluminum. Despite all the rhetoric, I suspect that more U.S. steelworkers lost jobs to the aluminum industry than to the Japanese. In other areas we've satisfied the primary demand for steel.

In 1980, when I asked a cousin how many farmers in Mercer County, Ohio, needed as much equipment as they had, he replied, "None." At the time, he had five tractors for two drivers. We now have as many cars and trucks in this country as we have people over the age of 18. So we don't need more cars. When I first mentioned this five years ago, my 19-year-old daughter said it couldn't be true because she didn't have one. But since then she bought a car, so now the set is complete.

And we no longer make automobiles from iron ore. We make new cars from old cars. Because the new ones are smaller, lighter, and better designed and use higher-strength steel, we can make six or seven new cars from five old ones. If you go to a county fair, you will see men of all ages wrecking cars for fun. These cars are today's raw material.

Recently I was in Wal-Mart and decided to check how many products had steel content. Other than a few hand tools and bicycles, there were none. There was, however, steel in the building and in the shelving. The consumer doesn't care what the product is made of. Connie has never sent me to the store for a pound of steel.

So, if I wanted to sell steel, I'd look to the people who want cars and appliances but don't yet have them. Frankly, Mexico comes to mind. In 1983, Caterpillar sold 12 machines in Mexico. In 1991, Caterpillar sold 1,200 machines in Mexico. In 1991, $486 million in goods were exported from Pennsylvania to Mexico, of which $154 million were primary materials. Also, I wouldn't worry too much about losing steel jobs to the Mexicans. Mexico wants jobs that are labor intensive. Steel is capital intensive.

Last month I was told by the spokesman of a specialty steel company that many steel mills in South America are for sale and that every specialty steel mill in Europe as well as some in Japan are looking for partners. These mills were all built with government money and can't compete in today's market. In the 1950s and 1960s, emerging countries wanted their own steel mills and airlines as a matter of national pride. Countries today have different priorities.

Two weeks ago, I had a chance to meet with a delegation from Slovenia. Slovenia is about the size and population of southwestern Pennsylvania. They expressed no interest in having a steel mill or a national airline. They wanted to know how to set up their own stock exchange and a computer industry.

The Slovenians are learning what we've forgotten. We've forgotten that free markets benefit the individual consumer. We seem to have forgotten that free trade among nations makes the strength of each nation's producers available to all of their citizen consumers. Yes, it drives the producer to make ever better products at ever lower costs. Yes, it requires the retraining of workers for better jobs. But it does result in better products and better jobs.

One final point. As I said earlier, Connie and I have a son, Jeff, in the Army. Our other son, Tony, who's here today, served in the Marine Corps. With the recent "New World Order" and the downsizing in the military, Jeff called home one day and said, "Dad, things are really tough when you're in the army and have no job security." I said, "Son, I can sympathize, but not very much. As a human being, if there is one organization I'd like to put out of business, it's the Army. I'm sure you'll be able to get a job doing something else."

The second group I'd like to put out of work is underground coal miners. Early this year, there was a short note in the paper that 1991 was the first year in 100 years that no one died in an underground coal mine in Pennsylvania. I appreciate their pride in the work they do and their anxiety at being trained for other trades, but I have yet to meet the coal miner who wants his son or daughter to be a coal miner.

The third job I'd like to eliminate is the job my father had sorting hot castings in a foundry. Twenty years of sorting castings exhausted his body and destroyed his lungs. No father's son should have that job.

My grandfather was a farmer; he farmed with horses. My father helped build machines and farmed with the machinery he built. I sit and I think. I cannot honestly tell you that I deserve to live a better life than they did, but I do—and I'm grateful.

Editor's Note

NAFTA was signed in 1992, forming the world's largest free-trade zone. More than 15 years later, it is viewed by many as a great success—bringing economic growth and improved standards of living for the United States, Canada, and Mexico.

As for Ron's presentation, no one chased Ron back to Pittsburgh for sharing his beliefs on free trade. In fact, the audience response was "superb."

Personal Finances (Maxims, Part 2)

This essay was written in 1992 in response to questions posed to Ron by his nephew about personal finance. The essay lays out a simple, step-by-step plan to pay off high-interest-rate debts and to shift assets to high-return investments.

Dear Nephew:

Here are some additional notes and things I didn't cover in "Basic Financial Maxims I Want My Kids to Know."

1. There are books available that go into great detail (maybe too much) on a whole shopping list of items relevant to spending and saving money. Two that I think you will find useful are *Making the Most of Your Money* by Jane Bryant Quinn and *Wealth Without Risk* by Charles Givens. Both are probably available at your local library. (Givens is also willing to sell you a whole program of videos, audios, and workbooks for $900, but that seems to defeat its own purpose.) Their sections on spending and savings are quite good, while their sections on investing are less so—partly because investing must change as the financial climate changes.

To this end, *The New York Times Book of Personal Finance* by Leonard Sloane gives good descriptions of financial instruments all the way from CDs to stocks and annuities. The descriptions are concise and factual, and they focus on the inherent nature of the instrument, both pros and cons. In 10 minutes on any one topic, you will understand more about it than 95 percent of the salesmen who are trying to sell it to you. To determine which investment climate we are in, and therefore which instruments are not appropriate, your best bet is to ask me.

2. Make a list of your assets and debts and their relevant returns or interest rates. It may look like the accompanying table.

    Then work to move your assets toward the areas where returns are high and pay off debts where the costs are high. In this case, I would keep the emergency fund intact but would use the savings account to pay off the charge card debt and part of the auto loan or to fund the individual retirement account (IRA). I would continue to fund my IRA (rate 12 to 13 percent and tax-deferred) or pay off my auto loan (saving 13 percent interest) with money I had been depositing into my savings account or CD that earned only 4 percent interest.

Personal Assets and Debts

Asset	Value	Rate
Savings account—CD	$10,000	4%
Emergency fund	$10,000	2%
Personal goods	$20,000	Depreciating
Car #1	$10,000	Depreciating
Car #2	$5,000	Depreciating
House	$150,000	Inflation
Mutual fund	$10,000	12–13%
IRA Stock account	$20,000	12–13% and tax deferred
Pension or 401(k)	$30,000	Tax deferred

Debt	Amount	Rate
Charge card	$1,500	−18%
Auto loan	$6,000	−13%
Mortgage	$120,000	−9%

3. To make your savings plan seem more of a reality, keep a notebook and enter each prepayment just as you did in the savings account. When you want to feel like you are getting ahead, take a look at your notebook. It will read:

3/14/1992—Paid off charge card $1500 at 18%
3/14/1992—Deposited into IRA $500 at 12%
4/14/1992—Deposited into IRA $200 at 12%
5/15/1992—Extra payment on auto loan $200 at 13%

You should be more satisfied seeing that you have been saving money at 12 percent to 18 percent instead of 5 percent.

4. Be aware that when you go to the bank for a mortgage or for any other purpose, the bank will ask you to fill out a statement similar to the one in the table. They will look at all of your assets and liabilities. They will be more impressed by your prepaying or not having high-cost debt than they will be by your having a savings account while carrying the high cost of debt. When you get to the point that the bulk of your assets are high return and your debts are low cost, your financial position will improve rapidly.

If you really want to impress your banker that you're a good credit risk, put together these statements, jot down your plans for paying off debt, and set up your prepayment notebook. Then make an appointment with the bank president and ask his advice on what you've done. He will be impressed with your plan and will think you're very smart for asking his advice. He will also remember you when you apply for a mortgage. Of course, all of this can turn negative if you don't actually follow through on the plan. Note that one of the best ways to impress people with your intelligence is to ask for their advice. (Parents and uncles are absolute pushovers for this!)

Good luck,
Uncle Ron

Chapter 6

1993–1998: Bonds Are Flat; Stocks Do Well

With interest rates back to normal (driven by the mortgage refinancing of 1990–1993), the time to make money in bonds ended. Inflation remained stable. The economy continued to grow. Stocks continued to do well.

1993
- Nelson Mandela becomes president of South Africa.
- President Clinton issues an economic call to arms, asking Americans to accept a painful package of tax increases and spending cuts.
- Terrorists bomb the parking garage of the 110-story World Trade Center in New York City.
- The Martin Luther King Jr. holiday is observed in all 50 states for the first time.

1994

- The Federal Reserve increases interest rates from 3 percent to 5.5 percent—the first time in five years—triggering a huge sell-off on Wall Street.
- Orange County, California, files for bankruptcy protection due to investment losses of about $2 billion.
- Civil war erupts in Rwanda, and Hutu extremists kill a million people.
- Millions of Americans watch O. J. Simpson lead police on a slow-speed chase on Southern California freeways, ending in his arrest for the murder of ex-wife Nicole Brown Simpson and her friend Ronald Goldman.
- Microsoft Corporation reaches a settlement with the Justice Department, promising to end practices to corner the market for personal computer software programs.

1995

- The 104th Congress convenes, entirely under Republican control—the first time since the Eisenhower era.
- African American men gather in Washington, D.C., for the Million Man March, led by Nation of Islam leader Louis Farrakhan.
- Leaders of Bosnia, Croatia, and Serbia sign a peace pact.
- In Oklahoma City, a car bomb explodes at the Alfred P. Murrah Federal Building, killing 168 people and injuring 500, including many children in the building's daycare center. Within a week, suspect Timothy McVeigh is caught and charged.
- First-class postage rates increase from 29 cents to 32 cents an ounce.

1996

- Liggett, the nation's fifth-largest tobacco company, acknowledges that cigarettes are addictive and cause cancer.
- FBI agents arrest the Unabomber, Ted Kaczynski.
- *Forbes* magazine ranks Bill Gates (the founder of Microsoft Corporation) the richest man in the world with a fortune valued at $18 billion.
- A cloned lamb, named "Dolly" after Dolly Parton, is born in Edinburgh, Scotland.
- Bill Clinton is reelected U.S. president.

1997

- U.S. adults under only age 50 without children or jobs can now receive food stamps for three months in any three-year period.
- Hewlett-Packard, Wal-Mart Stores, Johnson & Johnson, and the Travelers Group replace Bethlehem Steel, Texaco, Westinghouse Electric, and Woolworth in the DJIA.
- Hong Kong reverts to Chinese rule after 156 years as a British colony.
- The Pathfinder spacecraft lands on Mars, yielding photographic evidence that colossal floods once scoured the Red Planet's now-barren landscape.
- Voters in Oregon affirm doctor-assisted suicides with a 60 percent approval.

1998

- Twelve nations launch the European Economic and Monetary Union; a French mint produces the first coins of Europe's single currency, the euro.
- Prosecutors in the Monica Lewinsky case question President Clinton's Secret Service protectors before a grand jury.
- The United States announces a $2 million reward for information leading to the conviction of terrorists who bombed U.S. embassies in Kenya and Tanzania, killing 224 people, including 12 Americans.
- Citicorp and Travelers Group announce a merger in an $82 billion deal that creates the world's largest financial services company.

And the Climate Is . . .

This essay was originally published in Muhlenkamp Memorandum Issue 25, January 1993, as an expansion of the "Investing and Farming: Know the Climate" essay (April 1992). It talks more about the investment climate changes from the 1970s to 1993. Of particular interest is the lag in perception of the changes by the public. In the 1970s, people used strategies appropriate in the climate of the 1960s, and lost money. In the 1980s, people used strategies appropriate in the 1970s, and lost money. You don't have to predict climate changes, but you must recognize them when they occur.

In our essay "Investing and Farming: Know the Climate" (see Chapter 5), we discussed the importance of recognizing the current investment climate. We would like to expand on that theme. Exhibit 6.1 is the best picture we have been able to construct to display the investment climate. The chart adjusts the nominal interest rates on mortgages for inflation and taxes. Thus, it is a chart of the net real cost of borrowing money. To an investor, it represents the net real return from lending money.

Exhibit 6.1 makes visible why my father, with a 4 percent mortgage in the 1950s, strove to pay it off early. This chart also makes visible why, in the 1970s, baby boomers made money buying ever bigger houses with ever bigger mortgages. Their net real cost of borrowing was dramatically negative. Exhibit 6.1 is why we've been telling clients since 1981 to prepay mortgages.

Alternatively, from an investor's perspective, the chart makes visible the 2 percent to 3 percent real returns on bonds from 1952 to the mid-1960s. It portrays losses suffered by anyone who owned bonds in the 1970s. By 1979, anyone who owned a long bond had a loss. Many bonds sold at 50 cents on the dollar. If, during this period, you avoided the losses of long bonds by keeping your money in passbook savings,

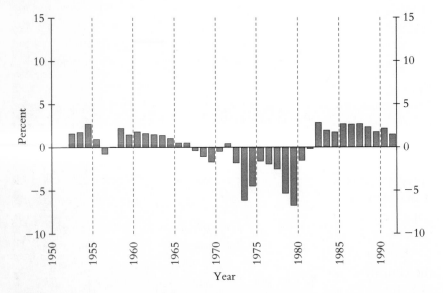

Exhibit 6.1   Real After-Tax Mortgage Rate, 1952–1992

you received 5.5 percent (pretax) while the value of your money shrank by 10 percent per year due to inflation. The chart also displays the unusually good returns to bondholders in the 1980s.

In short, the chart displays a change in the investment climate in 1968 and again in 1982. Each of these changes caught much of the public and many investors by surprise. Through the 1970s, people continued to use strategies appropriate to the climate of the 1960s, until the pain of 10 percent inflation became unbearable. Savers kept their savings in passbook accounts yielding 5.5 percent. Baby boomers who bought big houses (or farms) with big mortgages were warned by their fathers that they would never be able to pay them off. By the late 1970s, we all knew that we didn't want to pay off the mortgage early. And the savers, typically our parents, flocked to get the 14 percent rates offered by money market funds.

Meanwhile, the same pain that caused people to move their assets to 14 percent money market funds caused them to demand lower inflation, resulting in a new Fed chairman and a new occupant of 1600 Pennsylvania Avenue. Yet, while demanding and getting lower inflation, the public continued to follow the strategies appropriate to the 1970s. Our parents kept their money in CDs and money market funds to avoid any loss of principal, and were encouraged to do so by the experts. Baby boomers bought ever bigger houses with ever bigger mortgages, comfortable in the belief that doing so was a good investment and would make them money.

Yet the chart illustrates the heavy net cost of 11 percent mortgages in a 4 percent inflation economy. We've been warning our readers about this cost since 1987, but the public has only taken it to heart in the past two years. We had no influence on the timing of the change, but we believe the recession, exacerbated by the Gulf War, did. Anyway, it has finally happened. The bottom line is that the mortgaged American public has reversed its actions from "trading up on the equity" to "prepaying the mortgage." Folks, this change is a 180-degree turnaround; it is a complete reversal. And since a major segment of this public has gone from 30-year mortgages to 15-year mortgages, this new trend is unlikely to be reversed anytime soon.

Exhibit 6.2 is a plot of the DJIA over the same time span. We believe the climatic conditions you see in Exhibit 6.1 drove the prices you see in Exhibit 6.2, and the perception of the investing public lagged reality, just as the perceptions of the mortgaged public did. It's the same public.

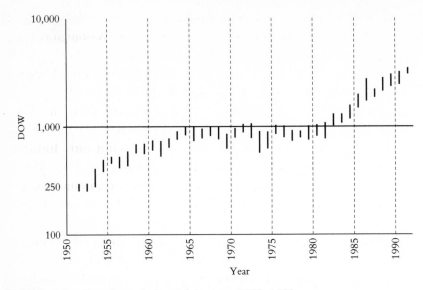

Exhibit 6.2   Dow Jones Industrial Average, 1952–1992

In 1934, Ben Graham co-authored the book *Security Analysis*, which is the definitive work in the field. In the 1951 edition, he said the stock market was overpriced, but (as Exhibit 6.2 shows) the market went up. In the 1962 edition, he upped his valuation criteria by 50 percent but still concluded that the market was overpriced. The market rose for another four years. By 1972, the public's confidence in the market had become so strong that a group of us working for an insurance company were nearly fired because we sold half of the stockholdings and went to cash; our criteria told us that, at that time, stocks were overpriced, but our boss did not agree. In 1973–1974, reality caught up with the market and stock prices dropped.

Today (1992), people who compare stock prices to the past decade say the market is too high. Yet our evaluation criteria, which flagged stocks as expensive in 1972, indicate that prices are now fair. After the experience of the past 10 years, we find it fascinating that there is still faith in real estate, but owning stocks is still considered risky.

Weathering the Cycles

In our weather analogy, while Exhibit 6.1 shows the investment climate, the seasons correspond to cyclicality in the economy and the markets.

Since World War II these seasons have been determined by cyclical patterns in monetary and fiscal policy emanating from Washington, D.C.

In the 1970s, people talked about a four-year cycle in the stock market. Such a cycle is visible in Exhibit 6.2 from 1954 to 1982. I believe the cycle was determined politically. After being elected, each president from Eisenhower through Ford (with implicit help from the Fed) squeezed the economy to contain inflation and then goosed it to get reelected. Jimmy Carter didn't read the script: He goosed it early. Inflation ran up, and he lacked maneuvering room in his final two years. Responding to popular demand, Reagan and the Fed squeezed the economy to lower inflation but did not goose it later, giving us a good economic decade. My advice to Bill Clinton would be to talk about stimulus but to save any action for 1995–1996. We're already set up for good economic numbers for the next couple years. (No, he hasn't asked.)

Finally, just to complete our picture of investment markets and the analogy to weather, daily stock price fluctuations correspond to daily rainfall. Whether stocks run up or down 30 points today is no more important than whether we get a half inch of rain. Today, such fluctuations correspond to human moods and to the passage of weather fronts across the landscape. Such movements give people in the media/entertainment business (and pilots of small planes) something to talk about but have very little importance.

2005 Update

We continue to find our weather analogies useful in describing the economy and the stock market.

The long-term picture, the investment climate, remains positive as inflation continues at about 2 percent and the economy continues to grow on a secular basis. Within that climate, the investment seasons continue. Although the economy is now expanding after recovering from only the second recession since 1982, the market has witnessed corrections in 1987, 1990, 1994, 1998, and 2002. So the markets have approximated a four-year cycle even though the economy hasn't. But the most recent years have had some added twists.

In our weather analogy, we sometimes witness daily weather patterns that seem to defy the season. Sometimes the anomaly is temperature;

sometimes it's rainfall. We've recently witnessed years when the November–December temperatures were unseasonably warm. In 2002 we talked about a drought in western Pennsylvania, but it was less a drought than a shift in the timing of the rainfall—more than normal rain in April and May, followed by almost none in June and July. The point is that we can have unusual daily weather without negating the normal seasons or the underlying climate. Similarly, in investing, the psychology (hopes and fears) of the investing public can result in security prices seemingly at odds with the values determined by the investment climate and the business cycle.

In 1999, the Fed raised interest rates to slow the economy. Similar action in the past resulted in declining stock prices. In fact, in 1999 on the New York Stock Exchange, the number of declining stocks exceeded the number of rising stocks. But a group of stocks, including Internet and technology stocks, caught the fancy of a group of investors and set dramatic new highs. For a period of about 18 months, psychology overwhelmed fundamentals for their select group, allowing prices to rise longer and much further than normally expected. Prices of some securities reached absurd levels based purely on hope. Those prices had to come back down to reflect reality. While doing so, investor psychology was pummeled by a litany of fears that sometimes seemed overwhelming, from the terrorist attacks of September 11, 2001, to fears of war in Iraq, to domestic snipers, to crop failure, and so on.

By July 2002, these fears coalesced to the point where many investors just wanted out—regardless of price. This psychological reaction was repeated with less intensity (albeit at lower prices) in September–October. We believe that the headlined prices of 1999 and 2002 were driven by the psychological hopes and fears of some investors. We don't believe that these hopes and fears have a major lasting effect on the underlying strength of the American economy, which has since recovered from a normal cyclical recession.

2007 Update

2006 was an interesting year. The prior setup looked much like 1994. After an economic recovery from a recession four years earlier, the Fed was raising interest rates to slow down economic growth and to contain inflation (for reasons we spell out in our essay entitled "Where To from

Here?" (See Chapter 9).We judged the odds as favoring a slowdown or soft landing, rather than a recession. And, economically, that's what we got.

But the psychology of the market added a few wrinkles. People looking for yield(s) drove up the prices of low-rated bonds, utilities (up 30 percent for the year), and REITS (up 37 percent for the year), to the extent that they no longer look attractive on a value basis. And the prices of Chinese stocks rose more than 100 percent.

As often occurs, psychology (short-term weather) can overwhelm the seasonal patterns, for a while.

Beware of Good Yields

This essay was originally published in Muhlenkamp Memorandum *Issue 26, April 1993. Investors had just come through a period when many of the risks of fixed-income securities had become apparent, but this did not stop them from continuing to look for high yields in fixed-income securities. This essay explains the yields and risks of fixed-income securities so that investors can know what to expect and what to watch out for. Remember, if it seems too good to be true, it probably is. Look for the hidden risks.*

Recently, the American investing public has learned several lessons in fixed-income investing. The first was the lesson of bankruptcy risk. Several years ago when CD and money market yields fell from 12 percent to 8 percent, much of the investing public (in an effort to maintain this income) went shopping for high-yield securities. The financial community, from banks to savings and loans to brokers, responded with various programs and securities that promised high yields.

Investors later learned that, all too often, high yields meant junk because the assets behind these securities were of poor quality. The recession of 1990–1991 drove the weakest companies into bankruptcy, and default rates on junk bonds rose from 4 percent to 10 percent. In addition, allegations of wrongdoing were brought against the prominent junk bond financier, Michael Milken, who subsequently pleaded guilty to securities fraud in 1990. Many investors and many in the financial community said, "Never again," but it is happening again—with a twist. Today, the goal is to get 8 percent returns in a 3 percent market, but the risk in doing so has changed (more on this later).

The second lesson was reinvestment risk. Throughout the 1980s, savers were told by investment professionals that CDs were riskless, only to find interest rates on CDs dropping from 8 percent to 3 percent. So when their 8 percent CDs matured and they wanted to reinvest that money, they found that only 3 percent CDs were available. Trying to predict rates is unreliable. Yet because CDs and bonds have fixed maturity dates, they require an investor to try to do just that. (To minimize risk for themselves, the issuers have created "callable" CDs and bonds, but investors face penalties if they want to cash in early.)

The third lesson was that international money market funds have currency risk. Since September 1992, the U.S. dollar has risen, and many investors in international money market funds have seen their principal shrink by 15 to 20 percent. Why? Let's use an example. Let's say you buy a 100-yen bond when the exchange rate between the U.S. dollar and the yen is 1:1. You spend $100 U.S. for a 100-yen bond. Then the dollar appreciates, and now 100 yen is only worth $80 U.S. If you sell that 100-yen bond, you will get 100 yen, which is worth $80 U.S. Your principal shrank 20 percent in U.S. dollars. So remember, if you own foreign bonds and the dollar appreciates against the currency of your bonds, you will receive fewer dollars per unit of currency when you sell. As an investor, you'd rather own foreign currency and foreign bonds during a time when the dollar is falling relative to foreign currency. Like many of the characteristics of bonds, this is counterintuitive for most people.

We believe that the public is about to learn another lesson in fixed-income investing—the risk of callability on corporate and municipal bonds and on corporate preferred stocks. Once again, the investing public is looking for "high yields." During the junk bond craze of the late 1980s, the primary risk on most corporate high-yield securities was corporate bankruptcy. High-yield securities were issued by companies with weak balance sheets at a time when the Federal Reserve System was squeezing the money supply and the economy was slowing down, making bankruptcy more likely.

Today (1993), bankruptcy risk among the issuers of high-yield securities is lower for four reasons:

1. The Federal Reserve is expanding the money supply.
2. The economy is expanding.

3. The current lower interest rates benefit big borrowers the most.

4. Investors and underwriters are very sensitive to the risk of bankruptcy.

What many investors don't realize is that the decline in interest rates that has lessened bankruptcy risk has also increased the number of bonds selling at premium prices and the risk of callability.

Exhibit 6.3 is a small section of a table that appears in the *Wall Street Journal* every day[1] under the heading of "Treasury Bonds, Notes and Bills." The table lists the Treasury bonds currently outstanding along with the latest Bid and Ask Prices. The final column gives the yield-to-maturity based on the Asked Price. The yield-to-maturity is the total return (annualized) if the bond were bought today at the Asked Price and held to maturity.

Thus, if you buy a 7.25 percent U.S. Treasury that matures in May 2016, you can expect to pay 104 cents on the dollar. From now to May 2016, you will receive interest payments of $7.25 per hundred (7.25 percent) each year; and in May 2016, you will receive the bond principal of 100 cents on the dollar. Therefore, you will have a guaranteed loss of 4 cents on the dollar of principal.

The final column shows that although the interest payment is 7.25 percent, once you adjust for the loss of principal the annualized yield-to-maturity on the asked price is 6.82 percent.

Most of us wouldn't worry too much about losing 4 percent of principal over 23 years; but let's look at the 11.25 percent Treasury bond of February 2015. To get an $11.25 interest payment each year would cost 151 cents on the dollar. Thus, we would receive a current yield of $11.25/151 or 7.5 percent; but when the bond matures in February 2015, we won't receive the 151-cent cost. We will only receive the 100-cent par value, a loss of principal of 51 cents—guaranteed.

Exhibit 6.3   Treasury Bonds, Notes, and Bills

Maturity Rate	Month/Year	Bid	Asked	Ask Change	Yield
11.250	Feb 15	151:01	151:03	−11	6.74
10.625	Aug 15	144:05	144:05	−9	6.76
9.875	Nov 15	135:15	135:15	−11	6.78
9.250	Feb 16	128:08	128:08	−8	6.80
7.250	May 16	104:30	104:30	−9	6.82

The final column shows that although the interest payment is 11.25 percent, once you adjust for paying 151 percent of par and losing that principal, the annualized yield-to-maturity on the asked price is 6.74 percent. In effect, the market price of the two bonds has been adjusted so that the expected return on the 7.25 percent and the 11.25 percent bonds are nearly the same.

If you scan the full table, you will see that, with a few special exceptions, the market has adjusted prices of all Treasury bonds so that the yield-to-maturity numbers are merely a function of time-to-maturity.

When you consider non-Treasury, fixed-income securities, you find a further complication because most corporate and municipal bonds and corporate-preferred stocks are callable. Just as you and I can pay off or refinance our home mortgages when we choose to do so, with little or no penalty, corporations and municipalities can pay off (or "call in") their bonds or preferreds when they choose to do so.

The following is a recent example that crossed my desk. In 1990, a local company, in need of equity capital, marketed a preferred stock to the public. The preferred paid an annual dividend of $2.60, and the stock was sold at $25 for a yield of 10.4 percent. Sounds good, right?

It is good enough that since 1990, the market price of the preferred has been bid up to 29.50. Note that at 29.50, the current yield on this preferred is $2.60/29.5 or 8.8 percent. Still good, right?

Yes, but if you read the prospectus on this preferred stock, you learn that the company can call it back in 1995 at $26.30 per share. Should the company not call in this preferred, its annual cost will be 9.9 percent.

Thus, if today's rates hold, it is likely the company will call in this preferred issue, and the current holder will lose 11 percent in principal ($29.50 to $26.30) in the next two years. When combined with the dividends received over these two years, the investor's "yield-to-call" or total return over that two years is 3.5 percent per year, which is to say the return is comparable to other securities maturing in two years.

The Treasury yield curve in Exhibit 6.4 is also printed in the *Wall Street Journal* every day.[2] It is simply a plot of the yield-to-maturity rate from the "Treasury Bonds, Notes, and Bills" exhibit excerpted earlier. As a rule of thumb, any security that seems to provide a yield of more than 1 percent above this curve (at the appropriate time span) carries a risk that you haven't been told about.

Be careful out there!

Treasury Yield Curve

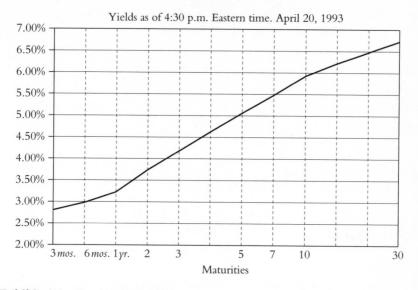

Exhibit 6.4   Treasury Yield Curve
SOURCE: *The Wall Street Journal*

2007 Update

At various places in this book, I've stated that in 2007, long-term Treasury bonds are fairly priced. I state that because they're priced at an interest yield of 4.75 to 5.25 percent, which I consider fair when inflation is 2 to 2.25 percent. However, that doesn't mean that all bonds are fairly priced. I find the incremental yields on lower-quality bonds to be inadequate, well below the levels that historically have been necessary to take the risk of lending to low-quality borrowers. As I write this update in August 2007, these quality spreads are widening (the prices of low-quality bonds are falling) back toward normal levels.

Editor's Note

Remember that bonds are traded in an open market, just like stocks. Therefore, they are subject to the influences of the market. With this in mind, let's take one more look at bonds. Since the coupon (the rate) of a bond is fixed, when interest rates are rising, the bond becomes less attractive to investors (they can get better rates elsewhere) and the price of the bond will fall. (This is what happened in the 1970s.) When

interest rates are falling, the fixed rate of the bond makes it more attractive to investors and bond prices rise, but only until they reach a price at which they are callable.
Then the bond will be called because the company that issued the bond will want
to refinance its debt at the lower rates that are now available. So no matter if interest
rates are rising or falling, the bondholder faces significant risks.

If this seems one-sided, consider this: In the bond market, the borrower issues
the bonds, and therefore writes the rules. Consequently, bonds are designed to
make money for the borrower, not the lender. Buyer beware!

What Is Risk? (Part 2)

This essay was originally published in Muhlenkamp Memorandum
Issue 28, October 1993. *At that time, one of Ron's largest clients
(a pension fund) was being told by a stock brokerage firm to increase
its investment allocation to bonds, since bonds were "guaranteed" and
the returns for the prior 10 years had been nearly as good as the
average for stocks. Ron didn't think the prior 10 years was
the appropriate time to consider. In this essay he looks back to 1952
to examine the long-term performance of stocks and bonds. In doing
so, he illustrates why the brokerage firm's advice to invest in more
bonds was misguided.*

*We have kept the original 1993 data and added updated data for
2002 in parentheses. The year 2002 provides an interesting comparison
because the recession in 2001 and its impact are quite similar to the
economics of a decade earlier.*

Much has been written about the "riskiness" of stocks and the "safety"
of bonds. But the data seems to focus on only the recent history, a time of
falling interest rates and capital gains in bonds. Our discussion has a
more long-term focus.

Risk versus Return

To get a little longer history on the riskiness of stocks and bonds, we
have plotted the annual returns from stocks and bonds for 1952–1992
(2002) in Exhibits 6.5 and 6.6.

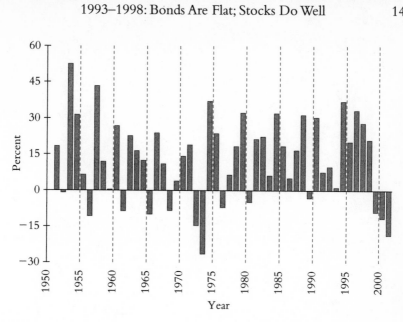

Exhibit 6.5   S&P 500 Index Yearly Total Returns, 1952–2002

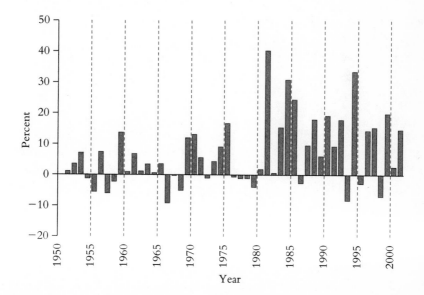

Exhibit 6.6   Long-Term Government Bonds Yearly Total Returns, 1952–2002

In 41 (51) years:

- Stock returns averaged 11.7 percent (11.2 percent) per year with 10 (13) down years;
- Bond returns averaged 5.6 percent (6.8 percent) per year with 13 (16) down years;
- Inflation averaged 4.2 percent (3.9 percent) per year.

We are not convinced, however, that a one-year period is the appropriate time frame to judge long-term investments. So we've smoothed the annual returns of stocks and bonds by computing three-year trailing averages. These averages are shown in Exhibits 6.7 and 6.8. Note that a three-year average does not change the average annual return.

On a three-year basis, stocks have had one (two) down period(s), and bonds have had three (three) down periods. So, if your definition of risk is the probability of losing money, the difference is small, but it favors stocks.

When people on Wall Street talk about risk, they really are talking about the variability of returns, not the probability of losing money. Wall Street maintains that stocks are riskier than bonds simply because there is a greater variation in the *one-year* return.

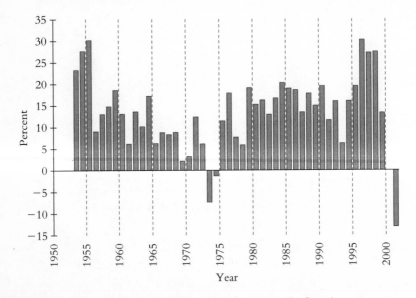

Exhibit 6.7 S&P 500 Index Total Return Three-Year Trailing Average, 1952–2002

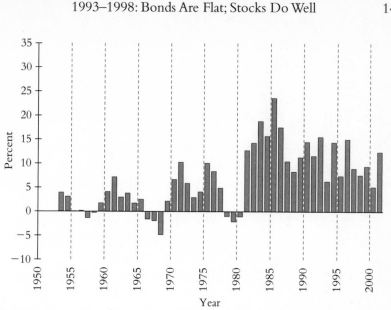

Exhibit 6.8   Long-Term Government Bonds Total Return Three-Year Trailing Average, 1952–2002

By Wall Street's definition, even if returns were positive each year and had the same pattern for stocks and bonds, but stocks varied between 0 percent and 20 percent while bonds varied between 0 percent and 10 percent, stocks would be considered riskier because the variation was greater. We think the problem is in the definition. Over 41 (51) years:

- Stocks averaged 11.7 percent (11.2 percent) per year, which was 7.5 percent (7.3 percent) over inflation, netting a total of 17 (33) times the original purchasing power;
- Bonds averaged 5.6 percent (6.8 percent) per year, which was 1.4 percent (2.9 percent) over inflation, netting less than two (four) times purchasing power.

Total returns from stocks consist of the dividends received and the change in price. Total returns from bonds consist of the interest received and the change in price. People seem to have forgotten that when interest rates go up, bond prices go down, and investing in bonds can lose you money. By 1980, 5 percent bonds bought in 1966 were worth less than 50 cents on the dollar. So, if you can predict interest rates, you will know when to own bonds.

We have found, however, that you don't need to predict interest rates to know when to own bonds. You only need to know whether current real returns are attractive.

Get the Real Story

At Muhlenkamp & Company, we define risk as the probability of losing purchasing power over time. When we look at bonds, we subtract the current inflation rate from the current yield level to get the expected *real* return.

We then set a hurdle rate of a 3 percent real return before we are willing to lend money by buying bonds. We've plotted nominal long-term interest rates in Exhibit 6.9 and real long-term interest rates in Exhibit 6.10. We have also indicated our 3 percent hurdle rate in Exhibit 6.10.

Exhibit 6.10 makes it apparent why from 1968 (when I entered the investment business) to 1981, I never invested in long-term bonds. Bonds didn't meet the 3 percent hurdle rate for real returns except for a brief period. This exhibit also illustrates why I was very comfortable

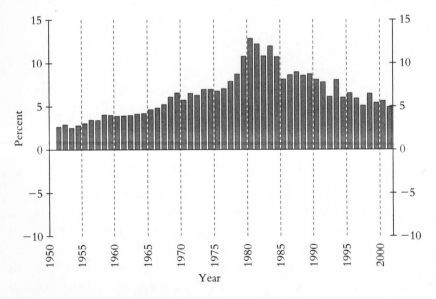

Exhibit 6.9 Nominal Long-Term Government Bond Rate, 1952–2002

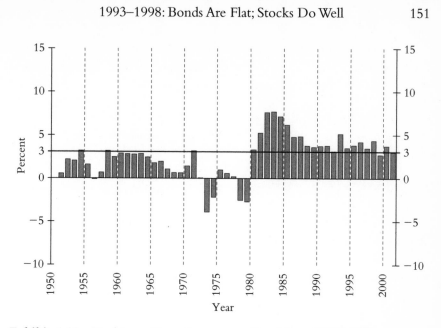

Exhibit 6.10 Real Long-Term Government Bond Rate, 1952–2002

investing heavily in bonds from 1981 through 1986. At that time, real returns on bonds were 6 to 8 percent, versus a hurdle of 3 percent. At various times during that period, corporate interest rates were higher than corporate returns on equity, meaning it was unprofitable for companies to borrow money and interest rates had to fall. But Exhibit 6.10 demonstrates more than that.

Exhibit 6.10 demonstrates three (four) distinct periods in the returns available from bonds:

- From 1952 to 1965, bonds promised average nominal returns of 3.5 percent and real returns of 2.1 percent. Hindsight and Exhibit 6.6 show that they actually provided nominal returns of 2.1 percent. We consider this period normal, at least in comparison to what followed.
- From 1966 to 1980, bonds promised nominal returns of 6.75 percent and very poor real returns of 0.1 percent. They produced nominal returns of 2.6 percent (because rates went up).
- From 1981 to 1993, bonds promised nominal returns of 9.5 percent and unusually good real returns of 5.0 percent. They produced nominal returns of 13.6 percent (because rates went down).

- (From 1994 to 2002, bonds promised nominal returns of 6 percent and real returns of 3.9 percent. They produced nominal returns at 9.2 percent—because rates declined.)

We consider both the 1966–1980 period and the 1981–1993 period to be unusual and not likely to be repeated anytime soon. For an explanation about why this happened, see our essay "And the Climate Is . . . " (earlier in this chapter).

If we also calculate the stock returns for these periods, we find that:

- In the 1952–1965 period, when bonds averaged a 2.1 percent return, stocks averaged 14.5 percent.
- In the 1968–1980 period, both stocks and bonds did poorly, but stocks did better than bonds: 6.7 percent compared to 2.6 percent.
- In the 1981–1992 period, when bonds did very well, stocks did better: 14.7 percent compared to 13.6 percent.
- (In the 1993–2002 period, stocks did 9.5 percent, compared to bonds' 9.2 percent.)

To understand why this is so, read our essay "Why the Market Went Down" (Chapter 4).

At Muhlenkamp & Company, we believe the reason stocks perform better than bonds is not because they are riskier but because corporate management works for the stockholder and against the bondholder.

Exhibit 6.10 also shows that, after an unusually good decade, real long-term interest rates have returned to normal levels of roughly 3 percent over inflation. Rates are now 6 to 7 percent (4 to 5 percent). Returns greater than 6 to 7 percent (4 to 5 percent) will require a continued decline in interest rates, either because inflation continues down or because public enthusiasm for bonds causes an overshoot beyond fair value.

While we believe each of these possibilities has a slightly greater than 50 percent probability (now less than 50 percent), bond returns will no longer be driven by the unusually high real interest rates of the last decade. The time to be heavily invested in long bonds has just come to an end (even more true today).

Exhibit 6.9 also can be read as the return investors expected from their purchases of bonds in each of the past 41 (51) years. In fact, these returns were guaranteed. Exhibit 6.6 shows the returns investors actually received. Realized returns were well below guaranteed returns until 1981.

Conclusion

Although we haven't yet constructed a chart for stocks similar to Exhibit 6.10, we judge the average stock to be priced to return 9 to 10 percent (8 to 9 percent). The caveat is that stocks are normally more sensitive to public hopes and fears than are bonds, so corrections of 5 to 15 percent can occur at any time. Partly, this is because stock prices are reported on the news every day and played up by the media and the brokerage community, while bond prices are largely ignored. Frankly, the most likely trigger for such a correction in stocks in the current environment would be an uptick in interest rates, and therefore, a decline in the price of bonds. When we put all of these factors together, we see the following current conditions:

- Inflation is 3 to 3.5 percent (approximately 2 percent).
- Short-term debt is likely to return a nominal 3 percent (1 percent), or 0 percent (−1 percent) real.
- Long-term debt is likely to return a nominal 6 to 7 percent (4 to 5 percent), or 3 to 4 percent (2 to 3 percent) real, with some volatility.
- Stocks are likely to return a nominal 9 to 10 percent (8 to 9 percent); 6 to 7 percent (6 to 7 percent) real, with greater volatility.

Therefore, for money with a horizon beyond three years, we find the real returns available on stocks to be double those available on bonds, and we find both stocks and bonds to be more attractive than short-term investments.

Editor's Note

So what's the bottom line? Looking at the performance of stocks and bonds from 1952 to 2002, we see that in the long term (three years or more) stocks have better returns than bonds. This is because the corporation works for the stockholder and against the bondholder. In other words, a company will doggedly try to increase its profitability but will not pay one penny more than it has to on its loans. So in a well-run company, you would rather be an owner (stocks) than a lender (bonds). You don't want to be either in a poorly run company.

Are Stocks Too High?

This essay was originally published in Muhlenkamp Memorandum
*Issue 29, January 1994. It looks at the assumptions behind stock
valuation models and why they often misprice the stock market. Using
the same data, but modifying the model, Ron creates a new valuation
model that better anticipates stock prices. Same data—different
perspective.*

For 10 years we've been hearing that stocks are "too high" and that
prices should decline. Yet during that time, stock prices have quadrupled.
In the early 1970s various studies showed that stocks normally sold at 17
times company earnings. So in 1973, when prices fell to 15, then 14,
then 13 times earnings, many advisers said that stocks were "cheap" and
should be bought. They kept saying this as stock prices fell all the way to
six or seven times earnings. Since then, when we hear that stocks are
"cheap" or "too high," our response is, "Relative to what?" It turned out
that in 1973, "Stocks are cheap" meant relative to recent price-to-earnings
(P/E) ratios. In the 1980s, "Stocks are high" meant relative to recent P/E
ratios and current interest rates. Let me explain.

Determining Fair Value

The models that seek to determine fair value for stocks use corporate
earnings and a capitalization rate (such as a P/E ratio) to arrive at fair value.
Nearly all such models use interest rates to set the capitalization rate. Current interest rates are *assumed* to be fair, as if there were no emotions in the
bond market. Interest rates themselves are never viewed as too high or too
low. (When I was doing basic evaluation work 20 years ago, I initially made
the same assumption, but soon found it to be a mistake. I then learned that
fair values are determined by inflation and that interest rates and bond
prices suffered from the same emotional swings that stock prices do.)

For the past 10 years, stocks have been viewed as too high in relation
to interest rates. In reality, interest rates have been too high. When short-
term rates fell in 1990–1991, the models that used short-term rates as a
base started to show that stocks were fairly priced.

As long-term rates have fallen over the past couple of years, the
models that use long-term rates as a base have begun to show that stocks

are fairly priced. One database that we purchase, Ford Equity Research, calculates a price-to-value ratio (PVA) for 2,000 stocks based on long-term bond rates. Ford's PVA ratio fell below 1.0 (indicating prices are at fair value) in August 1993 for the first time since July 1980 (except for a brief period during the Gulf War). During much of the 1980s stock prices frequently bottomed at a PVA of 1.2. At those levels, the model indicated that stocks were 20 percent overpriced, but the reality was that interest rates were too high; stocks were a good buy.

We recently received from Ford Equity Research a graph of their PVA for the period 1970–1993, as shown in Exhibit 6.11. Quoting Ford's explanation of their model:

> Ford's PVA is determined by comparing the price of a company's stock to that derived by a proprietary dividend discount model (DDM). A PVA greater that 1.00 indicates that a company is overpriced whereas a PVA less than 1.00 implies that a stock is trading below the level justified by its earnings, quality, dividends, growth projections, and prevailing interest rates. Each month Ford publishes the average PVA of all the companies in the Ford Equity Research data base.

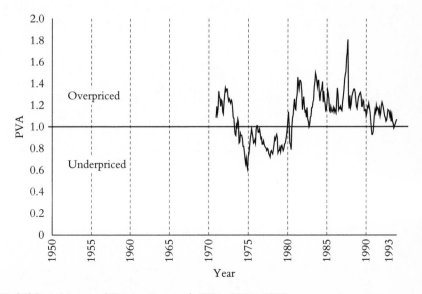

Exhibit 6.11   Ford Equity Research PVA, 1970–1993

For their "prevailing interest rates," Ford uses long-term interest rates. The structure of the model produces the result that, if all other things are equal, interest rates that are too low will depress the PVA ratio and indicate that stock prices are too low. Similarly, interest rates that are too high will boost the PVA ratio and indicate that stock prices are too high.

In Exhibit 6.12 we show Ford's PVA plot in line with plots of real (adjusted for inflation) long-term government bonds and the Dow Jones Industrial Average.

You can see that from 1973 to 1980 Ford's PVA is at or below 1.0 when real (adjusted for inflation) interest rates were unusually low. From 1981 to 1993 Ford's PVA is above 1.0 when real interest rates were unusually high. You can also see that when interest rates were unusually low, causing stocks to appear cheap, stock prices moved sideways. In fact, nominal (before inflation) returns in the 1970–1980 period were about 3 percent per year. Conversely, when interest rates were unusually high—causing many to conclude that stocks were too high—stocks in fact returned 15 percent per year for a quadruple return in 10 years.

We contacted Ford Equity Research and asked them to rerun their model, but instead of using prevailing interest rates, we asked them to substitute numbers equal to annual inflation plus 3 percent. This is equivalent to assuming that real interest rates were at a steady 3 percent for the period rather than the pattern depicted in the bar chart. For economy, we ran the numbers on an annual rather than a monthly basis. No other changes were made to the model.

This one change in the assumed interest rate (see Exhibit 6.13) resulted in the line labeled "PVA Revised" (line B) that we have overlaid on the earlier plot of PVA; the contrast is apparent. The revised PVA indicates that stocks were overvalued for most of the period 1970–1980, when nominal returns were 3 percent, and that stocks were very cheap in the early 1980s and have only recently returned to fair value, after quadrupling in price.

We believe that the revised PVA (line B) is a much better model than the original PVA (line A). It certainly has had much better results. The revised PVA approximates the model we've used for valuing stocks for the past 20 years. Note that when real interest rates are 3 percent, both models give the same values and recently indicated that stock prices are fair.

We're not denigrating Ford Equity Research; we find their data and many of their conclusions very useful. We're merely using their plot to

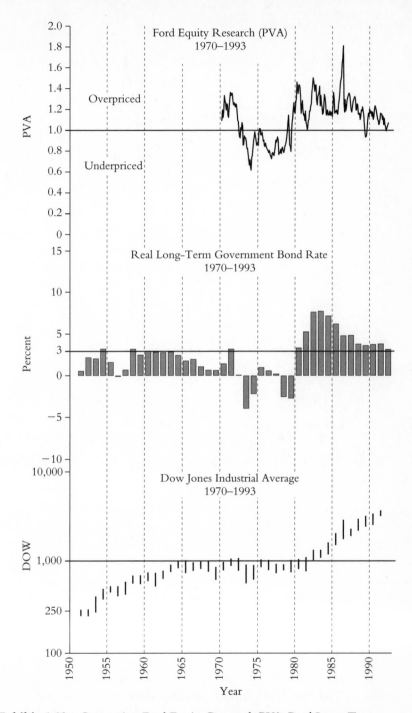

Exhibit 6.12 Comparing Ford Equity Research PVA, Real Long-Term Government Bonds, and the Dow Jones Industrial Average

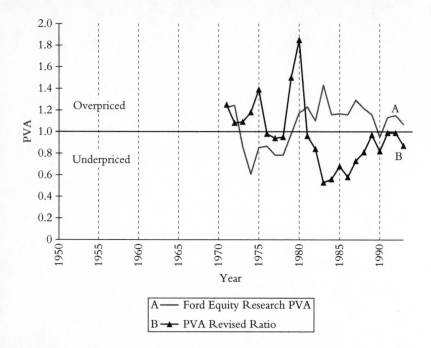

Exhibit 6.13   PVA Revised, 1970–1993

illustrate a fundamental flaw in most stock valuation models. Rather than taking inflation into account explicitly, such models use current interest rates and *assume* that such rates incorporate inflation. What we don't understand is why these assumptions seem to go unquestioned after 20 years of giving signals that are clearly wrong.

Editor's Note

When someone says stock prices are too high or too low, they are likely using stock valuation models that are based on current interest rates. These models have a very poor track record because often it is the interest rates that are too high or too low. Always understand the model behind the statements.

Diversification—Too Much of a Good Thing

This essay was originally published in Muhlenkamp Memorandum Issue 32, October 1994. At that time, there was an emerging trend in the investment advisory business to have a stockbroker or financial planner pick a broad array of investment managers in order to diversify your portfolio. Perhaps the planner would choose a dozen mutual funds for you to invest in. Those dozen funds might include growth funds, value funds, small funds, and large funds. That's what they meant by diversity—covering all the bases. Ron offers another perspective on diversity—an informed diversity where you diversify, but only among good investments.

We often hear the phrase "Don't put all your eggs in one basket." We think that's good advice. We always use at least 20 baskets, never putting more than 5 percent of our assets into any one of them.

But it's still important to check the quality of the baskets. Not all baskets are well constructed. Easter baskets are designed to be pretty. They are okay for carrying a few eggs which are already hard-boiled, but they are not suited to carrying a full load of fresh eggs on a daily basis.

Not all baskets are appropriate in all climates or for all purposes. A fiber basket that is ideal in a dry climate will disintegrate in a wet one. A plastic basket that cushions the eggs in a warm climate will turn brittle and crack in a cold one. A plastic-coated wire basket that is ideal for gathering eggs and transporting them a few yards is unsuited to transporting eggs long distances, where a cardboard box is much better.

In the investment business, a CD basket differs from a bond basket, which differs from a stock basket, which differs from a commodity basket, and so on. And the General Electric basket differs from the Ford basket, which differs from the Exxon basket . . .

Some people selling investment advice maintain that you should use all of these baskets *for diversity*. They speak or write of diversity as if it were the goal of investing. It's not! The goal of investing is to increase the purchasing power of your assets—to make you money. Any potential investment should be measured by its likelihood of making you money. Any potential investment that is unlikely to make you money should be discarded.

Diversification as a Safety Factor

The people who say you should own some of each investment *for diversity* are really telling you that they don't know how to judge a good investment from a bad one, or that they don't know what kind of investment climate we're living in. In one respect they are right. The less you know, the more you should diversify. If you don't know anything, you might as well own some of everything. But why should you pay a fee to people who don't know any more than you do?

Again, the goal of investing is to make you money. To do this, you can either take the time and make the effort to learn how to do it yourself, or hire someone to do it for you. If you had a perfect crystal ball, you would select the one best investment and put all your money into it. Nearly all great fortunes are the result of concentration, usually one person founding a company and focusing on one idea. But this is an all-or-nothing strategy, and no one has a perfect crystal ball. If you pick the wrong person or the wrong idea, you can lose your investment.

Warren Buffett (the most successful investor of our generation) operates one step removed from this. He has suggested that people would do better if they limited themselves to 20 investment selections in their lifetime. But he has also said that he wouldn't care if they closed the stock exchange for two years, and that he's willing to hold through price declines of 30 percent. Most investors are unwilling to take that 30 percent risk or to ignore the prices of their investments for two years. They lack the confidence to choose the one right idea or the one right stock or the one right time. So, for our clients, we diversify into 20 or more securities. We spend a lot of time and mental effort working to understand the securities available and the climate in which we live. We put what we learn on paper because, frankly, the better you understand what we are doing, the easier it is for us to make money for you.

When I was studying engineering, we were taught to include a "safety factor" in all of our designs. In many cases, the safety factor was 100 percent. One day, when discussing safety factors, our professor commented that a safety factor is really an ignorance factor. We used the safety factor to compensate for our ignorance of the material, the construction, the maintenance, and (of course) our design. Similarly, in investing, we diversify to compensate for our ignorance.

No matter how much work we do in getting to know a company, an industry, or an economy, we will still have a 20 to 30 percent chance of being wrong. No matter how well we get to know the people involved, there are some things they won't tell us. Often this is because they don't (or can't) know, but sometimes it is because they won't admit it. A certain small percentage will lie to us. So we check the statistic books and find that most of this risk can be neutralized (diversified away) by owning 15 to 20 securities. As a result, we plan to own 20 or more securities.

Based on some knowledge of basket/security construction:

- We avoid commodities and futures because they are a zero-sum game, and both the users and producers work to drive prices down.
- We are very skeptical of buying options and other derivatives because they are also a zero-sum game, and time works against you.[3]
- We avoid limited partnerships because the fees are too high.
- We know that CDs are guaranteed to lose you money after taxes and inflation (except for a brief period of time in the early 1980s).
- We are skeptical of debt instruments—bonds, mortgages, fixed annuities—because we know they are managed for the benefit of the issuers and against the interests of the investor.

Based on some knowledge of the current (1994) investment climate:

- We are avoiding real estate.
- We are very skeptical of foreign investing because the dollar is undervalued.[4]
- We are willing to own bonds at a price.
- We are not willing to confine ourselves to narrow categories of investments.

Generalists versus Specialists

When you check the history of the people who have good long-term records in investing, you will find that they are generalists. Warren Buffett concentrates his assets, but he chooses from a broad list of possibilities. So does (did) John Templeton, Peter Lynch, John Neff, and so on. If you read what they've said or written, each has strong convictions about how to choose investments and/or egg baskets. Each one has a consistent philosophy of investing and a documented track record of results. We would be comfortable having any one of these people managing all of our money.

But the recent, self-promoted fad in the investment advisory business is to have a journalist, a stockbroker, or a financial planner pick a broad array of investment specialists *for diversity*. They will tell you to own or hire a specialist in paper baskets, a specialist in cloth baskets, a specialist in metal baskets, a specialist in plastic baskets, and so on, in order to have diversity, as if that were your goal. They even document the success of each specialist in his or her field, but they don't show you their own past record at picking the specialists. Their selections are all hindsight. They imply that perfect hindsight equates to perfect foresight, but that's not often the case.

The Importance of Being Informed

So what should you do? Keep a diary of your thoughts on investing and the articles that make sense to you. Over time, you will learn what works and what doesn't.

You can shorten the learning curve by using your local library. The next time you are in the library, get the January 31, 1994, issue of *Forbes* magazine. On pages 132–133, Mark Hulbert lists the performance since 1983 of a number of investment letter writers.[5] Make a copy of the article and take it home. When you get a solicitation in the mail from a letter writer, check their track record.

In addition, when you read an article in a current magazine that seems to make a lot of sense, go to the library and see what the author or the magazine recommended three to five years ago. Use the same method for checking Morningstar's reviews of mutual funds.

Checking the record of your stockbroker or financial planner is likely to be more difficult. Most don't keep or publish a record of their recommendations or their results. Talking to a number of satisfied clients may be the best that you can do.

Finally, try to get differing opinions and question them all. This will broaden your perspective and help you make informed decisions.

Editor's Note

This trend to diversify among many investment managers specializing in different kinds of investments continues today. It allows investors to feel secure (they have covered all the bases) without knowing anything about investing. The drawback is that you are likely to get as many poor managers as good ones, and even the best managers will be constrained by the limitations imposed upon them by categorization of their investment fund. (See our essay "How Much Money Are You Willing to Lose for a Theory?" in Chapter 8.) By trying to blindly eliminate risk, you've increased your probability of poor returns. You will do better to take the time to find a good manager whose investment philosophy makes sense to you and let that individual manage your money. (See our essay "How to Choose a Money Manager" in Chapter 7.)

The Game of the Stock Market versus the Business of Investing

This essay was originally published in Muhlenkamp Memorandum *Issue 33, January 1995. A client had asked Ron to summarize his investment philosophy. This was Ron's response.*

I entered this business in 1968. At that time, I had never owned a stock or bond, and I had never taken any courses in Wall Street finance. (I had taken courses in corporate finance.) So I began my studies with a clean slate.

I soon learned that there are an unlimited number of people with ideas about how to invest your money, and all the ideas sound good at the time. Some of these people are paid to sell newspapers and magazines; some are paid to entertain on radio or television; some are paid commissions to sell financial products; and some are actually paid to manage other people's money.

Only this last group publishes the results of their advice. The others tell me when they have been right, but I have to research what they wrote three to five years ago to get a complete picture. I also noticed that the gurus and the managers who were heroes in any one year seldom repeated; those who had good long-term records tended to stay on top, but they were seldom heroes in any one year.

Since my goal is good, reliable, long-term returns, I decided to study the philosophies of the people with good long-term records. I found that they all own corporate stocks, but their approach is to look at companies as businesses. And I learned that, over time, stock prices do reflect the values of the underlying businesses.

I also learned that these values and the resulting stock prices have increased by 9 to 10 percent per year, indicating that if I just buy good companies and hold them long enough, my returns would be 9 to 10 percent. By contrast, long-term returns on bonds have been 4 to 5 percent, and CDs have been 2 to 3 percent. So I have concluded that, as a long-term investor, my normal position is to be 100 percent invested in corporate stocks.

The Game versus the Business

All the problems with investing in stocks are in the short term, where changes in stock prices often seem unrelated to long-term values. Short-term prices are determined by whatever hopes and fears are currently driving the American public to buy and sell stocks. These hopes and fears are fanned by the media, the brokerage community, and various pundits with a short-term agenda.

But it is also true that much of the public insists on this short-term agenda and revels in the drama of it. I call it *The Game of the Stock Market* (as opposed to *The Business of Investing*), and it is very entertaining. The game focuses on the most dramatic and volatile aspects of price movements. Even the language is borrowed from gambling, focusing on winners and losers. The game can also be quite profitable, but it requires an iron stomach and an *against-the-crowd* discipline that few people have.

A Reliable Business

Identifying a top or a bottom does no good unless you have the intestinal fortitude to act decisively on it. Professionals face the same problem. In mid-1987, Elaine Garzarelli became justly famous when she identified a short-term market top and avoided the decline in October of that year. But she then failed to buy in a timely fashion, even though her research told her to do so. Consequently, her advantage was dissipated as the market recovered to new highs in 1988 and 1989.

For most people The Game of the Stock Market is a distraction that prevents them from making money in The Business of Investing. Periodic setbacks and a focus on the game result in their selling stocks when they should be buying, and vice versa. We focus on the long-term business of investing because we have found it to be more profitable and more reliable.

Fund Your IRA Every Year, or How to Retire Wealthy by Driving Used Cars

This essay was originally published in Muhlenkamp Memorandum *Issue 34, April 1995.*

Recently, I commented to a friend that most investors buy stocks the way teenagers buy clothes. He responded, "How should they buy stocks?" Being a slow thinker, I didn't have a ready answer then, but I do now. Buy stocks the way you would buy used cars. The truly amazing fact is, if you also buy used cars, you can get rich on these two actions alone.

It is not hard to save $2,000 per year by driving a used car. Exhibit 6.14 shows that by investing $2,000 in an IRA every year, you can accumulate $1 million (at 12 percent) in 37 years or $885,000 (at 10 percent) in 40 years.★

There are three keys to saving $2,000 per year by driving a used car:

1. Insure only for liability. This alone will save you more than $600 per year.
2. Do not pay interest, which would cost you at least $130 annually per $1,000 borrowed.
3. Buy only what you can pay for in cash.

Exhibit 6.14   Investment of $2,000 per Year Compounded at 10 Percent and 12 Percent

Year	10%	12%
5	$12,210	$12,706
10	31,875	35,097
15	63,545	74,559
20	114,550	144,105
25	196,694	266,668
30	328,988	482,665
35	542,049	863,327
40	885,185	1,534,183

★Beginning in 2005, the allowance for IRA contributions was increased to $4,000, along with a catch-up contribution of $500 for people 50 years old and older. In 2006, the catch-up contribution amount was increased to $1,000.

Do Your Homework

So how do you buy a *good* used car, or a *good* stock? In each case, start at your local library. There you will find books titled *How to Buy a Used Car* (or something similar), which can be read in a few hours. Read one of them. It will give you criteria to use and a framework to work from.

For stocks, you need to be a little more careful. The principal difference between buying used cars and buying stocks is that, with stocks, many more of the charlatans write books. Be sure the author has a successful history of making money by investing, not just by selling books or magazine articles. These authors will also give you criteria to use and a framework from which to work. Peter Lynch's *One Up on Wall Street* is among the best I have found. Beyond that, read Ben Graham, Irving Fisher, and Warren Buffett. (Do not confuse the recent best seller *about* Buffett with the writings *by* Buffett.) Jim Roger's *Investment Biker* is a must for anyone considering foreign investing. It also provides an interesting perspective for those who are not.

When shopping for cars, your next step is to check out the data in *Consumer Reports*. Their data is based on consumer surveys and is so organized that in 20 to 30 minutes you can rule out the 80 percent of cars you do not want to own and focus on the 10 to 20 percent that you might want to own. If you want to refine the *Consumer Reports* data, talk to your mechanic (or, as my neighbor did, to your tow truck driver). If you do not yet have a mechanic you respect and trust, ask your neighbors with an interest in cars whom they trust. Do not be afraid to ask several neighbors. I have never met a person who resented being asked for advice, and just because you get several opinions does not mean you have to follow all of them.

When shopping for stocks, I begin with the *Value Line Investment Survey*, looking for companies with good balance sheets and a good return on equity capital (ROE). The ROE should be 15 percent or better; an ROE of 10 percent or less is not worth their being in business. I don't like to state rules of thumb because they are subject to change with inflation and interest rates, but today I would like the price-to-earnings ratio (P/E) to be less than the ROE and the expected growth rate.

Next, call the company to get its financial statements. Check the numbers and the footnotes in the annual report (it is audited) to be sure the *Value Line* numbers are accurate.

At this point, you will have identified up to a half-dozen car models that satisfy your criteria. Now it's time to shop the newspaper, because you would like to buy from a private individual. You would rather avoid a dealer because dealers dress up the cars they sell and know how to disguise problems. But the main reason you want to buy privately is because you would like to judge the current owner as well as the car. The degree of care the car has received can enhance or negate the record that you got from *Consumer Reports*. There are no used cars I would buy sight unseen, but there are people (very few) whose used cars I would buy sight unseen. In such cases, I would be buying based on my knowledge of the owner. Once you have identified a model that fits your criteria and a car that appears to be in good shape, be willing to pay your mechanic to check it over (it is cheap insurance).

Similarly with stocks, you would like to talk to the management of the companies you are interested in buying. For the individual, this is not always practical, but you can often get a reading on management from the company's annual report. The letter to shareholders should give you a summary of what management sees in their markets and what they are trying to accomplish. The best management will spell out the company's goals in specific terms. The proxy material will tell you how much stock management owns and whether they are compensated in ways that encourage them to work for the shareholders. In nearly all cases, the quality of the company's management is more important than the characteristics of the industry they are in. Finally, check with the company's customers. If the customers are happy, the company is doing something right.

The Winners, the Losers, and the In-Between

With both used cars and company stocks, you will find that junk is junk; there are many models and many companies you do not want to own at any price—so don't! Good is good; you will find some that you would like to own at a fair price. And there are a few gems that are worth paying a premium. (Warren Buffett has suggested that you should expect to find fewer than 20 gems in a stock-picking lifetime.) With both cars and stocks, look for the gems, but expect to compromise, particularly on the nonessentials. If you accept only perfect gems, you will miss a lot of good stocks and do a lot of walking.

Finally, be aware that no matter how much effort you put into it, on occasion you will get a lemon. When this happens, sell it and go on to the next vehicle. Selling a lemon may be a blow to your ego, but it's a lot less painful than keeping it. You will find that commissions for selling a stock are low. You will also find that selling a lemon you paid $3,000 for is a lot less painful than the new lemon your neighbor bought for $20,000.

How long will all this take? My daughter-in-law knows nothing about the mechanics of cars and knew nothing about shopping for them. Using the preceding advice, she spent four hours in the library and five or six hours shopping. In the end, she bought a good used car for $4,500. On stocks, I spend 40-plus hours per week.

The Road We've Traveled

Out of curiosity, I decided to check my own record. In 32 years, I have bought and sold 24 cars. The total of the purchase prices minus the sales prices is less than $20,000. If you adjusted this for inflation, it might be $30,000. So, our annual depreciation cost has been less than $1,000, and we've been a two-car family since 1970. Today, a more realistic depreciation would be $1,000 per car per year.

In the meantime, I have been fully funding my IRA since the law became effective in 1981. I have contributed $29,500 (in 1981, you could only contribute $1,500). I have not done anything fancy or heroic, just put the money in two good no-load, total-return mutual funds. As of March 31 of this year (1995), the market value was more than $76,000. A glance at Exhibit 6.14 shows that it has been compounding at better than 12 percent per year, and I am on track for a prosperous retirement.

We've seen some articles making the case that not everyone should fund their IRAs. We agree. The value of a traditional IRA or other tax-deferred asset is that the taxes are deferred. The negative is that when the assets are drawn out to be spent, they are taxed at the rates applicable to ordinary income, even if the returns were earned through capital appreciation. This has the effect of converting capital gains to ordinary income, so when your tax-deferred assets reach a level resulting in withdrawals being taxed at a rate over 30 percent, we believe it no longer makes sense to fund them. As a rule of thumb, when you become confident that your tax-deferred assets (pension plan, profit sharing plan, and IRA) will exceed $1 million by the time you reach 60, it makes sense to cease funding your IRA (and to take a full measure of comfort in what you have accomplished).

2007 Update

In line with the preceding paragraph, I have not contributed to my IRA since 1995. As of December 31, 2006, the market value was more than $340,000. A glance at the exhibit shows that it has been compounding at better than 12 percent per year, and I remain on track for a prosperous retirement.

Estate Planning for Generations

This essay was originally published in Muhlenkamp Memorandum *Issue 35, July 1995. It is the first in a series of three that discuss estate planning. In this essay, Ron sheds new light on the problem of estate planning by stretching his time horizon. Most estate planners look ahead 30 years (one generation) to develop an estate plan. Ron chooses to look ahead 90 years (three generations) to see the long-term impact of estate planning decisions.*

Last quarter, we wrote an essay titled, "Fund Your IRA Every Year, or How to Retire Wealthy by Driving Used Cars." We could have called it "How to Get Started on the Road to Wealth." Once started on that road, there is an ongoing need for intelligent investment management, which is a topic we address in most of our essays. But there is also a need for an intelligent finish, and for the management of assets you have accumulated but are not likely to spend during your lifetime. This endeavor is called estate planning, and I explore this topic in the next few essays.

Any useful estate plan must begin with the goals and priorities that you are trying to accomplish with your accumulated assets. We have found that most of our clients' goals and priorities approximate the following:

1. Provide for client and spouse during their lifetimes.
2. Allow for disasters.
3. Move assets to heirs.
4. Bequeath assets to charities or other organizations.

5. Buy insurance company products.

6. Pay taxes.

Be aware that you do have an estate plan. It was written for you by the U.S. Congress and the legislature of your resident state. But this plan puts taxes as the first priority. Basically it says that when you go to meet your ancestors, these governments will take as taxes 50 percent of everything you own over $600,000. If paying taxes is your first priority, you need no other estate plan. But if you have over $600,000 in assets (including the death benefit on your insurance policy), and you prefer that a greater portion of your assets go to your heirs or to charities, then you need to take positive actions to accomplish it. The earlier you start to do this, the more options you have. (Refer to "2007 Update" for current information.)

We have included insurance company products among this list of priorities because most of the estate plans we have seen place a high priority on making money for an insurance company, usually moving it to priority number three and often to priority number one.

When I worked for an insurance company 20 years ago, such a priority drove the accepted answers on the Chartered Life Underwriters (CLU) and Fellow, Life Management Institute (FLMI) exams that I took at the time. I am not surprised to see such recommendations from insurance agents. I have been surprised in the past 20 years to see most lawyers, accountants, and financial planners adopt the insurance company's pitch. There is a place for insurance in many estate plans, but most of the plans I have seen misuse insurance—often putting the clients' goals at risk. Insurance plans will be covered in detail in a future newsletter.

At an estate planning seminar that I attended a couple of years ago, one of the speakers said that when he did estate planning he looked ahead 30 years. It occurred to me that 30 years is only one cycle—that is, one generation. Years ago, I was taught that, to begin to understand something, you need to look at more than one cycle, so I constructed the chart in Exhibit 6.15. It illustrates what happens to your taxable assets (assets in excess of the $600,000 unified credit) under various assumptions.

Line A is the effect of estate taxes alone. Line A assumes that each generation grows the family assets at an after-tax rate that offsets inflation, but that estate taxes take 50 percent of the assets at the end of each generation.

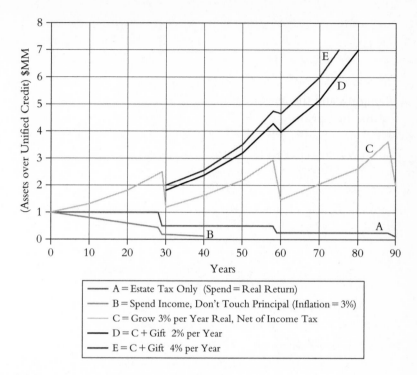

Exhibit 6.15 Long-Term Financial Planning Overview

Line B assumes that each generation spends the income but preserves the (nominal) principal and that inflation is 3 percent per year. A 3 percent inflation rate cuts the purchasing power of the principal by half in 25 years, and then estate taxes take half of that. The family loses three-quarters of the purchasing power of the assets in one generation. Note that in the past 25 years, inflation averaged 6 percent, so a family following this seemingly conservative advice lost 87 percent of the purchasing power of its assets in one generation.

Line C assumes that the assets grow by 3 percent per year over inflation, net of income taxes. This allows the assets to double in 25 years, but then estate taxes take half—so the next generation is back to where it started. Knowledgeable investment management makes the difference between line C and lines A or B.

Lines D and E involve gifting strategies to minimize estate taxes, allowing the family's assets to grow over time. To be most effective, these strategies must be in place long before the assets move from one generation to the next. In total, the chart makes plain that both knowledgeable investing and effective estate planning are necessary if your assets are to have much value for your heirs or other beneficiaries.

2007 Update

The argument in this essay remains valid, but the numbers have changed. In 2007, the unified credit is $2 million, not $600,000, and is legislated to change over the next several years. The tax rate will also change over the next several years, but will still be near 50 percent (in 2007, the maximum tax is 45 percent). To get a list of these changes in detail, ask the IRS for a copy of Publication 950.

Problems with Investing for Income

This essay was originally published in Muhlenkamp Memorandum *Issue 36, October 1996, and has been updated to 2007. It is the second in a three-part series on estate planning.*

In this essay, Ron shows how investing for "income" is flawed. What investors should do is invest to grow their assets. Though it may seem like semantics to some, it is a fundamentally different approach to investing and will lead to better investments and lower taxes.

In the preceding essay, "Estate Planning for Generations," we began a discussion on the effective integration of good investing and good estate planning. The following continues that discussion.

To the extent that any of us received instructions from our parents on the preservation of family assets, it was probably the maxim, "Protect the principal—spend only the income." For most people, it is the cardinal rule; it goes unquestioned. But if you are going to preserve your principal for any period of time, you need to understand why this rule is/was useful, when it works, and how things may have changed since your parents or grandparents found this to be a useful maxim.

The first major problem with the rule is one of definition. The investing public and their paid advisers have allowed the IRS to set the definitions of *principal* and *income*. We find the IRS definition to be worse than useless for investment purposes. In essence, the IRS defines principal as those assets on which you've already paid taxes. Investors define principal as the assets they started with. Any increase in assets the IRS defines as either *income* or *capital gains*.

Consider the following example. (The numbers are real, but approximate.) Mr. Jones had a pension plan funded with pretax dollars. When he retired at age 62, he rolled it over into an IRA; the value was $100,000. We view the $100,000 as assets. Mr. Jones views the $100,000 as principal. The IRS doesn't define it.

In the next eight years, the IRA grew to $250,000. Question: Is the additional $150,000 classified as principal, income, capital gains, or assets? Since the money is in an IRA and not taxed, the IRS doesn't define it. Therefore, it doesn't matter.

At age 70½, Mr. Jones begins withdrawing funds from his IRA. Is he withdrawing principal, income, capital gains, or assets? For tax purposes, the IRS says the money he withdraws from his IRA is all income. The point is that the IRS defines principal, income, and capital gains only to determine your tax bill. Their definitions have no other function, and there is no reason for the investor to be governed by the IRS definitions.

Preserving Purchasing Power

For most people, protecting the principal means preserving the number of dollars you started with. We believe protecting the principal means preserving the *value* (or purchasing power) of the assets you started with. When inflation is zero, the two are the same. But when inflation cuts the purchasing power of the dollar in half (as it did from 1968 to 1978 and again from 1978 to 1993), the number of dollars must double (and double again) to preserve the purchasing power of the principal.

The "spend only the income" part of the rule is so ingrained that when people need spending money, they don't say, "I need spending money"; instead they say, "I need income." This wouldn't matter except that their accountants, their stockbrokers, and their financial planners use the IRS definition of income, and the IRS often taxes income at a higher rate than capital gains or principal.

When we ask our clients whether they are allowed to spend capital gains, we often get a blank look. The rule doesn't say. But they are certain that they aren't allowed to spend principal. By following the rule as they understand it, people end up paying the maximum tax rates on their returns.

The following is a summary of tax rates (updated to 2007):

1. Estate taxes at 45 percent on assets over $2 million.
2. Income taxes at 10 to 35 percent on income and interest.
3. Income Taxes at 15 percent maximum on dividends.
4. Capital gains taxes at 15 percent maximum on long-term capital gains but:
   - You pay no capital gains taxes until you sell an asset.
   - You pay no capital gains taxes when you give an appreciated asset to charity.
   - You assign a stepped-up basis to assets you inherit.[6]

As an investor, it profits you to lower your tax bill by earning returns in ways that the IRS taxes at a lower rate. An 8 percent return in capital gains will often cost you less in taxes than an 8 percent return that is classified as "ordinary income." In addition, the capital gains tax can be deferred until you sell the asset; ordinary income will be taxed in the year you receive it. When capital gains tax rates were significantly lower than ordinary income tax rates, legitimate tax shelters benefited investors by converting ordinary income into capital gains.

The Problem with Investing for Income

In order to get more spending money, we now see people demanding more income and demanding that corporate management convert capital gains or principal into income by paying higher dividends. This does nothing to raise investors' returns; it merely raises their tax bills.★ But paying the higher tax rates on income is the smaller part of the problem.

The greater problem occurs because the focus on "income" causes investors to choose the wrong investment vehicles. Income vehicles— whether short-term debt, long-term debt, or preferred stocks—are not designed to protect the purchasing power of your principal. They are merely designed to pay you an interest or dividend stream for the use of your assets. While the level of these interest and dividend streams (on new issues) normally rise (and fall) to adjust for the level of inflation

---

★In 2007, dividend income is taxed at a maximum rate of 15 percent (the same as capital gains). Interest income continues to be taxed at the ordinary income rate of 35 percent (maximum).

plus a rate of interest, both the IRS and the public view the returns as income. In 1980, when inflation was 10 percent and interest rates were 14 percent, the IRS taxed the full 14 percent, and people spent the full after-tax returns. They did this even though their principal needed to grow by 10 percent to offset inflation if they were to keep the purchasing power of their assets intact. In effect, the IRS taxed 10 percent of their principal, and investors spent 10 percent of their principal.

Common stocks are designed to protect the purchasing power of your assets. Common stocks represent company ownership. One of the obligations of the company's board of directors is to (profitably) reinvest funds back into the company. Dividends to shareholders should be paid from the income remaining after this reinvestment. However, in many cases, the shareholders' demands for increased dividend income have been so great that directors raise dividends to levels that bleed the company of necessary capital. This either stunts the company's growth or results in the company issuing more stock to fund the company's needs. Such actions have been particularly common among electric utilities.

"Protect the principal—spend only the income" is a useful discipline only when:

- Inflation is near zero, or
- You are invested in the common stocks of companies in which the boards of directors view it as their primary responsibility to preserve the real value of the company (and thus, the value of the shareholder's stock) in an inflationary environment.

We have consistently maintained that normal market valuations (pretax) are:

- Short-term interest rates roughly equal to inflation, for a 0 to 1 percent real return.
- Long-term interest rates exceeding inflation by 3 percent.
- Stocks priced to provide returns over inflation of 5 to 6 percent.

Many of you are familiar with the chart published by Ibbotson Associates that shows compounded returns of stocks, bonds, Treasury bills, and inflation since 1925. Ibbotson recently adjusted these returns for taxes and inflation. The results are listed in Exhibit 6.16.[7]

Exhibit 6.16   Compounded Annual Rate of Return, 1926–2006

	Before Taxes and Inflation	After Taxes and Inflation
Stocks	10.4	5.1
Bonds	5.4	0.4
T–Bills	3.7	−0.7
Inflation	3.0	N/A

Hypothetical value of $1 invested at the beginning of 1926, with taxes paid monthly. No capital gains taxes are assumed for municipal bonds. Assumes reinvestment of income and no transaction costs. This is for illustrative purposes only and not indicative of any investment. An investment cannot be made directly in an index. © 2007 Morningstar, Inc. All rights reserved. 3/1/2007. Used with permission.

Exhibit 6.16 indicates that bond returns have been below our estimates, while stock returns have been a bit above our estimate. Specifically, neither bonds nor T-bills provided a significantly positive return.

During that 80-year period, which included a lot of good years, as well as a depression, several wars, and most of the disasters that people worry about, the only time you could have made decent money investing for income was during the depression and during the period of 1981 to 1993. Both periods are now over! The rest of the time, if you invested for income, you were unable to protect (the purchasing power of) your principal. We believe this is also true today. If you invest for income, you will lose (part of) your assets.

Redefining the Maxim

It's almost poetic—the public adopts a rule of thumb based on one time period and one set of circumstances, but it continues to use this rule of thumb after the circumstances have changed. Wall Street creates products that promise to generate returns in the form the public wants, but it doesn't tell the public what they are giving up to generate returns in this form. The media trumpets those strategies that would have worked well over the recent past. Meanwhile, the government is happy to increase the tax load on the favored forms of investments.

This was the pattern in real estate and other tax shelters; this is currently the pattern in variable annuities (which convert capital gains into income). This is also the net effect of paying Social Security benefits to wealthy retirees; many of these benefits will eventually be taxed at estate tax rates.

We believe that an investor's only recourse is to invest his assets to grow more assets (on an after-tax basis). Spend whatever portion of those assets is needed or desired to maintain a given lifestyle. Move the remaining assets to heirs or charities in concert with your goals and priorities. Periodically review and adjust to reflect changing markets, changing tax laws, and changing personal goals and priorities.

The Fundamentals of Life Insurance

This essay was originally published in Muhlenkamp Memorandum *Issue 37, January 1996. It is the third in a three-part series on estate planning. It shows why Ron disagrees with conventional wisdom with respect to life insurance and irrevocable trusts.*

As professional investors our perspective and conclusions differ from the conventional wisdom in several areas. One important area of difference is life insurance, which plays an important part in many financial plans. The following is a discussion of life insurance from an investment perspective.

Any whole-life policy has two parts. The first part is pure insurance, just like a term policy. The second part is a savings account (the insurance company calls it *cash value*). The savings account is designed to equal the death benefit of the policy at the end of the insured's life expectancy. As the savings account grows, the amount of pure insurance declines. (See Exhibit 6.17.)

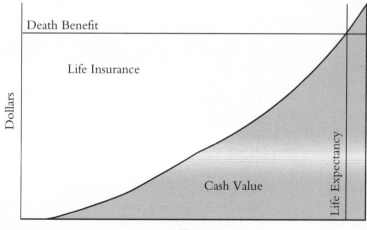

Exhibit 6.17   Whole-Life Policy

The insurance company estimates the interest rate it will earn during the life of the policy to determine the amount of the premium required to fund the savings account. They then add on the insurance premium that is required to offset the risk that the insured dies early. The sum of the two is the annual premium. Thus, the policy illustration is based on the premium and the assumed interest rate. If future interest rates match the estimated rate, the cash value of the policy will match the illustration.

But if future interest rates do not match the estimated rate, the insurance company will adjust premiums or the value of the policy to reflect the actual rates. When estimating future interest rates, most insurance companies use a rate similar to what they are currently earning. This rate reflects securities that they have bought and still hold. Since companies don't replace their entire holdings each year, their response to changing interest rates tends to be gradual and to reflect market changes with a lag. As rates moved up in the 1970s, this lag was reinforced by the reluctance of companies to sell bonds at a loss. As rates have moved down since 1981, the lag has been determined largely by *call protection.*

The bonds and the mortgages that insurance companies own are callable. *Callable* means that the companies issuing these securities can "call" or refinance them when interest rates drop. As interest rates fell over the past 15 years, many of us benefited by refinancing our mortgages. But this benefit was at the expense of the holders of these mortgages, including insurance companies. Much of the mortgage refinancing has been completed, but the bond refinancing is still going on. This is because most bonds have 5 or 10 years of call protection; therefore, the call response lags the market by 5 to 10 years.

How do these changes in interest rates get reflected in individual policies? In the 1970s, interest rates rose, exceeding rates that had been estimated in the 1960s. See Exhibit 6.18. As a result, the death benefits on two policies that I bought in 1964 and 1970 were upped by 40 percent in the early 1980s. This sounds impressive until you recall that the consumer price index (CPI) doubled during that period.

But since 1984, interest rates have fallen well below the levels that insurance companies estimated in the early 1980s. If you bought a whole life policy 10 or 15 years ago, you have probably received a statement in the past two to three years saying that the insurance company needs

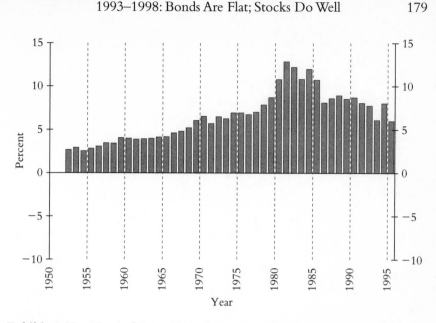

Exhibit 6.18 Nominal Long-Term Government Bond Rate, 1952–1995

more money, or they will decrease your death benefit. But this statement only reflects the decline in interest rates that occurred from the early 1980s to the late 1980s. The decline in rates that has occurred since the late 1980s means that three to five years hence (due to the call lag), you will get another statement saying that the insurance company needs more money *again*.

The people who have bought policies since 1985 will also receive statements asking for more money. And we believe there is a 50 percent probability of a third adjustment 5 to 10 years down the road. We estimate that the decline in the value of the policy will approximate 20 percent each time, for a *cumulative 40 to 60* percent *decline*.

The problem is that old and obsolete interest rates are still being used in policy illustrations. We recently reviewed a policy proposal in which the cash value illustration was based on interest rates credited to the policyholder of 8 percent. Yet a footnote stated that the actual rate credited will be 2 percent less than the company earns on its investment portfolio. The illustrated numbers were obsolete the day they were printed. In any other business, such illustrations would be considered fraud.

Policies are sold on the basis of illustrated growth in the cash value. In recent years, disclosure has improved and these tables usually include a footnote that states that in fact the interest earned will be 2 to 3 percent less than what the company earns on its investment portfolio. So the company is telling you up front that your assets with them will earn 2 to 3 percent less than the company earns *with your money*.

Since the bonds and mortgages they invest in normally earn about 1 percent more than Treasury bonds, you can expect to earn about 1 to 2 percent per year less than if you had simply bought long-term Treasury bonds.

The conclusion is that any money set aside to accumulate in an insurance policy or a fixed annuity will earn returns of 2 to 3 percent a year less than corporate bonds, which means it will earn 1 to 2 percent a year less than Treasury bonds. It also means it is likely to earn about 1 percent more than passbook savings and 4 to 5 percent a year less than common stocks. It *cannot* do better. When insurance commissions are figured in, the results become significantly worse.

If you are 35 years old, have few or no assets, and have people dependent on you, buy life insurance to cover the risk of early demise. We strongly recommend term insurance. But if you are 55 years old and have assets sufficient to care for your dependents, you don't need life insurance. Under these circumstances, buying cash-value life insurance merely prevents earning a decent return on your money. We call that a poor investment.

A second area where we disagree with the conventional wisdom is in the use of irrevocable trusts. (The following comments do not apply to revocable trusts.) The use of irrevocable trusts is driven by three factors:

1. IRS regulations that gifts to charities or heirs be irrevocable to qualify for charitable deductions or for exclusion from the donor's estate.
2. Donors' belief that they can only spend "income" during their lifetime; therefore, they believe they must keep their assets in their name.
3. A desire to control assets from the grave, either to protect irresponsible heirs from themselves or to benefit from the donor's superior investment acumen.

Our objection to irrevocable trusts is that they are irrevocable. The trust may not be able to adapt to changes in the world or in people. We've seen trusts that irrevocably stipulated:

- Trustees who became senile or died.
- Bank administrations whose trust departments became incompetent or were so careful to protect principal that inflation destroyed the assets. (See our essay "Estate Planning for Generations," Exhibit 6.15, line B.)
- Charities whose later administrators adopted policies counter to the donor's intent. (Henry Ford II resigned as trustee of the Ford Foundation—which his grandfather's will created—in disgust.)
- Investments that became obsolete. (I had a college classmate whose wealthy grandfather, observing the need for good public transportation, stipulated that his assets should always be invested in streetcar companies. His grandson was as broke as I was.)

Meanwhile the IRS discounts the value of any charitable gift to its *present value* in calculating any tax deduction. We've seen present values as low as 5 percent of the intended gift. The donor and the charity would have been better served with a present gift of 5 percent of the expected future gift. This would allow the remaining 95 percent to be invested (or gifted or spent) in concert with a changing world.

Why I Like the Flat Tax

This essay was originally published in Muhlenkamp Memorandum *Issue 38, April 1996. It was an election year, and Steve Forbes was making his first bid for president. He promised to energize the American economy by implementing a 17 percent flat tax (dubbed the postcard tax because it would be so simple, the tax form would fit on a postcard). This brought the idea of a flat federal income tax into the national spotlight.*

The first reason I favor a flat tax is because I just did my taxes. Despite my being fairly knowledgeable about taxes and my having a fairly simple tax return, it took me the better part of a day to do it. This day's work produced nothing of value to me, to the government, or to anyone else. It didn't affect what I earn or what I pay in taxes. It was simply the time I spent in calculating the tax. And I am not alone.

Form 1	Federal Income Tax		1996
First Name	Last Name	Occupation	Social Security Number
First Name of Spouse (if applicable)	Last Name	Occupation	Spouse's Social Security Number
City	State	Zip Code	

1. Wages, Salary and Pensions	1.
2. Personal allowance	
a. $25,200 for a married couple filling jointly	2a.
b. $13,100 for a single person	2b.
c. $17,200 for a single head of household	2c.
3. Number of dependents, not including spouse	3.
4. Personal allowance for dependents (line 3 multiplied by $5,300)	4.
5. Total personal allowances (line 2 plus line 4)	5.
6. Taxable wages (line 1 less line 5, if a positive number; otherwise zero)	6.
7. Tax (17% of line 6-multiply line 6 by 0.17)	7.
8 Tax already paid	8.
9. Tax due (line 7 less line 8, if positive)	9.
10. Refund due (line 8 less line 7, if positive)	10.

Exhibit 6.19 Proposed Flat Tax Form—1996

The Tax Foundation estimates that in 1994, individuals spent more than 1.8 billion hours and businesses spent more than 3.6 billion hours preparing tax returns. At the simplest level, the IRS notes proudly that it should take taxpayers "only" two hours and 42 minutes to complete the 1040EZ. The instructions for the 1040EZ are 36 pages long. Had we a flat tax, I could have filled out the Proposed Flat Tax Form in 10 minutes. See Exhibit 6.19.

The second reason I like a flat tax is that it isn't flat. The sales tax is a flat tax. In Pennsylvania the state sales tax rate is 6 percent. Someone who buys a Cadillac for $30,000 pays 6 percent or $1,800 in tax, twice the $900 paid by someone else who buys a Chevy for $15,000. Those who spend more pay more in taxes, at a directly proportional rate. The real estate tax is also a flat tax. Each homeowner in an area pays the same rate on the appraised value of their house. Those who live in larger houses pay proportionately more.

But the proposed flat income tax has personal allowances on which the taxpayer pays no taxes, making it a progressive or graduated tax. A family of four with an income of $36,800 pays no tax. A family of four with an income of $73,600 would be exempt from paying tax on the first $36,800, and pay 17 percent tax only on the remaining $36,800.

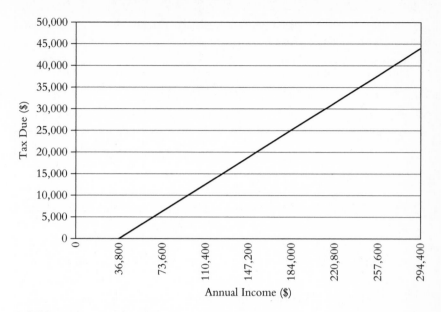

Exhibit 6.20   Results of Flat Tax on a Family of Four

This works out to 8.5 percent of their total income. Similarly, a family of four with an income of $110,400 would pay 17 percent on $73,600, or 11.33 percent of the total, and so on (see Exhibit 6.20).

But the main reason I like a flat tax is the same reason the politicians don't. When the rules are clear, it's hard for the public to cheat. It is also more difficult for the politicians to write rules making it legal for parts of the public to pay less taxes without cheating. Two hundred years ago, the authors of the *Federalist Papers* warned:

> It will be of little avail to the people that the laws are made by men of their own choice if the laws be so voluminous that they cannot be read, or so incoherent that they cannot be understood.

The warning remains valid!

The sales tax is simple and straightforward in its calculations. Few people cheat on their sales tax. Real estate taxes are straightforward. Attempts to pay less real estate tax usually focus on the appraisal, which is the part of the calculation where judgment is involved. But when tax laws are complicated (the Federal Income Tax Code is over 10,000 pages), it pays to hire lawyers to find exceptions in the law. When tax laws are complicated, it pays to hire politicians to write exceptions into the law.

Following are four common objections to the flat tax.

1. *The rich won't pay enough taxes.* Folks, the truly rich don't need taxable income—they have assets. They can either live off their assets or invest in municipal bonds, which are exempt from income taxes. Income taxes don't tax the rich; income taxes tax those who are trying to get rich.

2. *High-income people won't pay enough taxes.* When Ronald Reagan was elected president, the top marginal tax rate was 70 percent. Because of the rate, many high-income people used various schemes (tax-sheltered investments, salary deferral plans, etc.) to lessen the tax bite. One day I asked two doctor clients how much time they spent being doctors and how much time they spent avoiding taxes. Their response: "We spend about a day a week avoiding taxes." What an incredible waste of time and talent.

   After Reagan lowered the top tax rate, the tax avoidance schemes no longer made sense. So the doctors went back to being full-time doctors. They made more money and as a result paid more in taxes than they did before the Reagan tax cuts. So did a lot of other highly productive people, which gave us the strong economy of the 1980s. This strong economy produced tax receipts to the U.S. Treasury much higher than those of the pre-tax-cut era.

   Similarly, when the minimum rate on capital gains was 20 percent, we told our clients to ignore taxes in their investing. More recently, with the help of George H. W. Bush's and Bill Clinton's tax increases, ordinary income tax rates have climbed to 39.6 percent and capital gains tax rates are 28 percent. As a result, high-income earners and investors have modified their behavior, and U.S. economic growth has slowed.

3. *Losing the mortgage deduction will result in a decline in the value of housing.* Pure nonsense! Losing the mortgage deduction in concert with making interest income tax free would cause mortgage rates to fall to the level of municipal bond rates. The reason mortgage rates are so high is because the people who receive the interest must pay taxes on it. This same argument was made before Reagan cut tax rates. House prices didn't fall, but mortgage rates did.

4. *People will have less incentive to give to charities.* More nonsense. People give to charities because they believe in the charity and because they have the money, not because of the tax deduction. The same argument was made concerning the Reagan tax-rate cuts in the early 1980s. To my personal knowledge, M.I.T., Penn State, and Duquesne University each started aggressive multiyear fund drives in the early 1980s. The response was so good that each of them reached their original goals well ahead of schedule and increased their targets. Charitable giving as a whole reached an all-time high in the 1980s.

If you are interested in the views of others on the subject of flat tax, you may find one or more of the following books useful:

Flat Tax Primer: A Nonpartisan Guide to What It Means for the Economy, the Government—and You, by Douglas Sease and Tom Herman of the *Wall Street Journal* (Viking, 1996).
The Flat Tax: Freedom, Fairness, Jobs, and Growth, by Daniel Mitchell of the Heritage Foundation (Regnery, 1996).
The Flat Tax: A Citizen's Guide to the Facts on What It Will Do for You, Your Country, and Your Pocketbook, by Dick Armey, House Majority Leader (Ballantine, 1996).
Unleashing America's Potential, by the National Commission on Economic Growth and Tax Reform (St. Martin's Press, 1996).

The Trouble with Government Spending

This essay was originally published in Muhlenkamp Memorandum *Issue 40, October 1996. It was a presidential election year. Bob Dole and Jack Kemp were running on the Republican ticket against incumbents Bill Clinton and Al Gore. As in any election year, there was much discussion of taxes and government spending. But the discussion often dissolved into political attacks and sound bites instead of furthering any true understanding of the underlying economic issues. So in this essay, Ron offers his own perspective on taxes, federal spending, and their effects on the economy.*

When Bob Dole won the Republican nomination for president, it looked like a victory for the old-guard Republicans, à la George H. W. Bush, and a defeat for the growth Republicans, à la Ronald Reagan. The argument within the party appeared to be over for this election cycle. Then Bob Dole proposed a 15 percent cut in income tax rates and named Jack Kemp as his running mate. This decision seemed to resolve the argument (within the Republican Party) in favor of growth and smaller government.

Based on this, I had renewed hope that the presidential campaign would focus on the benefits of a smaller federal government. I believe this argument needs to be put directly before the American people. But so far, I have been disappointed in the presentation of the argument. So I will attempt to make the argument myself. The argument has two parts. The first part focuses on who is better able to spend our money, the federal government or individual citizens. The second part of the argument focuses on how to best generate more money to be spent by the citizenry and by the federal government.

Who Is Better Able to Spend Our Money?

In 1980, I spent an afternoon with my old college roommate, Mike, and his wife, Cindy. Cindy and I got into an argument that Mike finally summed up (and thankfully ended) with, "Ron, you believe that the average person, dumb as he may be, is better at making his own decisions and spending his own money than a highly educated, well-meaning person in Washington, D.C., can do it for him." I said, "Absolutely!" He continued, "Cindy, you believe that an intelligent, highly educated, well-meaning person in Washington, D.C., can spend the average person's money better than that person can do it for himself." She said, "That's right!" I can't summarize the argument any better than Mike did.

President Clinton's health care plan was based on his belief that the politicians in Washington, D.C., could spend our money better than we can. On his four-day train trip to the convention in Chicago, he proposed $8 billion a year in new government spending based on this same belief. Bob Dole now says, "We believe/trust the American people are capable of spending their own money a whole lot better than politicians can." (Yes, this is a change from his votes and actions in years past!) So the question is: Who do you believe is more capable of spending your money? I believe the issue from an economics standpoint is more a matter of incentive than it is of knowledge. Individuals are most capable of spending their own money regardless of knowledge, because when individuals spend their own money, they have better incentive to earn more money. Let me explain.

How Do We Best Generate More Money to Spend?

The trouble with government spending is that the government doesn't have any money. Every dollar spent by the government must be raised— either through taxes or through borrowing. We've heard a lot about the borrowing to cover the federal deficit, but we don't hear much about the taxes. For most of us, we only see the taxes that are on our annual tax return and our W-2 forms. The W-2 lists our gross pay along with deductions for Social Security (FICA) and state and local taxes. But this is only part of the story.

The other part is the taxes paid by the employer, which the employee never sees. Exhibit 6.21 shows the W-2 numbers for someone making a gross income of $36,000 per year. The exhibit also shows the amounts paid by the employer for FICA, various unemployment taxes, health

Exhibit 6.21 Employment Costs (W2 Filing: Married, Two Children), January 1996

Employee's Deduction		Employer's Costs	
Gross wages[1]	$36,000.00	Gross wages[1]	$36,000.00
FICA (Social Security and Medicare)	$2,754.00	FICA (Social Security and Medicare)	2,754.00
Federal withholding (0 exemptions)	3,696.00	Health insurance	4,207.32
State withholding	1,008.00	Unemployment taxes (federal and state)	167.52
PA State unemployment	10.80		
Occupational tax	10.00	Employee's cost to company	$43,128.84
Employee's take-home pay	$28,521.20		

[1]Based on the U.S. median income.

care, and so on. As you can see, for the employee to take home $28,521 it costs the employer $43,128. Specifically, for my son to take home $1.00 it costs me (his employer) $1.51. So he must produce $1.56 of value for me. The 5 cents is my return for hiring him. (In fact, the average profit to payroll in the U.S. economy is 5 to 6 percent.)

If the employee doesn't produce $1.56, he won't have a job. So the way to encourage job creation is to allow the employer to keep the nickel. If you tax away the nickel, you tax away the job. In the 1970s, we taxed away the nickel (inflation raised income taxes, and the government raised Social Security taxes) and businesspeople quit hiring.

Although Ronald Reagan didn't cut federal spending, he did cut tax rates, encouraging us all to earn more money (and, incidentally, to pay more taxes). So the question becomes, "What rules give people the greater incentive to produce and earn more—and to spend more effectively?" I have observed the following.

People have three working speeds:

1. They work for someone who can't/won't fire them, typically the government.
2. They work for someone who can fire them, typically a business.
3. They work for themselves.

People have four spending modes:

1. Spend their own money (money they've earned) on themselves (private economy).
2. Spend money they've earned on someone else (private charity).
3. Spend someone else's money on themselves (see the Senate office building).
4. Spend someone else's money on someone else (government programs).

Based on these observations, I would suggest that personal and national wealth production only occurs in the private (nongovernmental) market because when the government gets involved, work incentives decrease and spending becomes less efficient.

The most obvious example of this is in food production and farm policy. The consumer is quite willing to pay for food, and therefore to pay farmers to grow food. Only government would pay farmers to *not* grow food. By giving incentives to *not* produce goods and services, the government actively lowers the total wealth of the nation.

Summary

So what's the problem with government spending? It moves resources from the private sector (slowing the economy and decreasing employment) into the government sector where work incentive is poor and spending is inefficient. It assumes a well-meaning individual in Washington can spend our money better than we can, but government spending has none of the incentive effects that drive the economy. Which is more likely to get you to work overtime: the thought of a nice house, car, or vacation, or the thought of paying more in taxes so the government can buy another ship or build another bridge?

Editor's Note

We've updated the employment costs exhibit (see Exhibit 6.22). You'll notice several changes from the original. First, the median income has increased from $36,000 in 1996 to $40,000 in 2006. We've also added pension and profit-sharing contributions under employer's costs. These were not included in the original essay, but they constitute a significant portion of employer costs after the first year of employment, so they are included here. And though they are benefits to the employee (just as health insurance is), they are not part of the employee's take-home pay and therefore not apparent to most employees.

The updated exhibit shows that the costs of employment have risen since 1996. In 1996, for an employee to take home $1.00 in pay it cost the employer $1.83, so the employee had to earn $1.92 (remember, the employer wants his 5 percent). In 2006, for the employee to take home $1.00 in pay it costs the employer $2.12 so the employee has to earn $2.23 for the company. The change from 1996 to 2006 is partly due to taxes and partly due to health care costs.

If we want our economy to grow, and we want to reduce unemployment, we need to keep the cost of employment low. We need to allow the workers to keep enough of what they earn that they will continue to work to their full potential. We need to allow the employers to keep enough of their profits that they will create new jobs. More jobs mean more income, which means more income tax revenues (even at lower rates). Therefore, keeping employment costs low not only grows the economy and reduces unemployment, it also generates more revenue for the government.

Exhibit 6.22   Employment Costs (W-2 Filing: Married, Two Children), Updated

Employee's Deductions	January 1996	January 2006
Gross wages[1]	$36,000.00	$40,000.00
FICA and Medicare	$2,754.00	$3,060.00
Federal withholding (0 exemptions)	3,696.00	$4,056.00
State withholding	1,008.00	$1,228.00
PA State unemployment	10.80	$36.00
Occupational tax	10.00	$10.00
Employee's take-home pay	$28,521.20	$31,610.00
Employer's Costs		
Gross wages[1]	$36,000.00	$40,000.00
FICA (Social Security and Medicare)	2,754.00	$3,060.00
Health insurance	4,207.32	$13,765.20
Unemployment taxes	167.52	$266.94
Pension contribution[2]	3,600.00	$4,000.00
Profit-sharing contribution[3]	5,400.00	$6,000.00
Employee's cost to company	$52,128.84	$67,092.14

[1]Based on the U.S. median income.
[2]Based on the maximum allowable by law: 10 percent of gross wages.
[3]Based on the maximum allowable by law: 15 percent of gross wages.

Every four years the discussion of taxes and government spending comes into the spotlight as the Democratic and Republican parties vie for our votes. That means that we, the voters, get to tell the politicians who we think is better able to spend our money, and how we think our economy can best generate more money to spend. These questions are still alive and well.

Thoughts on the Future

This essay was originally published in Muhlenkamp Memorandum *Issue 41, January 1997.*

I have been asked by a local paper to write a short essay on the future.

The future is good! The future is good because large parts of the world population are adopting freer markets. In Asia, in Eastern Europe, and in much of South America, the move from state-controlled economies to free-market economies is now irreversible.

In a free market, the consumer is king. Each individual can choose whether to buy, what to buy, and at what price. No producer can make a consumer buy its product. Instead, producers must compete for the consumer's business. This competition can take many forms, but it is all aimed at serving the needs and desires of the consumer. Because of this, the true value of free markets comes to fruition.

The true value of a free market is that it provides incentives for each person to serve his fellow man. If you serve the needs of your fellow man, he will pay you. If you don't serve someone's needs, no one will pay you. Thus, the way to better yourself economically is to provide goods and services that other people desire. In fact, you can get rich by providing others with what they want. Furthermore, you can *only* get rich by providing what others want. Whether providing new or imaginative goods and services (from microwave ovens to the Internet) or existing goods and services at cheaper prices (read Sam Walton's autobiography), the standard for an individual's economic success is the degree to which he serves the needs and wants of others. As a consumer, I will pay only those who provide what I want. As a producer, I will be paid only by those to whom I provide a service that they want.

To criticize some consumers because their choice of incentive is different from mine is shortsighted. Every business transaction in a free market has a dual outcome. The buyer gets the product he chooses, and the seller gets paid for the product or service. The buyer sets the agenda because the product must be chosen before it is bought; otherwise it will rot on the shelf. Thus, consumers have the ultimate say in what is produced, and only those goods and services of value to consumers will be rewarding to producers.

These consumer-driven, free-market rules know no boundaries of geography or politics. No American was forced to buy a Sony or a Toyota. We did so willingly, because we perceived a better value for ourselves. In a free market, no one is forced to buy an airplane from Boeing, a soft drink from Coca-Cola, or a computer chip from Intel. Consumers do so willingly because they perceive a better value to themselves. As the number of people participating in free markets expands, we will each have access to the greater values produced by all of us.

Much of the focus on free markets has been on the loss of jobs to the producer/worker as a result of the constant changes driven by the consumer. This focus has two major faults. It ignores the fact that all workers are consumers, and it focuses on the transition rather than the result. The transition can be traumatic, but it is temporary. In the United States, we have accomplished exemplary results. Each generation's living standard has improved over the prior one; this will continue. What we must improve upon are the methods and the attitudes that we use to help people through the transition.

A second focus has been on the failure to fulfill all our desires at once. But this is simply a matter of priorities. In 1954 Abraham Maslow published a treatise positing a hierarchy of human needs. After the basic needs of food, shelter, and safety, he listed the needs of love, esteem, and self-actualization. He went on to state that, "As each need is satisfied, the next higher level dominates conscious function." In the United States today, it is not difficult for each of us to provide for the basic needs of food, clothing, and shelter. They are available to anyone willing and able to work. And in concert with Maslow's hierarchy, the discourse on human needs for much of the population has shifted to higher-order needs such as love and self-esteem.

Human concern for the environment, for example, will always be subordinate to food, clothing, and shelter. Only after these needs are met (and taken for granted) will secondary needs be addressed. That is why the air and water in the United States is cleaner today than in the past and is cleaner than in most developing countries. The very prosperity of the United States has moved clean air and water to a dominant position in the public's consciousness. Economic prosperity doesn't solve all problems, but it does provide the means to solve many of them.

Our remaining problem is that we haven't learned to live with our prosperity. Our economic well-being has progressed faster than our social theories on how to deal with discretionary time and money. Our attitudes toward work were appropriate to a time when work was drudgery. In most occupations, we've rid ourselves of the drudgery, but not the attitude. We've lost sight of the fact that useful work is also a way of serving others, and it is also a primary source of self-esteem. All too often, we teach our young: If it is useful, call it work and avoid it; if it's useless, call it play and pursue it. Then we complain that they have no self-esteem. I know many people who have found happiness in their work. I know none who have found happiness or self-esteem on the party circuit. Properly understood, the pursuits of economic prosperity and human fulfillment are complementary.

Why Did the Fed Raise Short-Term Rates?

This essay was originally published in Muhlenkamp Memorandum *Issue 42, April 1997. The Federal Reserve had just raised short-term rates in response to fears of inflation. Some people expected inflation because the GDP was growing, and Keynesian economic theory says that GDP growth causes inflation. The opposing school of thought, classical economic theory, says that printing money causes inflation. Since in 1997 the GDP was growing but the government wasn't printing money, it was a good time to take a look at the two theories.*

Recent Fed actions coincide with the debate in economic theory over the root causes of inflation. In each newsletter over the past year, we have related this debate to you, and it continues to command center stage in the stock and bond markets. Six months ago, we wrote:

> The debate is, "Does Economic Growth Cause Inflation?" Keynesian economic theory says growth causes inflation. Classical economic theory says that only the printing of money causes inflation. If you took economic courses 30–40 years ago, the odds are very high that you were taught the Keynesian theory (that growth causes inflation). I took these courses, and that is what I was taught (I'm 53). Most of the people who are now "chief economists" were also taught this theory.
>
> Economic history of the past 30 years has demonstrated that growth doesn't cause inflation. Specifically, the changes in policy by Paul Volcker and Ronald Reagan in 1979–1982 demonstrated that money growth, not gross domestic product (GDP) growth, causes inflation. But the evidence has not caused many economists to change their minds.
>
> More recent refinement of the theory states that growth greater than 2.5 percent per year will result in increased inflation after a time lag of about 18 months. We have now had GDP growth exceeding 2.5 percent for 18 months (which is why the issue is

front and center). So the Keynesians have been expecting increased inflation and have predicted higher interest rates as a result. Specifically, Morgan Stanley's chief economist has been predicting long-term U.S. Treasury rates of 8.5 percent by year-end 1997.

Conversely, at Donaldson, Lufkin and Jenrette (DLJ), their chief economist is predicting long-term Treasury rates of 4.5 percent by year-end 1997 (based partly on a belief that growth doesn't cause inflation and partly on his forecast of a recession in 1997). Folks, that is a huge difference! If rates go to 8.5 percent, a 6 percent 30-year Treasury that was priced at $1,000 on December 31, 1995, would be priced at $740 at year-end 1997. If rates go to 4.5 percent, the same 30-year Treasury would be priced at $1,230. Similarly, the S&P 500, which was priced at 620 on December 31, 1995, would be likely to sink to 550 or soar to 850 by year-end 1997. So the outcome is far more than academic.

An interesting side note is that these predictions were both made in early 1996 with a horizon of nearly two years. Two years is a short time in economics but a long time in the stock and bond markets. Two years is ample time for the markets to swing one way based on hope or fear, and then to swing the other way based on reality.

During the first half of 1996, the yield on long-term Treasuries rose from 6 percent to 7.25 percent. The price fell from $1,000 to $850. We believe this move was based on a fear of inflation in concert with the Keynesian theory. Evidence for this includes a 2 percent drop in bond prices and stock prices on July 5 when the government reported GDP growth for the second quarter of 4.6 percent.

Through the first nine months of 1996, the reported economic numbers have been mixed enough that neither economist saw a need to change his forecast—until now. The first change occurred on October 4, when in response to lower employment numbers (and an uptick in the unemployment rate), the economist at Morgan Stanley shifted his GDP growth prediction to 2 percent in the third quarter and 4 percent in the fourth quarter (from 3 percent in each quarter) and lowered his interest-rate ranges for 1996 from 8 percent-plus to 7.25 percent-plus.

That day, the bond market jumped over 1 percent and the stock market rose 1 percent. The numbers for the remaining months of 1996 will be key to determining which theory is accepted. We believe that the classical theory (growth does not cause inflation) will be affirmed once again, that interest rates will decline, and that the stock market will do well with a focus on individual stocks. Stay tuned.

Since we wrote the preceding account in October 1996, GDP growth has been greater than forecast, with the fourth quarter up nearly 4 percent, but without an increase in reported inflation. Nevertheless, the strong GDP numbers renewed the fears of inflation, resulting in renewed pressure on the Federal Reserve to raise short-term interest rates. The Fed raised rates by 0.25 percent on March 25, 1997. The Fed labeled the move "preemptive."

The strong fourth quarter also resulted in DLJ's economist extending his projections out three to six months, but he did not change his conclusion. Morgan Stanley's economist has also extended his prediction. So now both economists have extended their time periods, but they haven't changed their diametrically opposed forecasts. The strength in GDP and the fears of increased inflation have also moved the rates on long-term Treasuries to a range of 7.10 to 7.15 percent, up from less than 7 percent at year-end, but still below the 7.25 percent reached (three times) in 1996.

Normally we don't worry much about a difference in interest rates of 0.25 percent to 0.5 percent, and frankly we don't think current changes of this magnitude will have much effect on the economy. But in the current environment of well-balanced growth and fair stock prices, many market participants have focused on Fed actions and long-term interest rates as bellwethers for the next short-term move in the markets. In short, today the perceived signal may be more important than the reality.

Since World War II, each recession in the U.S. economy has been preceded by an increase from the Fed in short-term interest rates (although not all increases have been followed by recession), and each major decline in stock prices has also been preceded by an increase from the Fed in short-term interest rates. We believe we must respect this history and the Keynesian theories (and the amount of money responding to the theory) until we see further evidence (and *they* see evidence) that inflation is not increasing.

Two things that we are watching closely are long-term interest rates and the public's purchase of housing. Long-term interest rates directly reflect the fears of inflation. The reason the Fed raised short-term rates is to quell inflation and inflation fears, which should ultimately drive long-term rates down. When the Fed raised rates in March by 0.25 percent, rates on long-term bonds, which are determined in an open market, went up by roughly 0.125 percent.

The people who buy houses make their decisions partly based on the mortgage interest rates, which usually move parallel to other long-term interest rates. Since 1990, our observation has been that when mortgage rates exceed 8 percent (as they have just done), the public reduces its home purchases. Should it do so once again, long-term rates won't go much higher.

Meantime, we continue our normal course of identifying companies we would like to own, setting prices at which we like to buy their stocks, and investing some of our cash when those prices are met.

2007 Update

The top plot in Exhibit 6.23 illustrates the growth rates of gross domestic product (GDP) and the consumer price index (CPI)—inflation. In the bottom plot we've added interest rates on three-month Treasury bills (short-term rates), 20-year Treasury bonds (long-term rates), and 30-year mortgages. As you can see, the argument in 1996–1997 was merely a preamble to 1999–2000.

In 1997, despite GDP growth consistently above 3 percent, inflation did not pick up, but fell (contrary to Keynesian theory). This drop in inflation allowed long-term rates to fall to 5.5 percent by the end of 1998 (although not to the 4.5 percent predicted by the DLJ economist). Mortgage rates fell in concert with long-term Treasury rates.

In 1999, inflation did rise, causing increases in long-term rates and mortgage rates. In response to the rise in inflation, the Fed raised short-term rates through 1999 and early 2000. Then, as GDP growth declined, long-term interest rates rolled over and headed back down, while short-term rates and inflation continued to rise. Let me explain why.

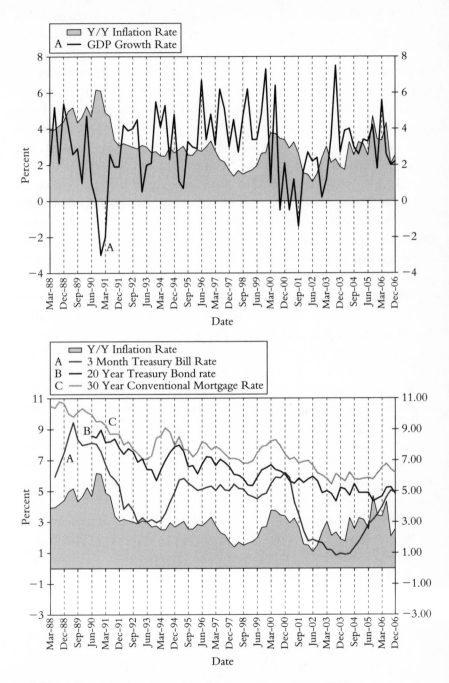

Exhibit 6.23   Inflation, Growth, and Interest Rates, 1988–2006

In 1999, Alan Greenspan, the Fed chairman, all but said that he'd take a recession rather than allow inflation to increase. So, once the markets concluded that the uptick in inflation was not a cause for alarm (the Fed was not going to let inflation get out of hand), long-term rates (which are determined in the marketplace) headed down, while short-term rates (which are heavily influenced by the Fed) were still rising. Mortgage rates followed long-term rates, although they lagged a bit at the time.

It has been 10 years since this essay was written, and inflation—after an uptick in 1999—has stayed in the 2 to 3 percent range. The Fed did what it said it would do: it has controlled inflation. Long-term interest rates have, in fact, dropped to the 4.5 percent levels predicted by the DLJ economist.

So what do we learn from this? First, classical theory (which says that excess money supply is the cause of inflation) has been a better guide to understanding inflation and interest rates than Keynesian theory. Second, on a monthly basis, the economic data that investors see move around a lot, giving ample opportunity for short-term swings in the bond and stock markets. So unless the investor has a long-term perspective and conviction as to which economic theory to follow, it's easy to get whipsawed in the markets.

Third, hindsight can be deceptive. We need to remember that investing is a real-time pursuit, and that the investor does not have the luxury of hindsight when making investment decisions. With hindsight, we know that the actions of the Fed in 1997 were a nonevent. With hindsight, we know that the actions of the Fed in 1999 heralded a recession. But *at the time*, how would an investor be able to judge the significance of what was going on? How would an investor know who to listen to? That is why the successful investor needs to have a core understanding of how the economy and the markets interrelate. Then he can hold steady in the midst of the debate and not get whipsawed by the market.

We have more to say about reading the economy on a real-time basis in Chapter 9.

Review of *What Works on Wall Street*

This essay was originally published in Muhlenkamp Memorandum
Issue 43, July 1997. A friend had asked Ron to review the book

What Works on Wall Street: A Guide to the Best-Performing Investment Strategies of All Time, by James P. O'Shaughnessy. In doing so, Ron illustrates common mistakes made by the investment community at large when evaluating investment strategies.

A friend asked me to review the book *What Works on Wall Street*, by James P. O'Shaughnessy. The book was published this year (1997) by McGraw-Hill and is subtitled *A Guide to the Best-Performing Investment Strategies of All Time*. These are my comments:

1. It is a useful book—chock full of data.
2. The book is limited in scope, focusing on the "Wall Street" in the title instead of the "Investment Strategies" in the subtitle.
3. The book is all hindsight. It should be titled *What Would Have Worked on Wall Street*.
4. The author briefly mentions the most interesting aspects of his data, but then ignores them.

I'll expand on each comment in turn.

The data is plentiful. The author uses Standard & Poor's Compustat Active and Research Database from 1950 through 1994. This gives 44 years of annual returns. He takes into account various biases (such as survivorship bias and inflation) that detract from the validity of most studies. Equally important, he is specific about how the data is used. He then analyzes this data by capitalization and by a number of popular investment strategies. The resulting tables alone are easily worth the price of the book. Chapter 4, which lists annual returns by market capitalization, is a must-read for anyone investing in small stocks because of their reported long-term outperformance.

O'Shaughnessy finds that the source of the small-stock outperformance was in stocks of less than $25 million capitalization. Even small cap funds invest in stocks averaging over 10 times $25 million.

The book is limited in scope. It looks only at stocks. Granted, that is the charter in the title, but at various times during the past 44 years, there have been periods when the best-performing investment strategies included real estate, gold, bonds, certificates of deposit, Chinese ceramics, oil and gas, and others. I mention this more as a reminder than as a criticism. If the data is available, which I doubt, a similar treatment of these vehicles would make a useful book.

The book is all hindsight. I believe Warren Buffett has said, "If the future were a repeat of the past, all librarians would be rich." The book should be titled *What Would Have Worked on Wall Street—If We'd Had a Crystal Ball 44 Years Ago*. But even a crystal ball is insufficient. As a practical matter, a profitable strategy is only useful if it was identifiable *at the time*, and if the strategy had a strong enough rationale to cause investors to believe in it with enough conviction to put money on the line *at the time*. Otherwise, saying low price-to-sales is a useful strategy is no more profound than saying, "I wish I'd have bought Coca-Cola."

O'Shaughnessy ignores prior attempts at determining "the best-performing investment strategies." These attempts include *Risk and Returns from Common Stocks* and *Security Prices in a Competitive Market* by Richard Brealy, which were published by MIT Press in 1969 and 1971, respectively. *Stock Market Logic* by Norman Fosback, first published in 1976, is a rational, comprehensive review of stock market indicators, econometrics, and stock selection theories, culminating in "A Total Financial Management System." If O'Shaughnessy's unstated premise (what has worked in the past will work in the future) is true, then *Stock Market Logic*, which described what works well on Wall Street, should have provided the key to wealth. Fosback now publishes *Mutual Funds Magazine*. It would be interesting to read his review of the current book.

However, my real criticism is this: *The book doesn't make good use of the data it presents*. O'Shaughnessy's conclusions are based on the results of the entire 44-year period. Yet on page 144, O'Shaughnessy prints tables showing the Compound Annual Rates of Return by Decade for the strategies of High and Low Price-to-Earnings, High and Low Price-to-Book, High and Low Price to Cash Flow, High and Low Price to Sales, and High Yield.

A quick look shows that none of the strategies was optimal for two successive decades. In the large stock universe, the optimal strategy in the 1950s was *low* price to cash flow. In the 1960s, it was *high* price to cash flow. In the 1970s, it returned to *low* price to cash flow. Note that each decade's optimal strategy was a *reverse* of the prior decade's optimal strategy. Someone using a strategy derived from O'Shaughnessy's methods, based on his data, over a decade, would have found their strategy to be backwards in the following decade. In Chapter 14, O'Shaughnessy reviews Returns on Shareholder Equity (ROE). In his "Implications" (summary) on pages 182 and 187, he points out that high ROE was a very successful strategy from 1952 through 1967—successful enough to make someone using an O'Shaughnessy method a true believer, only to have the strategy not work in the 1970s.

Presumably, this tendency for optimal strategies to change over time is the reason he uses the entire 44-year period. Unfortunately this averages out, and therefore hides, the most interesting aspect of the data. More to the point, it assumes that investors have such conviction in the conclusions of his studies that they are willing to stay with it through a decade or more of underperformance.

O'Shaughnessy never entertains the idea that shifts in markets and optimal strategies might be normal. An idea that such shifts are normal would make them expected, and possibly observable. We expect such shifts. We expect them to occur when there is a change in the *investment climate* (our phrase). We think that the shifts in the optimal investment strategies likely occurred in the periods 1965–1968, 1979–1982, and 1990–1993, when we believe the investment climate changed. It is our intent to do such a study, based on O'Shaughnessy's annual data, but we haven't done it yet. Stay tuned.

Editor's Note

No matter how good the data is, the analysis of the data determines whether you are successful. O'Shaughnessy's data is good but, like many analysts, he misses a critical point. He fails to recognize that investment climate changes. Therefore, the success of an investment strategy depends upon the climate in which it is used. A successful investor must recognize the climate (and changes in climate) and choose the appropriate strategy for that climate.

Competition for the Consumer

This essay was originally published in Muhlenkamp Memorandum Issue 44, October 1997. During much of the 1990s, companies focused on getting their costs down to be "competitive." Government discussed privatization to lower its spending. The media focus was on the detrimental effects of such actions to the employees. Ron wrote this essay to show the other side of the issue: the benefits to the consumer.

We often hear the argument that a company or a country must do certain things "to compete" or "to be competitive." This goal of being competitive is stated as the rationale for much of the cost cutting and downsizing in industry, as well as the privatizing of various tasks previously done by government, both in the United States and in other countries.

We agree that each of these entities should be competitive, but we think that much understanding has been lost because the sentence is seldom finished. The complete sentence would state: "We must take these steps to be competitive *for the consumer's business.*" Such a statement makes it explicit that the ultimate beneficiary, and the ultimate driver, of these corporate actions is the consumer. In a free economy, the consumer is *king*!

In a free economy, no person or company can make the consumer purchase its product; only government can do that. Producers can advertise, pitch, cajole, and sweet-talk, but they cannot force the consumer to purchase their product. Unless the producer offers a product the consumer wants, at a price the consumer is willing to pay, no purchase will take place.

Certainly, there are products the consumer must buy—food, clothing, and shelter—but in a free economy there is no requirement to buy these products from any one provider. As long as the market is open, multiple producers will compete for the consumer's business. Over time, most producers learn that the best sales gimmick is to provide a quality product at a cheaper price.

Years ago, I was taught that there are "natural monopolies" for some goods, but I no longer believe that. The only monopolies I can find are government sanctioned. In the current decade, we have opened up markets in natural gas and long-distance phone service and are currently opening electric power. Each of these markets was once viewed as a natural monopoly. Granted, transitions to freer markets can be confusing. The recent move to deregulate telephone and electric service in the United States has resulted in some confusion and complaints because people are now asked to make choices they didn't previously have to make. I am told that some people in Russia have similar complaints now that they have choices in buying food and clothing.

The beauty of a free market is that consumers who don't want to spend their time shopping to save the last nickel still benefit from the actions of their neighbors who do. This competition for the consumer's business drives all producers to produce better products at lower prices. I must admit that I didn't understand much of this until I read Sam Walton's autobiography. Sam Walton founded Wal-Mart. He perceived his job as that of a purchasing agent for his customers. There is nothing you can buy at Wal-Mart that you can't buy somewhere else. The only thing that Wal-Mart claims (or advertises) is lower prices. The sole task Sam set for himself was to bring existing products to his customers at a lower price. He did it well enough to become the richest man in the country.

As an investment manager, I am embarrassed to admit that I never bought a share of Wal-Mart. My rationale was that retailing is the world's second oldest profession; what can Sam Walton do that Kmart can't copy in six weeks or Sears copy in six months? It wasn't until I read Sam's book that I learned that Sam had worked for, and run a franchise store for, a discount retailer. He left because he thought his ideas for lowering costs and prices had merit, but the franchisor wasn't interested in his ideas. And Kmart chose to fight his ideas rather than co-opt them. (Remember that Kmart was the leading discount retailer at the time. Sam Walton and his ideas eclipsed Kmart in 20 years.)

In a free market, the consumer is king. If you serve the consumer by providing a product or service that he values, you can get rich. But of equal importance, you can get rich *only* by providing a product that the consumer values. Many is the inventor who created a new product he thought was great, but the consumer wasn't interested. Many is the engineer who improved an existing product (by his standard) only to be chagrined when the consumer didn't appreciate the improvement.

Several years ago, Intel launched a consumer advertising campaign identifying those computers with "Intel Inside." But when their next new chip, the Pentium, was found to have an arcane flaw, Intel found consumer awareness to be a two-edged sword. Intel found that statistical analyses and other explanations, which had been acceptable to their corporate and engineering customers, were not acceptable to the retail consumer. The retail consumer was a more demanding customer than the professionals! Intel's management finally realized that, if they wanted to sell consumer products, they had to accept the consumer's standard for performance. Andy Grove, the chairman of Intel, describes this realization as a major "inflection point" for his company. I would describe it as the realization that the consumer sets the rules.

In a free market, every improvement in quality or service becomes the new standard that all competitors are expected to meet. Similarly, each price decline becomes the new standard of competition for the consumer's business.

Chapter 7

1999–2001: The Fad Years (Some Call Them the "Bubble" Years)

From 1999 to 2001, we had a split stock market. Inflation was stable, interest rates were fair, but all the long-term economic indicators were overrun for a time by an investing fad. Tech stocks climbed dramatically, and then fell. Other stocks weathered the storm. The fad went round-trip in three years. The repercussions will be felt on two levels:

1. For the individual stocks involved in the fad, tracking for the next several years will be affected by the tax losses generated.
2. For the individual people involved, if the experience of 1968 is any guide, it will take a long time, maybe a decade, before they trust the stock market. They may, however, be susceptible to alternatives of various promise.

1999

- In Colorado, two Columbine High School students use guns and explosives to randomly kill 12 students and one teacher before killing themselves.
- The U.S. Senate impeaches President Clinton and, ultimately, acquits him on perjury and obstruction of justice charges in the Monica Lewinsky affair.
- The United States posts its second surplus in two years at $122.7 billion.
- NATO forces strike Serbian air defenses and other sites as Serb forces step up their efforts to crush resistance in Kosovo.
- The world population reaches 6 billion. The designated 6 billionth baby is born in Bosnia.
- In the United States married couples with children constitute 26 percent of the population as compared to 45 percent in 1972.
- First-class postage rates increase from 32 cents to 33 cents an ounce.

2000

- The world braces for software glitches due to Y2K.
- A decrease to a 35-hour workweek takes legal effect in France.
- The U.S. government reports a 3.9 percent jobless rate, the lowest in 30 years.
- The median price for a new house in the United States is $162,000; average size is 2,266 square feet. (This compares to a median price of $42,100 and an average size of 1,645 square feet in 1975, and a median price of $78,300 and an average size of 1,780 square feet in 1984.)
- The U.S. Senate votes 83–15 to end trade restrictions on China.
- The Russian government, under its new president, Vladimir Putin, approves a 13 percent flat tax on personal income, replacing the previous three-bracket system with a top rate of 30 percent.
- The Melissa computer virus infects e-mail in tens of thousands of computers, causing $80 million in damage.
- Election officials begin a recount of the U.S. presidential election; winner remains in suspense based on the Florida result.

2001

- Congress formally certifies George W. Bush the winner of the bitterly contested 2000 presidential election.

- In Afghanistan, the Taliban orders the death penalty for anyone who converts from Islam to a different religion.
- Pacific Gas & Electric (PG&E) files for bankruptcy with $9 billion in debt; California uses rolling blackouts to cut off power to hundreds of thousands of people.
- First-class postage rates increase from 33 cents an ounce to 34 cents an ounce.
- On September 11, terrorists attack the United States. At 8:45 A.M., American Airlines Flight 11 crashes into the North Tower of the World Trade Center in New York City. At 9:03 A.M., United Airlines Flight 175 crashes into the South Tower of the World Trade Center. At 9:38 A.M., American Airlines Flight 77 crashes into the Pentagon. At 10:10 A.M., United Airlines Flight 93 crashes southeast of Pittsburgh.
- On October 7, U.S. and British forces strike 31 targets in Afghanistan. Air defenses, communication nodes, and other large fixed sites are targeted.

Prosperity

This essay was originally published in Muhlenkamp Memorandum *Issue 52, October 1999. In this essay, Ron points out that for prosperity to be consumed, it must be produced. So if we want to enjoy the good life that comes with prosperity, we need to understand how prosperity is produced. What motivates the worker to work? What motivates the employer to hire the worker? How do we protect these incentives so that our economy continues to grow?*

I want to discuss how we produce prosperity. In this regard, the past 30 years have been fascinating.

Defining Prosperity

What does *prosperity* mean to you?

When I ask this question, people respond in terms of a better lifestyle, home, car, or vacation; a secure retirement; funding college education; and so on. But these responses describe how we consume prosperity. I believe we can't consume prosperity unless we produce prosperity.

In the 1970s, we had stagflation. Stagflation is a combination of low growth (stagnation) and high inflation. According to the economic theories I was taught in the late 1960s, this wasn't supposed to happen. Inflation was supposed to be a result of too much growth. Low growth was supposed to result in lower inflation or deflation. So stagflation wasn't supposed to happen—but it did.

In the 1980s and 1990s we had accelerating growth and declining inflation, along with huge federal budget deficits. When Ronald Reagan proposed the tax cuts that resulted in budget deficits, conventional economic wisdom argued that the increased federal borrowing would result in higher interest rates, a crowding out of commercial borrowers, and a declining economy. It didn't happen; interest rates fell, and the economy expanded for nearly 20 years. What went right?

In the 1970s we had 10 percent inflation and a progressive federal income tax rate structure with a top tax bracket of 70 percent. Inflation of 10 percent meant that each individual needed 10 percent more money each year just to maintain his standard of living. The progressive tax rate meant that if you received a 10 percent raise (pretax), your taxes went up 20 percent. (These numbers are straight from the tax tables of 1979.) A 70 percent tax rate meant that after a certain level it didn't pay to work (and produce).

All Work, No Pay?

One day in 1980, I was visiting a couple of clients who are doctors. They had set up pension and profit-sharing plans, but they also had a plethora of other plans, including salary deferral, and so on, each of which was designed to minimize or defer their tax bill. I finally asked them how much of their time they spent being doctors and how much of their time they spent deferring taxes. They said they spent about a day per week deferring taxes. So here you have two highly intelligent, highly trained individuals who spent four days a week doing something useful and one day a week producing nothing, simply because of their high tax bracket.

The 70 percent tax bracket fed a tax shelter industry that funneled money into areas that were tax-favored rather than economically productive. And we got a glut of boxcars, barges, and see-through (empty) office buildings. Meanwhile, my friends who were farmers concluded that the way to get ahead was not to grow more food, but to borrow more money and buy more land. My suburban friends spent some of their working hours planning how to borrow more money and how to buy a bigger house.

At about this time, a friend of mine who taught at Duquesne University sketched the following scenario based on a five-day work week:

- Monday, you pay 10 percent in taxes on your earnings.
- Tuesday, you pay 20 percent in taxes on your earnings.
- Wednesday, you pay 30 percent in taxes on your earnings.
- Thursday, you pay 40 percent in taxes on your earnings.
- Friday, you pay 50 percent in taxes on your earnings.

How many of you would come to work on Friday? Over the years, I have asked several thousand people this question. I used to get 2 to 5 percent of hands going up. Lately, I'm getting zero. People are telling me that, at a 50 percent tax bracket, they will quit working. And you don't have to be an adult to come to this conclusion.

In the early 1980s, when my daughters were in their early teens, I hired them to keypunch for me. I paid them $5 an hour when they could make only $2.50 an hour babysitting. After watching their money go to early-teen things that I considered frivolous, I suggested that, henceforth, they should not spend half of what they earned working for me. But the next time I asked them to work, they were unavailable, and the next. I finally had to remove the restriction in order to get the work done. My early-teen daughters were unwilling to work under a 50 percent tax rate (as perceived by them) even though the net to them was as great as they could earn elsewhere.

I believe the reason we had high unemployment in the 1970s is simply that it didn't pay to work. Certainly there were people looking for jobs, nearly all of whom would not have been in the 50 percent-plus tax brackets. It would have paid for them to work, but it didn't pay a businessperson to hire them. Aside from the income taxes, there was a raft of other penalties.

When I hired my first full-time employee in 1981, I had to fill out seven different forms and pay seven different taxes. My friends who were running small businesses told me I was crazy to hire employees instead of temporaries. Yet few politicians seem to understand that taxing the employer is not conducive to creating jobs. The exception was Ronald Reagan.

In 1983, Ronald Reagan lowered the top tax rate to 28 percent. It paid businessmen to earn the incremental dollar, so they started hiring. Unemployment has fallen ever since. George H. W. Bush and Bill Clinton raised the top tax rate to 39.6 percent. Depending on the state and local rates, most people face an additional 3 to 8 percent in taxes. So we are once again flirting with the 50 percent rate at which people tell me they will quit working.[1]

Working: It's Not Just a Paycheck Anymore

Meanwhile, there is another dynamic that has changed in the past 30 years. If you work in a union shop, seniority (length of tenure) gives you preference on certain things. Thirty years ago, seniority gave a worker preference in working overtime (which pays one and a half or two times the hourly rate). Today, seniority still gives preference, but it is viewed as the right to not work overtime.

My father worked all the overtime he could. When I worked in a union shop for a couple of summers, I worked all the overtime I could. It was a chance to earn more money. Recently, I had a conversation with a man who has a tool and die shop in Vandergrift, Pennsylvania. I asked him if he has trouble getting employees. He said it isn't too bad. He pays less than Allegheny Ludlum (the big local mill), but people want to work for him because there is no compulsory overtime. Let me repeat. He can pay less because he has no compulsory overtime (which would allow employees to earn one and a half or two times the normal rate). Given similar choices, people have reversed their preference! What is going on?

I believe that many people no longer work just for money. While this may seem to contradict my earlier argument, I think the answer is a bit more subtle.

My parents and their peers, who lived through the Depression, were willing to work long hours and live cheaply to make things better for their children. People in Japan who survived the war were willing to work long hours and live cheaply to make things better for their children. When my son, Tony, was in Korea, he wrote home to say, "Dad, these people work 60 hours a week and live in rabbit hutches." My observation is that people who have been truly poor (without food, clothing, and shelter)—or who fear being truly poor—will do almost anything to avoid it. But those who have always had the basics, and take them for granted, have much different incentives.

Once you are able (or believe you are able) to take food, clothing, and shelter for granted, the willingness to work additional hours becomes a direct tradeoff between leisure time and additional goods or services. And it involves not just the hours of work, but also all the other facets of working, from a sense of challenge and satisfaction to the social and human aspects. Working becomes not just a means to feed and clothe yourself and your family; it also becomes a way to foster a sense of purpose and self-esteem. I know a lot of people who find purpose and self-esteem in their work. I don't know any who have found it in the party circuit.

One interesting aspect of the current U.S. economy is that many of the goods and services we now consume were unheard of just a generation ago. We use the word *need* to describe goods and services our parents viewed as luxuries and our grandparents never dreamed of. It has become apparent that there is no limit to the goods and services desired by the consumer, which means that there is no limit to GDP per capita from a demand or consumer perspective. The only limit to GDP per capita is what that same consumer is willing to produce.

If we want people to choose to work and produce increasing amounts of discretionary goods and services, we, as employers, must compensate employees in ways that are meaningful to them, not just in salary but also in the work environment.

Encouraging the Employer

At the same time, if we want people to choose to employ others and to produce increasing amounts of discretionary goods and services, we, as citizens and voters, must allow employers to earn returns that are meaningful to them, not only in money but in freedom from excess regulation.

If we raise taxes on employees, they're likely to quit working. If we raise taxes on employers, they're likely to quit hiring. And the margin of incentives is slim. In our economy, profit to payroll averages 6 cents on the dollar.

For my employee to take home $1, it costs me $1.84 (including the 401(k) contribution), which means that he has to produce $1.95 of value to provide me with the 6 percent profit. (For an update, see our essay "The

Trouble with Government Spending" in Chapter 6.) I believe much of the prosperity of the past 20 years rides on that 6 percent margin of profit.

As Abe Lincoln said, "You cannot help the wage earner by discouraging the wage payer."

Taxes—Choose Your Poison: Old Tax Return versus Proposed Tax Return

This essay was originally published in Muhlenkamp Memorandum *Issue 53, January 2000. Steve Forbes was campaigning to be the Republican candidate for president. One of his campaign promises was to reform the federal income tax, replacing it with a flat tax of 17 percent. Forbes proposed a similar tax plan in his 1996 bid for president (which Ron discusses in his April 1996 essay "Why I Like the Flat Tax," in Chapter 6). The twist here is that Forbes now proposes to let the taxpayer choose which income tax return to use.*

Exhibit 7.1 shows the tax return you would have to file should Steve Forbes be elected president and get his programs enacted. When you have completed your tax return for 1999, you might want to fill out the form to determine the difference in dollars, time, and frustration between his proposal and our current system.

I have been a fan of Mr. Forbes's flat tax proposal since he first proposed it, partly because I believe it will foster economic growth (for the reasons I gave in last quarter's essay, "Prosperity"). But even I was surprised when I heard Steve's response to presidential candidate Gary Bauer in a recent

Exhibit 7.1   Proposed Flat Tax Form for 1999 Individual Wage Tax 1999

1. Wages and Salary	1. _____
2. Number of adults in family	2. _____
3. Number of children in family	3. _____
4. Deductions for adults (multiply line 2 by $13,000)	4. _____
5. Deductions for children (multiply line 3 by $5,000)	5. _____
6. Total deductions (line 4 plus line 5)	6. _____
7. Taxable income (line 1 minus line 6)	7. _____
8. Tax (multiply line 7 by 17%)	8. _____

debate. Mr. Bauer took Steve to task for dropping the mortgage interest deduction and the charitable gift deduction in his flat tax proposal. Steve replied, "We'll give you the choice, file either the flat tax form or the old 1040 forms complete with the mortgage deduction and the charitable deduction. The taxpayer can file whichever one he chooses." Now I've known for a long time that Steve's program would allow you to do this, and that individual choice and responsibility are at the core of all his programs, yet I was surprised when I heard a presidential candidate say that an individual taxpayer could calculate his taxes in multiple ways and choose the lesser tax rather than the greater tax, as is now often required.

That Steve Forbes should be the only one of six Republican candidates (all of whom favor some tax cuts) who would allow the taxpayer this choice speaks volumes about how far we are from understanding what makes a free economy work. And it means that I must find better ways of explaining the ideas in my essay "Prosperity."

Editor's Note

When Steve Forbes offered the taxpayer the choice of which tax form to use, he sent a clear, if surprising, message. He was saying it's okay if the taxpayer chooses to pay lower taxes. It seems like a rash suggestion. After all, the government needs tax revenue to function. However, he was just taking the work incentive argument to its logical conclusion. By allowing people to choose, he was placing top priority on fostering work incentive. If people work more, the economy grows. Therefore, even at lower tax rates, the government will collect higher tax revenues.

Forbes withdrew from the presidential race in February 2000. With the end of his campaign, the national spotlight moved away from the flat tax. However, its supporters remain. They are encouraged not only by the attention Steve Forbes brought to the issue in 1996 and in 2000, but also by the gains the flat tax has made outside of the United States, particularly in the former Soviet bloc countries. Estonia established a flat tax in 1994, Latvia in 1995, and Russia in 2001. Ukraine and Slovakia each adopted a flat tax in 2003. Economist Bruce Bartlett has said this about the flat tax:

> A key factor driving all of these countries to adopt radical tax simplification and a lowering of rates is tax evasion. They were simply unable to collect sufficient revenue under their formerly complex, high-rate tax systems. In every case, implementation of a flat tax caused collections to rise, as the benefit of evasion was

reduced. (If the top rate is 50 percent, failing to report $1 of income saves you 50 cents in taxes. But if the rate is only 13 percent, as it is in Russia, evasion saves you only 13 cents—no longer worth the risk of getting caught for many evaders.) According to Hoover Institution economist Alvin Rabushka, inflation-adjusted personal income tax revenues in Russia rose 28 percent the first year the flat tax was in effect, and 21 percent the following year. So far this year (2003), real revenues are up about 17 percent. Revenues were flat or falling before the flat tax was imposed.[2]

Social Security by the Numbers

Ron first wrote about Social Security in his October 1992 newsletter. In 2000 he updated his 1992 argument, and then in response to the questions it generated, he wrote a follow-up essay entitled "Social Security Revisited: A Plan to Fix It." The two essays were then updated in 2005. We present here the 2005 updates to Ron's two-part series on Social Security.

This first essay in the two-part series discusses Social Security on a per-person basis. It shows why Social Security cannot continue the way it is and how it got into this mess, and discusses some of the options we face at this point.

In 1992 we published an essay entitled "Social Security by the Numbers." As with all government programs, the numbers are much more understandable when viewed on a per-person or per-family basis. So we set out to answer two basic questions: "What did I pay into it?" and "How much can I expect to get?"

As the topic of Social Security is now on the agenda in Washington, D.C., it seems like a good time to update the data. This is particularly true as increasing numbers of people are becoming aware that Social Security, as presently configured, is unsustainable.

First, the numbers.

What Did I Pay into It?

Exhibit 7.2 shows the maximum Social Security tax paid by an employee each year since the system started in 1937. Equal amounts were paid

Exhibit 7.2   Social Security Taxes

Year	Maximum Covered Earnings	Tax as % of Covered Earning	Tax ($)	Inflation-Adjusted Dollars for 2004
1937	$3,000	1.00%	$30	$384
1938	$3,000	1.00	$30	$379
1939	$3,000	1.00	$30	$386
1940	$3,000	1.00	$30	$391
1941	$3,000	1.00	$30	$388
1942	$3,000	1.00	$30	$369
1943	$3,000	1.00	$30	$334
1944	$3,000	1.00	$30	$314
1945	$3,000	1.00	$30	$309
1946	$3,000	1.00	$30	$302
1947	$3,000	1.00	$30	$278
1948	$3,000	1.00	$30	$243
1949	$3,000	1.00	$30	$226
1950	$3,000	1.50	$45	$342
1951	$3,600	1.50	$54	$406
1952	$3,600	1.50	$54	$376
1953	$3,600	1.50	$54	$369
1954	$3,600	2.00	$72	$488
1955	$4,200	2.00	$84	$566
1956	$4,200	2.00	$84	$568
1957	$4,200	2.25	$95	$630
1958	$4,200	2.25	$95	$608
1959	$4,800	2.50	$120	$752
1960	$4,800	3.00	$144	$895
1961	$4,800	3.00	$144	$881
1962	$4,800	3.13	$150	$909
1963	$4,800	3.63	$174	$1,043
1964	$4,800	3.63	$174	$1,030
1965	$4,800	3.63	$174	$1,017
1966	$6,600	3.85	$254	$1,459
1967	$6,600	3.90	$257	$1,437
1968	$7,800	3.80	$296	$1,609
1969	$7,800	4.20	$328	$1,707
1970	$7,800	4.20	$328	$1,619
1971	$7,800	4.60	$359	$1,674
1972	$9,000	4.60	$414	$1,852

(continued)

Exhibit 7.2   (*continued*)

Year	Maximum Covered Earnings	Tax as % of Covered Earning	Tax ($)	Inflation-Adjusted Dollars for 2004
1973	$10,800	4.85	$524	$2,268
1974	$13,200	4.95	$653	$2,664
1975	$14,100	4.95	$698	$2,565
1976	$15,300	4.95	$757	$2,550
1977	$16,500	4.95	$817	$2,600
1978	$17,700	5.05	$894	$2,673
1979	$22,900	5.08	$1,163	$3,231
1980	$25,900	5.08	$1,316	$3,284
1981	$29,700	5.35	$1,589	$3,493
1982	$32,400	5.40	$1,750	$3,512
1983	$35,700	5.40	$1,928	$3,618
1984	$37,800	5.70	$2,155	$3,919
1985	$39,600	5.70	$2,257	$3,938
1986	$42,000	5.70	$2,394	$4,032
1987	$43,800	5.70	$2,497	$4,126
1988	$45,000	6.06	$2,727	$4,341
1989	$48,000	6.06	$2,909	$4,447
1990	$51,300	6.20	$3,181	$4,640
1991	$53,400	6.20	$3,331	$4,595
1992	$55,500	6.20	$3,441	$4,577
1993	$57,600	6.20	$3,571	$4,568
1994	$60,600	6.20	$3,757	$4,666
1995	$61,200	6.20	$3,794	$4,579
1996	$62,700	6.20	$3,887	$4,577
1997	$65,400	6.20	$4,055	$4,649
1998	$68,400	6.20	$4,241	$4,781
1999	$72,600	6.20	$4,501	$4,995
2000	$76,200	6.20	$4,724	$5,134
2001	$80,400	6.20	$4,985	$5,274
2002	$84,900	6.20	$5,264	$5,466
2003	$87,000	6.20	$5,394	$5,497
2004	$87,900	6.20	$5,450	$5,540
		Total	**$94,925**	**$157,248**
2005	$90,000	6.20	$5,580	
2006	$94,200	6.20	$5,840	
2007	$97,500	6.20	$6,045	

SOURCE: www.ssa.gov.

by the employer. If you want the exact numbers for your account, call the Social Security Administration at (800) 772-1213 or visit their web site at www.ssa.gov to get a request form. (Note: It's unlikely that people paying Social Security taxes today also paid them in 1937—68 years ago—but we believe it's useful to print the entire exhibit.)

Our regular readers know that historic numbers must be adjusted for inflation. This we have done for you; thus, the 1937 contribution of $30 represents $384 in 2004 purchasing power. Totals for each column are shown at the end of the table.

How Much Can I Expect to Get?

The Social Security web site (www.ssa.gov) states that a single person retiring in 2004 at age 66, who had always paid in the maximum, would receive $21,924 per year. A married couple with a nonworking spouse (categorized as "Family") would receive $32,880 (see Exhibit 7.3). Those who paid less than the maximum would receive less. For current numbers, call the Social Security Administration at (800) 772-1213.

It's interesting to note that the average Social Security wage earner earned $34,731 in 2003; he and his employer would have paid 2 × 6.20 percent or $4,307 in 2003 to Social Security. Exhibit 7.3 also

Exhibit 7.3   Social Security Benefit Analysis

Maximum SSA Benefits 2004$

	Monthly	Annual	Years to Use Contributions
Individual	$1,827	$21,924	14.3
Family	$2,740	$32,880	9.6

Maximum SS Taxes Contributed
(assume contributing maximum since 1937):

	Tax $	2004 $
Individual	$94,925	$157,248
Employer	$94,925	$157,248
Total	**$189,850**	**$314,496**

Assumes normal retirement age 66, individual and family receives full benefit, and individual paid in maximum amount.

SOURCE: Information derived from www.ssa.gov.

demonstrates that dividing the maximum annual benefit into the inflation-adjusted total contribution from employee and employer of $314,496, an individual retiring today can expect to get all of his money back in 14.3 years, a married couple in 9.6 years. But the life expectancy of a male age 66 is 16 years, a female is 20 years, and these benefits are promised for life.

The Social Security problem is a result of two inherently incompatible viewpoints:

1. Social Security was established as, and is viewed as, social insurance—a way of providing for those in need. It is a Depression-era program designed to keep older people out of the poorhouse. Any discussion of benefits soon becomes a discussion of those who need the money for subsistence living.[3]
2. Social Security has come to be viewed as a pension plan whereby "I'm entitled" to benefits because "I paid in all those years."[4] This was not the original purpose of the program. In fact, FICA, which is the heading for your Social Security contribution on your W-2 form, stands for "Federal *Insurance* Contributions Act."

When we ask people to describe the primary purpose of Social Security, those over 50 tend to focus on social insurance and those under 40 tend to focus on the pension plan, but nearly all believe that both aspects are important.

But insurance plans and pension plans are very different concepts using very different assumptions. A pension plan involves setting money aside over a period of years, investing it to grow its value in real terms (i.e., versus inflation and eventual taxes) so that assets available in retirement are a direct result of the assets set aside and the returns earned on those assets in the interim. The person receiving the pension can spend more than he put in (in real purchasing power), only if the invested returns exceed the interim inflation and the taxes paid upon withdrawal.

An insurance plan is entirely different. In an insurance plan, such as fire and casualty insurance, those who suffer the loss receive more than they paid in because those who don't meet the criteria (i.e., suffer the loss) receive nothing. I do not want to collect on my fire insurance, nor do I feel entitled to collect, unless I have a fire. Similarly, I do not want to *need* Social Security benefits, but they've been promised to me whether I need them or not.

In 1935, when the Social Security Act was passed, life expectancy was 63 years. Congress set the age at which benefits began at 65 in the full expectation that more than half the people would receive no benefits (because they would die before age 65). This is how an insurance plan works: A minority receives more than they paid in because a majority receives less than they paid in.

Back in the 1930s, there were 40 workers for each retiree, so it was easy to give a retiree a useful benefit because it was spread among 40 workers. Referring back to Exhibit 7.2, we see the rate of 1 percent on the first $3,000 in annual pay is equal to $30 per year or $384 per year in current dollars, matched by the employer. Sounds like a valid insurance plan, doesn't it? And it was, as long as the assumption held. But as life expectancies improved, the ratio of workers to retirees fell to 5:1 in the 1960s and 3:1 in the 1990s. That's why the contribution per worker increased by four times from 1937 to 1968 and has tripled since. In 30 years, the expected ratio of two workers per retiree will require a 50 percent increase from today's workers' contributions if current promises are to be kept.

But it's only a promise.

Social Security has never been run as either a pension plan or as an insurance plan. It has always been pay as you go, a transfer of money from workers to retirees. One man explained to me that it's both a pension plan and an insurance plan, "except for the fact that there are no assets, only IOUs in the trust. The IOUs in the trust will have to be paid with increased tax revenue or new taxes."

Exactly! Social Security has no assets. The benefits promised are simply a political promise—a political promise to raise taxes on our children and our grandchildren. But that assumes that our children will continue to work and continue to hire others, regardless of the tax rate.

But *we* didn't.

In the 1970s, when the top tax rate in the United States was 70 percent, we had 10 percent unemployment and a stagnant economy because it didn't pay the most productive members of our economy to hire other people. So they put their money into unproductive schemes designed to minimize taxes (tax shelters) and took time off to play golf. Over the past 20 years, I've asked thousands of people, "How many would continue to work at a 50 percent tax rate?" In the 1980s, 2 to 5 percent raised their hands. Lately I'm getting no one. If we aren't willing to work at a 50 percent tax rate, why do we assume our children will be willing to work at a 50 percent tax rate?

The real choice today is not how to save Social Security in its present form. It can't be done without driving us to the stagnation of the 1970s.

The real choice is: Would you rather live in the economy of the 1970s with 10 percent unemployment and rely on the promise of Social Security, or in the economy of the 1980s and 1990s and not need Social Security?

The benefits of Social Security can be saved by splitting it into two parts:

1. A *pension plan,* which allows private accounts that the individual owns and is able to invest for decent returns. While participation in the private plan can be voluntary, once chosen, the contribution would be mandatory (people must fund it) and carved out of the Social Security contribution. These accounts would look much like IRAs.

2. An *insurance plan,* for which the benefits are need-based. For example, anyone with annual income greater than twice the national average, or assets greater than 20 times that (which at a 5 percent rate would support spending at two times the national average income) would not receive Social Security. Should their income or assets fall below these levels, they would once again be eligible for benefits. Today, those levels for an individual would approximate $70,000 in income or $1.4 million in assets.

For the multimillionaire who reads this and fears that I'm cutting off your benefits, you're right. But consider that you're now paying income tax on these benefits at a rate of 28 to 35 percent and you can expect your estate to pay tax on the remainder at 30 to 48 percent. So each dollar that is promised to you will become $0.65 to $0.72 after income taxes, and $0.33 to $0.50 after estate taxes. Under my plan, the promise is more likely to be kept should you actually need Social Security.

Social Security Revisited: A Plan to Fix It

This essay was originally published in January 2001 and was updated in January 2005. It is a follow-up essay to "Social Security by the Numbers."

In the prior essay ("Social Security by the Numbers") we looked at Social Security from the point of view of the individual, specifically, "How much did I pay into it?" and "What can I expect to get out of it?" Our essay resulted in a number of comments and questions. In order to address these questions, we need to review Social Security in the aggregate—that is, what does the whole program look like?

In Exhibit 7.4 we've plotted the following for each year since 1940:

- The number of dollars workers paid into the program in taxes.
- The number of dollars retirees received from the program in benefits.
- The resulting assets in the "trust fund."

As you can see, the program currently looks pretty good. There is close to $1.2 trillion in the trust fund, roughly three years worth

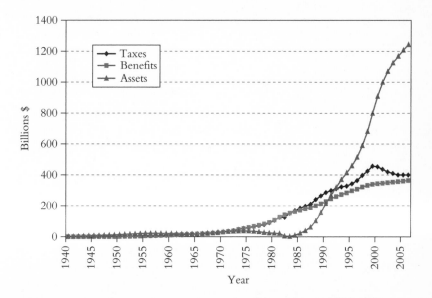

Exhibit 7.4   The Social Security Program Financial Status, 1940–2005

of benefits. This looks impressive until you realize that most people receive benefits for 20 years, not 3.

Most of you know that we don't like to make projections, but in the case of Social Security, it's pretty easy.

The benefits to be paid out each year will equal the number of retirees multiplied by the benefits promised to them.

The taxes paid in each year will equal the number of eligible workers, multiplied by the employment rate, multiplied by the withholding rate on their salaries up to a stated level.

Since nearly all the future retirees are already in the workforce and nearly all the eligible workers for the next 20 years have already been born, it's fairly easy to project the taxes, benefits, and assets for the next 20 to 40 years. In fact, our projections look just like the projections of the Social Security Administration (SSA). The projections are included in Exhibit 7.5, which shows why today's retirees over the age of 65 don't have a problem; there will be sizable assets in the program for the next 30 years.

But Exhibit 7.5 also shows why the children of today's retirees, people currently age 30 to 40, do have a problem: The program runs out of money in 2035.

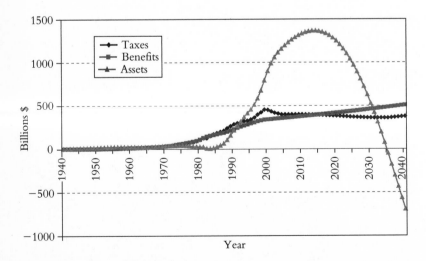

Exhibit 7.5   The Social Security Program—Projected Finances

Why has the program worked so far? When the Social Security program was initiated in 1937, the average life expectancy in the United States was less than 65 years. Eligibility for benefits was set at age 65 in the expectation that fewer than half of the workers would collect Social Security (because they wouldn't live long enough). Furthermore, when the program started, there were a lot of workers paying into the program and few receiving benefits.

In 1945, the ratio of workers to retirees was over 40 to 1; in 1950, over 16 to 1; and in 1960, the ratio was 5 to 1. Today, the worker-to-retiree ratio is a little over 3 to 1.

As the worker-to-retiree ratio fell, the SSA found it necessary to raise the tax rate from 2 percent in 1937–1949 (1 percent employee + 1 percent employer) to 6 percent by 1960, to 12.4 percent in 1990. The 12.4 percent rate remains today.

Furthermore, the SSA found it necessary to raise the level of wages on which the tax is paid from $3,000 in 1937 ($38,400 in 2004 inflation-adjusted dollars) to $87,900 in 2004.

We've plotted the applicable tax rate on Exhibit 7.6. We've also marked the years when the combination of tax rate and rate base first pushed the top payer over the levels of $2,000, $4,000, $6,000, $8,000,

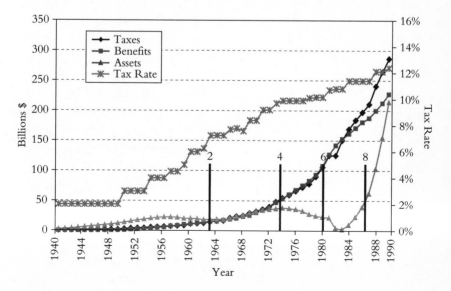

Exhibit 7.6   The Social Security Program, 1940–1990

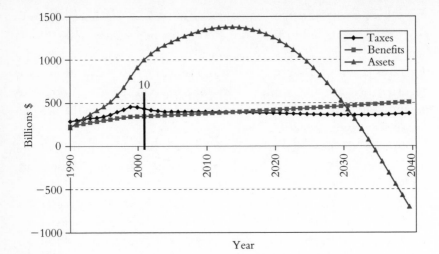

Exhibit 7.7   The Social Security Program, 1940–2040

and $10,000 (all numbers inflation-adjusted). Note that Exhibit 7.7 is a continuation of Exhibit 7.6, simply with a change in scale.

Also, starting in 1984, the Social Security Administration started cutting the value of retiree benefits. In 1984 it started taxing benefits; it began by taxing 50 percent of the benefit and it now taxes 85 percent of the benefit. More recently, it has been raising the retirement age. I was born in 1944; the age for me to qualify for full Social Security benefits is 66 years, not 65. If you were born in 1960, the age at which you will qualify for full benefits is 67 years, not 65.

Social Security benefits are calculated as a percentage of your qualifying pay prior to retirement. Currently, benefits are calculated at 90 percent of the first $627 of one's average indexed monthly earnings; plus 32 percent of one's average indexed monthly earnings over $627 and through $3,799; plus 15 percent of one's average indexed monthly earnings over $3,779. Since the average wage earner today earns roughly $34,731 per year ($2,894 monthly), the average retiree is promised benefits a little over 45 percent of their pay. See Exhibit 7.8 for details.

Three people each paying 12 percent in taxes can support one person taking 36 percent out in benefits. (Note that in 1960, five people each paying 6 percent in taxes could support one person taking 30 percent out in benefits.) The problem is that the ratio of workers to retiree will decline to just 2:1 by 2030.

Exhibit 7.8   Social Security Benefits

	Monthly	Annual
Average wage per SSA 2003	$2,894	$34,731
SSA Benefits Calculation		
90% of $627, plus	$564	$6,772
32% of earnings >$627 through $3,779 plus	$726	$8,706
15% of earnings >$3,779	$0	$0
Total	**$1,290**	**$15,478**
% of current wage	**45%**	**45%**

SOURCE: Information derived from www.ssa.gov.

At that point, the two workers would each have to pay 18 percent of their pay (nearly a 50 percent increase) into Social Security in order for one retiree to receive 36 percent. Some people believe this is a viable solution. I don't. In the 1970s, I saw what happens when people are pushed into ever-higher tax brackets. At some point, they quit working. Even if the employees want to work, if the employer quits, the employees are out of work.

A second solution is to cut benefits. (In fact, I've suggested cutting the benefits of millionaires, but there aren't enough millionaires to solve the problem.) Many retirees believe that their benefits can't be cut. They believe they're entitled to the promised benefits. But the Supreme Court (*Fleming v. Nestor,* 1960) has ruled that we're not entitled to the promised benefits. Some retirees were shocked when Medicare tripled the amount (from $10 to $30) of the co-pay for prescribed drugs. Folks, the rules on Social Security are set by the same people who make the rules on Medicare. If they believe it is necessary, they will cut your benefits.

But there is a third way to make Social Security viable for the next generation.

If a part of the taxes used to build the trust fund for the next 30 years could be invested to earn a reasonable rate of return, we could alleviate the problem. Some have suggested allowing people to invest part of their Social Security taxes in a Personal Security Account. To me, a Personal Security Account sounds a lot like an IRA (call it a PSA). So I took a look at my IRA to see how it has done.

Exhibit 7.9 is a plot of my personal IRA from 1981 through 2004. The bottom line is the total dollars I've paid in—$1,500 in 1981 plus

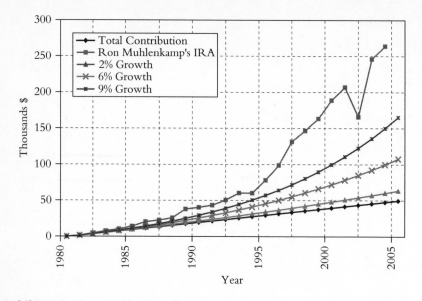

Exhibit 7.9　Ron Muhlenkamp's IRA

23 years multiplied by $2,000 per year is equal to $47,500. The middle lines are calculated: They show the assets I'd have if I'd earned 2 percent, 6 percent, or 9 percent per year. The top line is what my account has actually done. Exhibit 7.10 simply extends Exhibit 7.9 out another 20 years to show a typical working lifespan of 44 years.

The Social Security Administration recently sent me a statement that said my promised benefit upon retirement is $21,924 per year. The IRS says my life expectancy at age 66 is 16 years. So the SSA expects to pay me $350,784 over my retirement years. We've marked that on Exhibit 7.10.

Alternatively, an annuity that promised me $21,924 for 16 years would cost $240,000 at the start, if we assume an interest rate of 6 percent. We've marked that on Exhibit 7.10.

You'll note that at contributions of $2,000 per year, the return has to be 6 percent or greater to reach $350,000 in 44 years, but that it reaches $240,000 in 37 years. I've exceeded $240,000 in 24 years. The amazing thing is that the $2,000 per year that I put into my IRA is less than 30 percent of what I've paid into Social Security to date. So just by earning a reasonable return on my investment (it's been invested only in

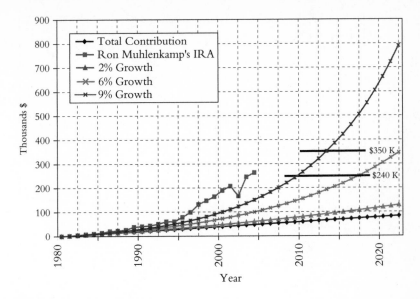

Exhibit 7.10 IRA Projections

two no-load mutual funds), I will be able to fund an amount equal to my promised Social Security benefits with only 30 percent of the Social Security taxes. This makes 70 percent of my Social Security taxes available to someone else.

One roadblock to the adoption of Private Savings Accounts (PSAs) for a part of Social Security is that the bookkeeping would show an interim loan during the transition. The latest estimate shows a loan of about $6 trillion, which is, of course, a huge number. But this loan would not be a new debt! It is simply admitting to the size of the promise (debt) that has already been made. It is simply the present value of the amount by which the assets in Social Security are below the promises made by Social Security. Further, $6 trillion spread among 100 million American families is $60,000 per family.

For most families, the first major step in building family assets is the purchase of a home, which is subject to a mortgage. The second major step is the building of a portfolio, typically of stocks and bonds, to help in funding retirement.

Today, approximately 70 million American families are homeowners. But most don't really own their home; their ownership is subject to them paying off their mortgage. People are willing to make mortgage payments (typically for 30 years) because the contract says when they've completed making their mortgage payments, they will, in fact, own their home; and they trust the courts to enforce that contract.

If you're one of these homeowners, would you prefer to make a similar (mortgage) payment to the government, in return, for a promise that the government will provide you with the same or a similar house at the end of 30 years? Would you trust the government to do so, even if the Supreme Court has ruled that the government is not required to keep its promise? Bottom line, which do you trust more—the law and the courts, or a political promise? To date, I've found no one who would prefer a political promise to the current laws on mortgaged home ownership.

For 70 years (since 1937), the government has mandated that workers pay into the Social Security system as a way of funding a part of their retirement. And it has made promises to pay benefits upon the worker reaching a defined age. But the government has been forced to change the terms of the promise as the demographics have changed.

PSAs would replace part of that promise with a package of individual ownership of the assets in return for a 30-to-40-year "mortgage" as those assets are funded to a sufficient size. These assets would be owned by the individual and could be sold or passed on to heirs just like a home or an IRA account. This is the method people prefer for the assets they live in. Why do some consider it so frightening for their proposed retirement assets?

From the preceding data I reach four conclusions:

1. The 65-plus-year-olds don't have a problem; their children do.
2. Using Personal Security Accounts for a part of the taxes can help alleviate the problem.
3. We have a fairly short period of time (the next 10 to 15 years while the assets in the trust fund are building) to implement the PSA. After 15 years the window closes.
4. Politically, it will probably not happen soon enough unless those over 65 push for it.

Folks, our politicians know the numbers. They expect to hear complaints from young workers who know the numbers, but they fear a backlash from retirees who don't know the numbers.

And they know that retirees vote in greater percentages than do younger people. Plus, the problem won't come to fruition for 30 years, which is 5 to 15 elections away.

So, in order to solve the problems, it is necessary for retirees to insist to their congresspeople that they reform Social Security for the benefit of their children and grandchildren.

Economics and Why Election 2000 Is Important

This essay was originally published in Muhlenkamp Memorandum Issue 56, October 2000. This essay is the capstone of Ron's writings on economics. It weaves together his theories on inflation and its effects on the bond and stock markets, interest rates and what drives them, taxation and work incentive, and government spending. The common thread is the idea that people drive the economy. The government influences that relationship. Therefore, when we make political choices, we are also making economic choices. This essay explains the effects of those choices. Read it again and again—at least every election year.

In the past 35 years I have witnessed a fascinating experiment in economics. In the mid-1960s, when I was in college, the U.S. Gross Domestic Product (GDP) was growing at 4 percent to 5 percent, mortgage rates were at 5.5 percent, and the unemployment rate was at 4 to 4.5 percent. Inflation wasn't even mentioned because it had been at less than 1.5 percent since the wars (World War II and Korea). All of this was considered normal.

The economics books I studied at the time discussed inflation in terms of "cost push" and "demand pull," with the underlying theme that inflation was caused by too much growth in the economy. The books also argued that government spending was at least as stimulative as private spending and was actually more effective at jump-starting an economy. As a capstone to all of this, I was taught that with the U.S. economy growing at 4 percent per year and the Soviet economy growing at 6 percent per year, GDP per capita in Russia would surpass GDP per capita in the United States in roughly the year 2000.

By 1968, the U.S. economy was enjoying its second-longest expansion ever. Consumer confidence was high, and Wall Street was booming. Stocks like Litton Industries, LTV, National Student Marketing, and

Equity Funding were making investors millionaires almost overnight. A book, *The New Breed on Wall Street,* featured the "hot" mutual fund managers of the day including Fred Mates, Fred Alger, and Fred Carr.

Economists were so confident of their ability to fine-tune the economy that some university economic departments cancelled their courses on the business cycle. The point is—we've been here before, but we blew it.

Just 11 years later, in 1979, inflation was 10 percent, GDP growth was 2 percent, unemployment was 10 percent, and mortgage rates were 11 percent on their way to 15 percent. President Carter complained about a malaise in the American public.

What Happened?

In the mid-1960s President Johnson wanted to fight the war in Vietnam and the war on poverty at the same time, but he didn't want to raise taxes to pay for them. In order to finance the spending, the U.S. Treasury and the Federal Reserve expanded the money supply at a rapid rate (they printed excess money). As is usual, the early effects were beneficial; the negative effects took a little longer (sort of like using a credit card—the payments are delayed).

Gradually, as we kept printing more dollars, the value of those dollars fell. By 1973 the value of the dollar (relative to its 1965 value) had fallen 31 percent. Compared to other benchmarks, it had fallen 33 percent vs. the Deutschmark, 22 percent vs. the Japanese yen, and 67 percent versus gold. All this time we were buying ever larger quantities of oil from the OPEC nations and were paying for it in ever depreciating dollars. So, in 1973, OPEC raised the price of oil. This gave our politicians a scapegoat for inflation, but the politicians didn't change their policies. Why should they? Popular economic theory, which I was taught at the time, held that inflation was caused by supply and demand constraints, not by printing money.

By 1979, the dollar (relative to its 1965 value) had fallen 59 percent. It had fallen 57 percent versus the Deutschmark, 44 percent versus the Japanese yen, and 88 percent versus gold. The dollar was so weak that President Carter deemed it necessary to appoint an independent central banker as chairman of the Federal Reserve Bank. In order to rebuild confidence, President Carter had to choose someone whom our trading partners would trust to support the value of the dollar as his first priority. He chose Paul Volcker.

Also in 1979, I wrote an essay titled "Why the Market Went Down" (see Chapter 4) to explain the impact of inflation on the stock and bond markets. Based on this paper, we told our clients in 1980 that if Reagan and Volcker were successful in getting inflation under control, we'd have a good decade in the stock and bond markets.

Paul Volcker soon made it clear that he planned to grow the money supply at a rate of 6 to 8 percent rate, and economic commentary hit the fan. The economic community argued as follows: Inflation is 10 percent and is intractable. If you only grow the money supply at 6 percent, the economy will be forced to shrink at a 4 percent rate $(6 - 10 = -4)$. Volcker did it anyway, and by 1982 inflation fell to 4 percent with GDP growth of 2 percent.

Volcker's action and the ensuing economic numbers demonstrated that inflation is caused by printing too much money, not by too much growth. He also demonstrated that GDP growth competes with inflation for money and that GDP growth can outmuscle inflation for the available money supply. Inflation was not intractable. In fact, for a given growth in the money supply, higher growth in GDP actually causes lower inflation!

While we still have some economists and a lot of commentators believing that growth causes inflation, central banks have learned the lesson. As evidence of this, I'll cite the central banks of Europe. When their governments decided to adopt a single currency, the euro, it was necessary to bring the inflation rates in several countries down to the level of Germany. They didn't even attempt supply/demand management. Each country set out to lower its inflation rate by controlling the growth in its money supply, and each was successful in lowering its inflation rate.

Today inflation is under control in each of the major countries and each of the major currencies of the world. Inflation is coming under control in a list of countries from Brazil to Chile to Greece, and the sensitivity to inflation of investors in the stock and bond markets gives me confidence that it will remain under control for the foreseeable future. We've learned the lesson that Paul Volcker taught us.

But the second lesson of the past 35 years, the lesson of Ronald Reagan, we haven't learned.

In 1960, real economic growth had slowed from the 4 to 5 percent rate of the 1950s. President Kennedy was advised by some economists to increase government spending to jump-start the economy. He was advised by a few others to cut taxes to jump-start the economy. He did both, choosing to go to the moon and to cut taxes. The economy resumed 4–5 percent annual growth.

As we said earlier, President Johnson simultaneously fought the Vietnam War and the war on poverty. He sought to pay for them by inflating the money supply. The first effect of this inflation was a decline in the value of the dollar, but another effect was on income tax rates.

In the United States, we have progressive income tax rates. The tax rate progresses higher, as your income progresses higher. So as your income increases, your taxes increase faster. In the 1970s, these rates were not indexed for inflation. In fact, in the 1970s, if your income went up 10 percent, your federal income taxes went up 20 percent; in other words, a worker who got a raise equal to inflation pretax was still losing ground after tax. It also meant that professional people got bumped into ever-higher tax brackets, the highest being 70 percent.

At a 70 percent rate, individuals gain more by avoiding taxes than they do by producing more income. Many people resorted to "tax shelters," which were designed to take advantage of provisions in the tax law rather than produce useful or desired goods and services.

With the average wage earner falling behind and the top wage earners discouraged from producing more, or from hiring others to produce more, is it any wonder that we had a malaise in the economy?

Ronald Reagan changed all that. He cut the top income tax rate to 28 percent. Tax shelters went away, and the top earners went back to producing useful goods and services and hiring others to help them. But when Reagan announced his tax cuts, economic commentary hit the fan. Many economists maintained that his tax cuts would cause federal deficits, which would cause government borrowing and rising interest rates. Rising interest rates would crowd out private borrowing and shut down the economy.

They were right on the first part. Government deficits ballooned. But they were dead wrong about interest rates and the economy. Interest rates fell and the economy boomed.

In June 1991, at an M.I.T. reunion, I had a long discussion/argument with an old classmate who graduated in economics and was, and is, the chief economist at a major consulting firm. He argued that the government deficits would drive interest rates higher. I argued that people's response to rates (by not buying ever larger houses with ever larger mortgages) would drive rates lower.

Long-term Treasury rates at the time were 9 percent. By late 1993 (two and a half years later), they had fallen to 6 percent. In late 1993, we concluded that the bond rally was over.

The best explanation I've found for the "Reagan Lesson" came from a friend of mine, a professor of economics at Duquesne University. In 1980, he shared with me the five-day workweek analogy (which was described in the "Prosperity" essay). The analogy culminated in this question: "If on Friday you had to pay 50 percent taxes on your earnings, would you come to work?" Most people say no. Clearly, you *can* tax away work incentive.

Here's a real-life example. At one time, I tried to teach my teenage daughters about saving money by insisting they save 50 percent of their earnings. (I thought they were spending frivolously.) But the next time I asked them to work, they refused. It seems they had a lesson for me. I learned that what I thought was "frivolous" spending was, in fact, their incentive for working. Think of it this way. What encourages you to work overtime and produce more? Is it basic food, clothing, and shelter; is it discretionary goods like a better car, a better house, or a better vacation; or is it so you can pay more taxes and the government can spend more money? In Japan, for 10 years the government has tried to jump-start the economy by building more roads and bridges. The strategy is straight out of my economics book from the 1960s. It hasn't worked. It's why I believe Japan needs a Ronald Reagan.

Ronald Reagan understood the economic incentives of tax rates. He understood that if you lower the tax burden, people will produce more, the economy will expand, and over time, tax receipts will also expand. George H. W. Bush did not understand this, and he allowed conventional economic arguments to convince him to break his pledge and raise taxes. President Clinton doesn't understand it, which is why he could make the statement, "We could cut taxes, but you might not spend it right." I didn't think my daughters were "spending it right," but I learned that there is no "wrong" spending in the private economy, because that spending is the incentive for more production.

Reagan's tax cuts did create a deficit, but deficits per se are not the problem. The question is what you use the money to accomplish.

Personally, I've used deficit spending in 17 of the past 38 years: six years when I was in college, eight years when my kids were in college, and three years when we bought houses. Each worked out well. I have not borrowed money to take a vacation or buy a new car, nor to buy things that depreciate. Ronald Reagan borrowed money to get the economy moving again and to win the Cold War. Both worked very well.

Today we're hearing the same arguments against tax cuts that we heard in 1980. Politicians believe they can spend our money more wisely than we can. That is no surprise. What's surprising is how many economists still believe this after the evidence of the last 20 years.

But the pertinent question is not who can spend the money more wisely. The pertinent question is which spending results in the greater incentives for more production and thus more prosperity for ourselves, our kids, and our grandkids? With the top income tax rates (including state income taxes) at 40 to 50 percent we are once again at risk of killing the incentive for economic growth.

We need only to look at estate taxes to see the result. Estate tax rates are at 37 to 55 percent. And today we're seeing schemes for avoiding estate taxes that rival the tax shelters of the 1970s in complexity and nonproductivity.

To me, elections are not about Democrats versus Republicans. Elections are about politicians versus taxpayers and consumers. Elections are about choosing bigger government versus choosing smaller government.

I'm amazed at the number of intelligent people who tell me they're not likely to vote because they "can't get excited about either candidate." Folks, it's only the free market that offers you 15 choices of cereal or toothpaste so you can get exactly what you want. Government is different from the free market because it insists upon only one solution for all people. In the upcoming election, our choices are down to two. We will have a president, and he will have an agenda. If we don't choose the better agenda, we will have to live with the other one.

2007 Addendum: Expanding on the Five-Day Workweek Analogy

Let's take our five-day workweek analogy one step further. Remember that most people said they would not work at a 50 percent tax rate. Well, here's a new proposition.

Pick a person whose name you know, a friend or a stranger. For the next 20 years you will be a partner of that person in a one-way partnership. You have your choice of two sets of terms, as follows:

A. You will receive 30 percent of everything that person earns over $30,000 per year.

B. You will receive 30 percent of everything that person earns from $30,000 to $100,000 per year; and 70 percent of everything he/she earns over $100,000 per year.

Which do you choose, A or B?

It's easy to see why many people might choose B, expecting to get more money. But remember what we saw in our five-day workweek analogy: people say they won't work at a 50 percent tax rate, so they certainly won't work at a 70 percent rate. And to your partner, the proposed one-way partnership looks like a 70 percent tax rate. So if people do what they say they'll do, at the 70 percent rate you will receive 70 percent of nothing. And 70 percent of nothing will always be less than 30 percent of something.

President Reagan faced this choice in 1981. The existing top tax bracket was 70 percent. It resulted in people in the top tax bracket taking time off, investing in tax shelters, and not expanding their businesses. In short, it resulted in 10 percent unemployment. President Reagan chose A—a top tax bracket of about 30 percent—and the U.S. economy has led the developed world for 25 years. Japan and Western Europe have not made a similar choice. As a result, their economies have been slow or stagnant for over a decade. Unemployment in Western Europe is over 10 percent today compared to 5 percent in the United States.

The key to the one-way-partnership analogy is perspective. To choose the terms that make you the most money, you must consider the perspective of your partner. Though *you* are setting the terms, your *partner* is the one producing the wealth. I find this analogy useful because our tax system is set up the same way. The politicians set the terms, but the taxpayer produces the wealth. Some of our politicians would do well to more carefully consider the perspective of the taxpayer.

About a year ago, a U.S. senator said that if he had to choose between a rich man buying a new Mercedes or Congress taxing that man to buy a new school bus, he, the senator, would vote to tax the man to buy the school bus. The senator is assuming that the choice is between the Mercedes and the school bus. But a Mercedes is discretionary. The man could live without it. At a 35 percent tax rate, a man who wants a $65,000 Mercedes must earn $100,000 and will pay $35,000 in taxes toward the school bus. At a 50 percent tax rate, he has to earn $130,000 for that same Mercedes. People tell me that at tax rates of 50 percent or higher they will not work. In other words, instead of earning that $130,000 for the Mercedes, the rich man might just stay home and relax, which means that at a higher tax rate you will get neither the Mercedes nor the school bus. I believe this is what happened in the 1970s, and I believe this is what would happen should we raise taxes much beyond their current levels.

Bottom line, economics is about people and their choices. The easy way to understand economics is to put yourself into someone else's shoes. If you want to grow the economy, consider the perspective of the people who make the economy grow. What are their needs? What are their wants? Under what terms do they have the greatest incentive to work? When you allow people to benefit from their own efforts, the economy grows, creating more prosperity for everyone—worker, business owner, and politician alike.

How to Choose a Money Manager

This essay was originally published in Muhlenkamp Memorandum Issue 59, July 2001.

One of the most common mistakes that investors make is that they move their money from one manager to another frequently, and often at the wrong times. There is a tendency to choose a money manager based on good performance in the preceding year or two. But then when the manager has a bad year, the investor takes his business elsewhere. The problem with this approach is that, in essence, the investor has bought high and sold low. The solution is to do a better job choosing your money manager in the first place so you are confident staying with him in the down years. Ron shows us how.

Choosing a professional money manager has much in common with choosing professionals in other fields. As in selecting a lawyer or accountant, it is difficult to judge basic competence and integrity without a lengthy professional history or personal relationship. Therefore an investor must rely on references from existing clients or other professionals.

Money manager referrals can usually be obtained from members of the brokerage community, or from accountants and lawyers, preferably those serving the manager's present clientele.

Beyond the determination of basic integrity and competence, the investor's real need in choosing a money manager is to find a manager with a consistent investment philosophy that the investor is comfortable with. Consistency and comfort are the keys.

There are a number of profitable investment philosophies. Some of the better known are fundamental value, contrarian (which is simply acting in opposition to the conventional wisdom), and earnings momentum. Any of these, if consistently applied, can make money.

The difficulty is in the consistency of application. No matter how good the underlying philosophy, there will be periods when it appears not to be working. It is during these periods that it will be very tempting to try a different philosophy, usually just as it ceases to work. Thus, to a great extent, successful investing depends on standing firm in the face of the current emotional fashion. This can only be done if both the investor and the manager are comfortable with, and have conviction in, what they are doing.

We call this the "sleep factor." People who hire money managers pay them a fee not only to earn a healthy return, but to do so in a fashion that allows the investor to sleep at night. A philosophy or methodology that keeps an investor awake has obvious ill effects on physical and mental health, effects that eventually flow over into the investor's financial health as well.

People who are uncomfortable will change to become comfortable again, so it is critical that the philosophy and methods used for investing be comfortable to the investor so he can stay with them in the face of adversity.

For this reason, a true meeting of the minds must occur between the manager and the investor. The manager must explain his philosophy and methods in terms that the investor understands, and this dialogue must be ongoing; there should be no surprises.

Because there will be periods when the chosen philosophy appears not to be working, there must also be an understanding between the investor and manager of a reasonable period of time for judging whether the manager is in fact doing what he said he would. Is he fulfilling the investor's expectations? Are the expectations consistent with the philosophy and methods chosen?

A long-term, value-oriented philosophy, for example, will not normally outperform the market averages during short-term market upswings. If the investor is unaware of this tendency, he may begin to second-guess his selection of a value manager during a roaring bull market. He may become uncomfortable and consider changing horses in midstream, when all he really needs is a better understanding of the horse he is riding.

Again, this sort of indecision can be especially deadly in the investment business, as this year's hero (or bum) rarely repeats. To continue the analogy, often the investor leaps upon a horse which is about to go under, just as his original mount gets a second wind. To avoid these disasters, the investor and manager must share investment goals and perspective.

The final factor in the manager-selection equation is client reporting. An often abused area for many managers, the client reporting jungle is proof positive that the biggest computer doesn't necessarily produce the best reports.

Thirty pages of printout is no good to a person too intimidated by investment jargon to read beyond page one. Designed more to inundate than educate, these elaborate productions often hide poor performance in a tangle of statistics and bond duration equations.

A good and useful report, by contrast, tells the client the value of his portfolio on the day he started with the manager, the change in value over time, and the value today.

It shows the percentage return generated by the portfolio for the given period and, if the client desires, may include a comparison of the client's return with that of market averages (Dow Jones Industrial Average, S&P 500, etc.), or any other bogey the client selects. It shows the securities held, their market value, and their yield. If the account pays taxes, the report also provides realized gain and loss data for use in preparation of tax returns.

Nothing else (unless the client specifically requests it) is required. Simple, straightforward reports are read and understood by clients. Complex, cluttered ones go straight into the (circular?) files.

In summary, a successful investment manager needs a consistent investment philosophy, a sense of perspective, and the confidence and discipline to carry it through. The investor, in turn, must understand and be comfortable with the manager's philosophy. He must know why it works and when it won't work, so he too has the confidence to see it through. A wise investor once said that in the money management business the only surprises are bad surprises. He was right.

Chapter 8

2002–2006: Back to Normal, a Normal We Haven't Seen since 1965

During this period, inflation is stable at about 2–3 percent, and has averaged 2 percent for the past 10 years. Most industries have ample capacity. This is *normal*—a normal we haven't seen since 1965. In a normal economy, how well a company does (and, therefore, how well its stock does) depends on how well it is run. Short-term variations in the market will always be driven by hype, hope, and fear, but the long-term investor can go back to choosing stocks based on company performance, price, and value.

When some people read the above, they are concerned that history is going to repeat itself and we will have the same rising inflation and poor stock performance that we saw in 1965–1980. But that is like expecting a depression after World War II because we had one after World War I. The situation after World War II was not the same as after World War I, primarily because after World War II the public (and therefore the government) feared another depression and took actions to prevent it. Likewise, because we have experienced the inflation of 1965–1980, we are sensitive to the problems of inflation. Today, we are not going to inflate the money supply because we still fear inflation. In 1999, Alan Greenspan all but said that he would take a recession rather than inflate the money supply. And he did! In 2004–2006, the Fed again raised interest rates for the express purpose of slowing the economy and keeping inflation under control. When people are worried about something, they, and their governments, take actions to avoid it.

When we look at the past, we must remember that history seldom repeats itself *exactly*. We cannot extrapolate the past in its simplest terms and expect to predict the future. Elements of history are relevant today, but we must understand the past *in context* to understand its implications for the present.

2002

- President George W. Bush singles out Iran, Iraq, and North Korea as an "axis of evil"; the Bush administration announces a five-color code system to alert Americans about the danger level posed by terrorists.
- Kmart, the third largest U.S. discount retailer, files for bankruptcy protection.
- Arthur Andersen is convicted of obstructing justice by shredding Enron-related documents in a verdict that boosted prosecutors' efforts to get to the bottom of the Enron scandal.
- With $107 billion in assets, WorldCom files for Chapter 11 bankruptcy, the largest U.S. bankruptcy ever. (The number-two U.S. long-distance phone company said it discovered $3.8 billion in improperly booked expenses.)
- The U.S. trade deficit climbs to $35.9 billion, the highest on record.
- John Allen Muhammad, an army veteran, and John Lee Malvo are arrested near Frederick, Maryland, in connection with the sniper shootings that left 10 dead and three wounded.
- The U.S. Congress gives President Bush authorization to use armed forces against Iraq.
- After shutting down, West Coast dockworkers and shipping lines reach a tentative six-year contract.
- World AIDS Day marks 42 million HIV-positive people around the world, with 75 percent in sub-Saharan Africa.

- First-class postage rates increase from 34 cents an ounce to 37 cents an ounce.

2003

- Inflation is stable, averaging 2 percent for seven years; long-term Treasury bonds yield 5 percent; and average price-to-earnings ratios (P/Es) for equities are at 17.
- The U.S. Labor Department reports that unemployment is at 8.6 million (6 percent), an eight-year high; President Bush signs an emergency extension of federal unemployment benefits.
- Space shuttle Columbia breaks apart in flames over Texas, killing all seven astronauts just 16 minutes before they were supposed to glide to ground in Florida.
- On March 20, the U.S.-led ground war in Iraq begins; a "shock and awe" strategy is planned. On May 1, President Bush announces, "Major combat operations in Iraq have ended."
- The U.S. Congress gives its final approval to $330 billion in new tax cuts for families, investors, and businesses, accelerating cuts in income tax rates, reducing federal taxes on stock dividends, and boosting the child tax credit by $400 per child.
- California's first statewide recall election ousts Gray Davis and lands actor Arnold Schwarzenegger in the governor's office.
- The U.S. Federal Reserve cuts short-term interest rates by 0.25 percent; the new 1 percent rate is the lowest since 1958.
- The last Concorde flight takes off from London's Heathrow Airport on November 26.

2004

- A national monument to the 16 million U.S. men and women who served during World War II opens to the public in Washington D.C.
- In Madrid, al-Qaeda claims responsibility for a series of bombs that blow apart four commuter trains, killing 190 people and wounding over 1,450.
- The United States hands over power to Iraqi interim government; Iyad Allawi becomes prime minister.
- Pilot Mike Melvill steers the SpaceShipOne rocket plane skyward, soaring 62.5 miles above Mojave, California, to become the first private-sector astronaut.

- Chechen terrorists take almost 1,000 schoolchildren hostage at an elementary school in the Russian province of North Ossetia. Attackers force hostages into a gym rigged with explosives. Over 300 people die; more than half are children.
- Hamid Karzai is elected president of Afghanistan during the country's first presidential election; millions of Afghans cast votes despite the threat of Taliban violence.
- President George W. Bush is re-elected for a second term in the White House.
- A massive earthquake near the Indian Ocean island of Sumatra sparks a wave of deadly tsunamis, causing one of the worst natural disasters in living memory.

2005

- In January, millions of Iraqis vote in their country's first free election in 50 years.
- Pope John Paul II, whose papacy was marked by his efforts to end communism, dies on April 4; German Cardinal Radzinger emerges as Pope Benedict XVI.
- On July 7, terrorists detonate bombs in London's crowded subways and one double-decker bus, killing 56 people and injuring another 700, the largest attack on Great Britain since World War II.
- Hurricane Katrina slams into the Gulf Coast on August 29, causing massive damage to New Orleans and the coasts of Mississippi and Alabama. An estimated 1,300 people die; damages total $150 billion.
- Riots break out across the suburbs of Paris, triggered by teens, frustrated by years of high unemployment. One person is killed and 126 police and fire personnel are injured; nearly 9,000 cars and at least two buildings are set ablaze.
- Muslims in India's Kashmir region go on strike, closing schools, shops and businesses, in protest of newspaper cartoons published in far-away Denmark depicting the Prophet Mohammed.
- The continuing threat of avian or "bird" flu requires China and other nations to impose more rigorous measures to contain the lethal virus. Nations around the world scramble to assemble viable containment plans and amass stockpiles of antiviral drugs.

2006

- The conflict in Iraq gets bloodier and more entrenched. A vicious skirmish erupts between Israel and Lebanon. A war drags on in Sudan. A tin-pot dictator in North Korea gets nuclear bomb capability, and the president of Iran wants to go nuclear too.
- The compendium of information known as Wikipedia, the people's video network YouTube, and the online metropolis MySpace emerge as seminal forces in the ever-evolving World Wide Web.
- Leading astronomers declare that Pluto is no longer a planet under historic new guidelines that downsize the solar system from nine planets to eight.
- Bosnians vote in historic general elections that will choose the first government to run the country without international supervision since the end of the 1992–1995 war.
- Democrats sweep elections in both the U.S. House of Representatives and the Senate.

Consumer Spending

This essay was originally published in January 2003 with data through 2000. In 2007, the data have been updated through 2006 and additional charts added.

Consumer spending and consumer debt are often used as indicators of the health of the economy. If consumer spending is strong, the economy continues to grow. If consumer debt is under control, then the consumer spending is sustainable. In this essay, Ron takes a look at consumer spending over the last 55 years to gain perspective not only on the strength of the economy overall, but to evaluate changes in spending patterns over those 55 years. He then looks at consumer debt in terms of debt payments as a percentage of disposable income. In other words, how much of a burden are the debt payments in each household's budget? This debt burden indicates whether the level of consumer spending is sustainable.

I've been carrying Exhibit 8.1 in my briefcase for several years. Taken directly from the U.S. Bureau of Economic Analysis, the most recent

Exhibit 8.1 Personal Consumption Expenditures (PCE), 1950–2005

	1950	1955	1960	1965	1970	1975	1980	1985	1990	1995	2000	2005
Total PCE (Billions of Current $)	$192.70	$259.00	$332.30	$444.30	$648.90	$1,030.30	$1,762.90	$2,712.60	$3,831.50	$4,969.00	$6,683.70	$8,745.70
Total PCE (Billions of 2000 $)	$1,336	$1,616	$1,876	$2,354	$2,798	$3,200	$3,576	$4,209	$4,907	$5,523	$6,684	$7,792
U.S. Population (Millions)	151	165	179	191	203	215	227	238	249	265	281	296
PCE per Capita (Thousands of 2000 $)	$8.8	$9.8	$10.5	$12.3	$13.8	$14.9	$15.8	$17.7	$19.7	$20.8	$23.8	$26.3
Consumer Spending (as % of PCE)												
Durable goods	15.9%	15.0%	13.0%	14.2%	13.1%	13.0%	12.2%	13.4%	12.2%	11.9%	12.0%	11.7%
Motor vehicles and parts	7.1%	6.8%	5.9%	6.7%	5.5%	5.3%	4.9%	6.5%	5.4%	5.0%	5.0%	5.1%
Furniture and household equipment	7.1%	6.3%	5.4%	5.6%	5.5%	5.3%	4.9%	4.7%	4.5%	4.5%	4.6%	4.3%
Other	1.7%	1.8%	1.7%	1.8%	2.1%	2.3%	2.3%	2.2%	2.3%	2.3%	2.4%	2.4%
Nondurable goods	51.0%	48.1%	46.0%	43.1%	41.9%	40.8%	39.5%	34.2%	32.5%	30.1%	29.5%	29.3%
Food	28.0%	26.5%	24.8%	22.7%	22.2%	21.7%	20.2%	17.2%	16.6%	15.2%	14.3%	13.9%
Clothing and shoes	10.2%	9.0%	8.1%	7.7%	7.4%	6.9%	6.1%	5.6%	5.3%	5.0%	4.7%	3.9%
Gasoline and oil	2.9%	3.3%	3.6%	3.3%	3.4%	3.9%	4.9%	3.6%	2.8%	2.3%	2.5%	3.3%

Fuel oil and coal	1.8%	1.5%	1.1%	1.0%	0.7%	0.8%	0.9%	0.5%	0.3%	0.3%	0.3%	0.3%
Other	8.2%	7.9%	8.3%	8.5%	8.3%	7.6%	7.4%	7.3%	7.4%	7.4%	7.8%	7.9%
Services	33.1%	36.8%	41.0%	42.7%	45.0%	46.2%	48.4%	52.4%	55.3%	58.0%	58.5%	58.9%
Housing	11.3%	13.3%	14.5%	14.7%	14.5%	14.3%	14.5%	15.0%	15.3%	14.9%	14.4%	14.7%
Household operation	4.9%	5.5%	6.1%	6.0%	5.8%	6.2%	6.5%	6.7%	5.9%	6.0%	5.8%	5.5%
Transportation	3.2%	3.3%	3.4%	3.3%	3.7%	3.5%	3.7%	3.7%	3.7%	4.0%	4.0%	3.7%
Medical care	3.7%	4.4%	5.3%	6.3%	7.8%	9.1%	10.3%	11.9%	14.1%	15.7%	14.8%	17.3%
Recreation	2.0%	2.0%	2.1%	2.2%	2.3%	2.5%	2.4%	2.8%	3.2%	3.5%	3.8%	4.1%
Personal Business	3.4%	3.9%	4.4%	4.7%	5.0%	5.2%	5.9%	6.9%	7.4%	8.2%	9.5%	7.5%
Other	4.5%	4.6%	5.2%	5.6%	5.9%	5.5%	5.2%	5.4%	5.7%	5.7%	6.2%	6.3%
Government Receipts from Social Insurance* (% of PCE)	2.9%	3.5%	4.9%	5.3%	7.2%	8.7%	9.4%	10.4%	10.7%	10.7%	10.5%	9.9%

*This percentage is based on the total dollars contributed to the Government by employers and employees for: Social security; Medical Insurance; Unemployment; Worker's Compensation; etc. For more information, visit the web site Bureau of economic Analysis: www.bea.gov. This data was taken from the following table: Table 2.3.5. *Personal Consumption Expenditures by Major Type of Product.*

SOURCE: U.S. Bureau of Economic Analysis, www.bea.gov.

edition lists personal consumption expenditures (PCE) in the United States for the past 55 years. It then breaks down overall spending as a percentage of the total for broad categories of spending. I've added three lines near the top of the table.

1. First, I adjusted the PCE for inflation, bringing all numbers to year 2000 dollar values.
2. Next, I listed the U.S. population for each year.
3. Finally, I calculated PCE per capita.

I've also extracted the personal consumption expenditures data and plotted it in constant dollars on a per capita basis, as shown in Exhibit 8.2.

The data tell me a number of things. The first is that the U.S. economy has experienced tremendous growth from 1950 to 2005. Personal spending went from less than $200 billion to over $8,700 billion ($8.7 trillion) in 55 years. That's a multiple of 45 times. When we adjust for inflation of 7.7 times, we're left with a growth in spending in real dollars of 5.8 times. When we adjust for population, personal consumption expenditure per capita multiplied three times. Net, we are three times as prosperous in 2005 as our grandparents were in 1950.

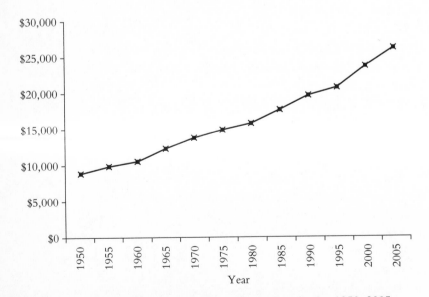

Exhibit 8.2   Personal Consumption Expenditures Per Capita, 1950–2005

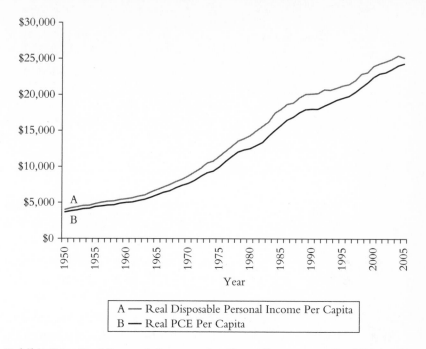

Exhibit 8.3   Real Personal Consumption Expenditures versus Real Disposable Personal Income, 1950–2005

Now some people will say, "That's spending—that's not income." And that is true. So in Exhibit 8.3 I have shown personal disposable income alongside personal consumption expenditures.

So now let's break down the expenditure data into four categories: durable goods, nondurable goods, services, and government social insurance (as shown in Exhibit 8.4). Since 1950, the percentage that is spent on durable goods is pretty steady, on nondurable goods it has gone down, on services it has gone up, and government social insurance is up. I'll break each of those down in turn.

Let me start with nondurable goods, specifically food and clothing; (refer to Exhibit 8.5). To me, the interesting thing about food is that, try as we might, we can't consume much more of it per person than our grandparents did. So food consumption is relatively stable. Yet the percentage of consumer disposable income spent on food has been cut in half (from 28 percent to 14 percent) in the past 50 years, despite the fact that half the money we currently spend on food is outside the home, and

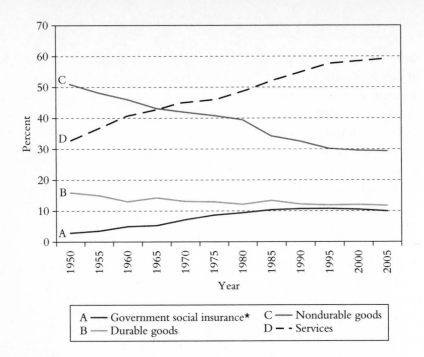

Exhibit 8.4 Personal Consumption Expenditures by Category (as a Percentage of the Whole)

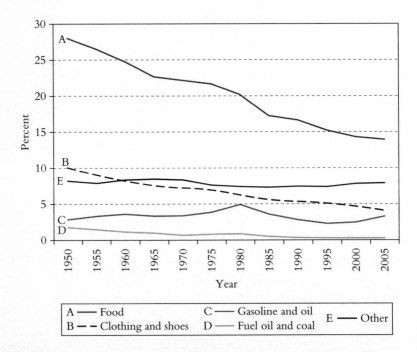

Exhibit 8.5 Personal Consumption Expenditures—Nondurable Goods

therefore includes preparation costs. Clothing has gone from 10 percent of our disposable income to 4 percent. And our wardrobes are bigger today than they were 50 years ago. If you doubt it, just compare the size of closets in an old house to the walk-in closets of today. Added together, food and clothing has gone from 38 percent of our budget in 1950 to just 18 percent in 2005. That's 20 percent of our budget that is available to us to spend on other things that wasn't available to our grandparents.

Looking at durable goods, as shown in Exhibit 8.6, motor vehicles and parts went from 7 percent to 5 percent even though in 1950 the typical family had one car and in 2007 the typical family has two. (In fact, today we have more cars and small trucks than we have people with driver's licenses.) Furniture and household appliances has gone from 7 percent to 4 percent, despite our having more of each (to fill our larger houses) than our grandparents did.

In services, housing has been stable (in percentage terms) since 1960, as shown in Exhibit 8.7. Today, however, new houses average over 2,000

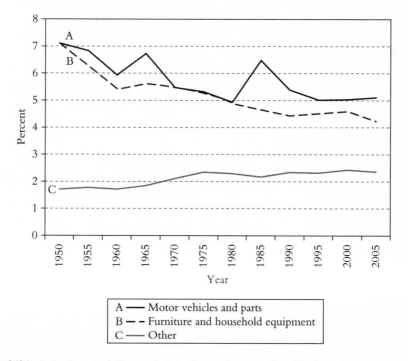

Exhibit 8.6   Personal Consumption Expenditures—Durable Goods

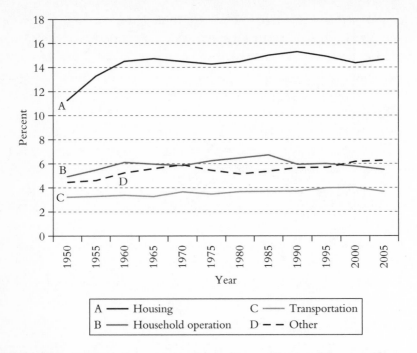

Exhibit 8.7   Personal Consumption Expenditures—Services (Housing, Household Operation, Transportation, and Other)

square feet. In 1960, they averaged about 1,000 square feet. So our houses are twice the size, even though our families are smaller. Similarly, household operation and transportation have remained stable (as a percentage).

Four items in the family budget have grown dramatically over the past 50 years—all service items, as shown in Exhibit 8.8.

First is medical care, which has grown from 4 percent to 15 percent. The fact that medical care expenses have grown doesn't surprise anybody, but the degree of growth often does.

Second is recreation, which helps explain why Las Vegas is the fastest-growing city in the country.

Third is personal business, which is primarily personal financial business—think brokers and mutual funds growing on a base of banks and insurance companies. While I suspect that the year 2000 might have had an increment due to the Wall Street fad of the time, it's been a steady uptrend for 50 years.

The fourth item, which the government doesn't include in expenditures but which I've added, is government receipts from Social Insurance

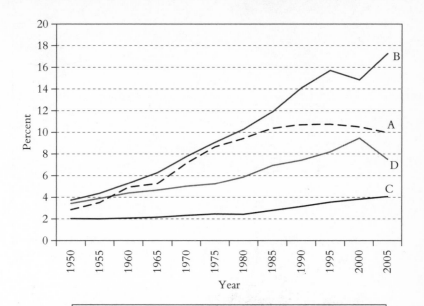

Exhibit 8.8   Personal Consumption Expenditures—Services (Government Social Insurance, Medical, Recreation, and Personal Business)

(including Social Security and Medicare)—which is up three and a half times from 1950 to 2005.

To an investor, these trends are intriguing. As investors, we tend to have a bias toward those areas where the long-term trends are up. But we're aware that it's also possible to make good money in the areas that are shrinking on a percentage basis. Think food stocks in the 1980s, or Wal-Mart since 1972.

Consumer Debt

I'm also hearing that the consumer is borrowed to the hilt and therefore can't sustain the current level of spending. I often see charts (like Exhibit 8.9) showing growth in consumer debt to income. But such a chart comparing debt (a balance-sheet item) to income (an income-statement item) ignores any changes in interest rates. I think a more useful comparison is debt-to-assets, as shown in Exhibit 8.10. Note that the "Total Debt" line in Exhibit 8.9 is the same as the "Liabilities" line in Exhibit 8.10.

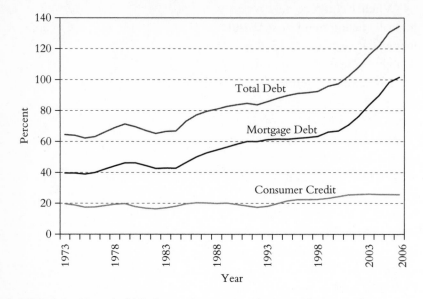

Exhibit 8.9   Household Debt as a Percentage of Disposable Personal Income

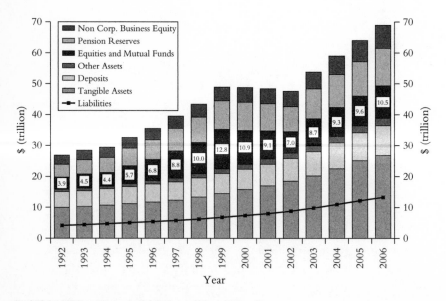

Exhibit 8.10   Household Balance Sheet Details

When I compare debt to assets, I find that the ratios have been in a gradually falling trend since World War II. In 1950, the amount of assets to debt was 4.5 times; in 2005, it is 5.5 times. (See Exhibit 8.10.) Note that the "Liabilities" line in Exhibit 8.10 is the "Total Debt" line of Exhibit 8.9.

The debt of Exhibit 8.11 also looks scary, but it ignores the fact that interest rates on mortgages have been cut in half since 1980 and that incomes have gone up.

When the payments on this debt are compared to disposable income, you get Exhibit 8.12.

Because interest rates are now lower, the current debt levels are less burdensome to the consumer. The chart says the household debt service burden has ranged between 14 percent and 18 percent for 25 years. Some believe that interest rates can only go up from here (I don't), but most mortgages are fixed-rate, meaning the debt burden for most homeowners won't increase involuntarily even if mortgage rates do increase. (For information pertaining to adjustable rate mortgages (ARMs), see our essay "Why Interest Rates Won't Go Back Up Anytime Soon," in Chapter 5.)

Folks, the consumer is not tapped out.

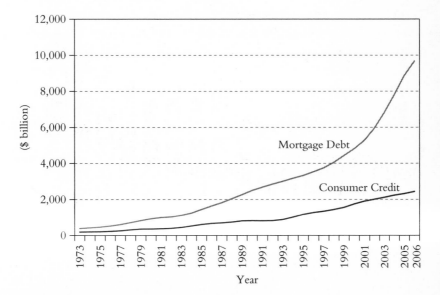

Exhibit 8.11   Debt

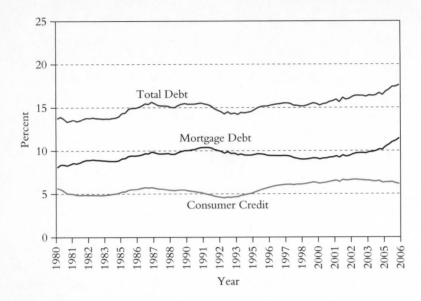

Exhibit 8.12   Household Debt Service Burden (Debt Payments/Disposable Income, Percent)

Editor's Note

So let's review: We eat out more than our grandparents did, yet we spend half as much (as a percentage) on food. We have more clothes, but spend half as much (as a percentage) on clothes. We live in bigger houses, filled with more stuff, but our cost for housing (as a percentage) is stable, and we spend less (as a percentage) on durable goods. Our medical-care costs are growing, but we are living longer. Our recreation expenditures are growing, which means we spend more of our money on play. In other words, in the United States not only is the consumer king, but the king continues to prosper.

Foreign Investing

Adapted from a presentation delivered at the December 2002 Muhlenkamp & Company Seminar. Just as many investors fail to take changes in inflation into account when evaluating investment choices, many also fail to take currency exchange rates into account when investing outside the United States. In this essay, Ron takes a sharp look at foreign investing by tracking not only foreign stock performance but currency exchange rates as well.

Exhibit 8.13   Comparative Returns, Domestic and International Equities, 1975–1994

Comparative Returns Domestic and International Equities

20 Years	Cumulative	Annualized
S&P 500	1,420%	14.19%
EAFE*	1,962%	16.05%

*Morgan Stanley International Europe-Australia-Far East Index

Year	S&P 500	EAFE*
1975	37.31	37.10
1976	23.99	3.74
1977	−7.19	19.42 ▮
1978	6.39	34.30 ▮
1979	18.65	6.18
1980	32.39	24.43
1981	−5.26	−1.03 ▮
1982	21.53	−0.86
1983	22.59	24.61 ▮
1984	6.3	7.86
1985	31.8	56.72 ▮
1986	18.67	69.94 ▮
1987	5.25	24.93 ▮
1988	16.61	28.59 ▮
1989	31.69	10.80
1990	−3.10	−23.20
1991	30.47	12.50
1992	7.62	−11.85
1993	10.08	32.94 ▮
1994	1.32	8.06 ▮

Note: The black bars on the right denote the years when the EAFE outperformed the S&P 500.
SOURCE: Morgan Stanley International Europe-Australia-Far East Index.

In 1995, we were told that we should be invested in foreign stocks because, as Exhibit 8.13 tells us, for the prior 20 years if you had invested in the S&P 500 you would have done 14.5 percent per year. If you had invested in the EAFE (which is Morgan Stanley's Europe, Australia, and Far East Index), you would have done roughly 16 percent per year. So people said that you've got to invest in foreign stocks.

We know that when you invest outside the United States, part of your return is due to the performance of securities in the local currency and part is due to the change in the currency values relative to each other. We wondered what happened to the currency during the years when the EAFE outperformed the S&P 500. So we constructed a chart of the trade-weighted dollar for the period (see Exhibit 8.14).

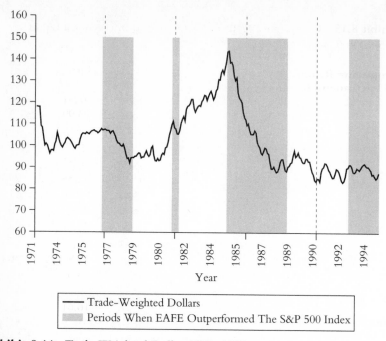

— Trade-Weighted Dollars
Periods When EAFE Outperformed The S&P 500 Index

Exhibit 8.14   Trade-Weighted Dollar, 1971–1995

We found that in each of those periods when the EAFE outdid the S&P 500 by more than 2 percent, the dollar was going down, and these were the *only* times when the EAFE outdid the S&P 500. In early 1995, it looked to us like the dollar was below where it should be, so we concluded that it wasn't a good time to invest in foreign securities.

So what has happened to the EAFE since 1995? Let's look at the updated data in Exhibit 8.15.

For the period from 1995 to 2002, the EAFE underperformed the S&P 500 as the dollar continued to strengthen against other currencies. Investing in foreign stock in 1995 would not have been a wise choice.

Exhibit 8.16 plots the trade-weighted dollar, the S&P 500, and EAFE from 1975 to 2006. Anytime you see the gray above the black, it's a period when the EAFE outperformed the S&P 500—and each of those is a period when the trade-weighted dollar is falling relative to other currencies. From 1995 to 2006, there have been two periods when the EAFE outdid the S&P 500.

Exhibit 8.15   Comparative Returns, Domestic and International Equities, 1975–2006 (Updated)

Comparative Returns Domestic and International Equities	Year	S&P 500	EAFE*
	1975	37.31	37.10
	1976	23.99	3.74
	1977	−7.19	19.42
	1978	6.39	34.30
	1979	18.65	6.18
	1980	32.39	24.43
	1981	−5.26	−1.03
	1982	21.53	−0.86
	1983	22.59	24.61
	1984	6.3	7.86
	1985	31.8	56.72
	1986	18.67	69.94
	1987	5.25	24.93
	1988	16.61	28.59

32 Years	Cumulative	Annualized
S&P 500	5,671%	13.45%
EAFE*	5,213%	13.15%

Year	S&P 500	EAFE*
1989	31.69	10.80
1990	−3.10	−23.20
1991	30.47	12.50
1992	7.62	−11.85
1993	10.08	32.94
1994	1.32	8.06
1995	37.58	11.55
1996	22.96	6.36
1997	33.36	2.06
1998	28.58	20.27
1999	21.04	27.37
2000	−9.10	−13.96
2001	−11.89	−21.21
2002	−22.10	−15.66
2003	28.68	39.17
2004	10.88	20.70
2005	4.91	14.02
2006	15.79	26.86

*Morgan Stanley International Europe-Australia-Far East Index

Note: The black bars on the right denote the years when the EAFE outperformed the S&P 500.
SOURCE: Morgan Stanley International Europe-Australia-Far East Index.

The lesson to learn is this. You can't just extrapolate the past to arrive at the future. You have to have some measure of value. This allows you to make a judgment as to whether recent price trends are sustainable or have

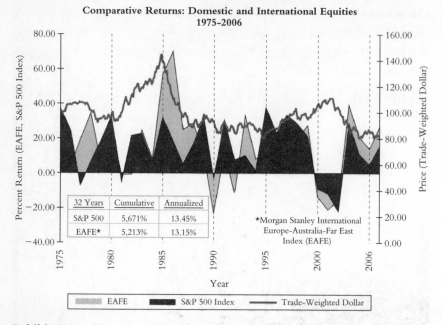

Exhibit 8.16 Domestic and International Equities, Comparative Returns, 1975–2006 (Updated)

overshot the mark, resulting in fundamental over- or undervaluation. Markets are partly valuation and partly trends and momentum. You want both working for you. Today (December 2002), it looks like the dollar is beginning to roll over. It looks like it is a little overpriced so, frankly, foreign stocks are looking interesting for the first time in a decade. So we are starting to do some work on them.

Any time you invest outside of the United States you take two additional risks. One is accounting risk (and with a little help from Enron, we're finding out that we have more accounting risk in the United States than we thought we did). The other is currency risk. Exhibit 8.16 shows us that when it comes to foreign investing, the currency is at least as important as an individual company's financial performance.

In roughly 1994 or 1995, Morgan Stanley came to town and talked about all these great companies they were going to bring public in India and China, and how we ought to invest in them and make a lot of money. What do I know about a company in India or China? What I concluded was that if they are going to bring all these companies public, the company that I know is going to make money is called Morgan Stanley. They get paid up front. So we bought Morgan Stanley, and it worked out rather well. Sometimes it helps to be a little simplistic.

The Fad, Recession, and Getting Back to Normal

Adapted from a presentation delivered at the December 2002 Muhlenkamp & Company Seminar. The investing community was still trying to come to grips with the dramatic fluctuations in some stock prices (commonly referred to as the tech stock bubble). Ron presents an argument of why those prices rose and fell, and what to make of it.

Starting late in 1998, the American public discovered the game of the stock market. A number of people bought computers, got onto the Internet, and discovered day trading. Being computer types, they fell in love with tech stocks, as well as online brokers, and tech stock prices climbed. They climbed so dramatically that more people joined the rush. And Wall Street, a superb marketing organization, helped and encouraged them in believing and buying more of what they wanted. For 18 months, the game of the stock market became a favorite American pastime. But it was a fad. The prices were inflated by the craze, and for the next 18 months, the tech stock prices gave it all back. See Exhibit 8.17. (The rise and fall of the tech stocks are shown by line B, the NASDAQ line. The rest of the market is depicted on the chart by the S&P 500 Index.)

Think about that. In a three-year period, a fad involving millions of people and billions of dollars went full circle. What made the whole thing even more dramatic was that many of the investors were new to investing. It's human nature that when we enter an unfamiliar area, like finance, we often assume that the time we enter is a normal time. It's like the traveler who visits another country and assumes that the weather they experience is normal for that region in that season. But when they ask the locals, they find out it is a record-breaking event. That's how it was for those who invested in tech stocks, and no one was listening to the locals who said it was a fluke.

Thus, many of the new investors believed that rapidly rising prices were normal and therefore were not prepared for the decline that

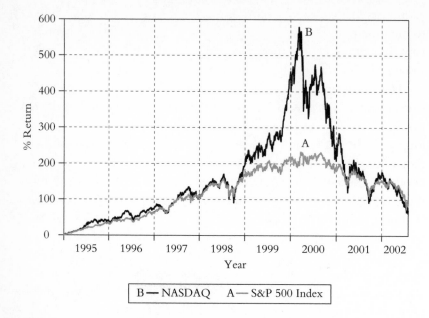

Exhibit 8.17 NASDAQ versus S&P 500, 1995–2002

followed. They were left groping for answers. "What happened? Why did my stocks' prices fall?" And the locals would answer, "They had to. Those prices were inflated." So then they ask hopefully, "When are the tech stocks coming back?" The local might reply dryly, "Not until you stop asking." And being new to the region, and still somewhat in shock, the newcomer laments, "But I did so well in 1999." The local looks them in the eye and says, "Well, 1999 is over. The best thing you can do is pretend that those prices never occurred because they weren't real to begin with."

So what were the more seasoned investors doing during this time? Well, many were playing the game as well. A Wall Street analyst's job is to make money for the investment firm he works for. That means bringing in clients. If an analyst or stock broker chose not to invest in tech stocks in 1998 and 1999, he lost clients. Besides, it was very hard not to get caught up in the fad. Tech stocks were climbing impressively, and many thought the tech rush was real and sustainable. The technology was real, though the prices paid for the companies were not. The Internet was viewed as the "new railroads" (railroads having been a great economy-changing industry in the 1800s). Few commentators bothered to mention that the average railroad in the United States has been bankrupt four times. People wanted to believe that the tech fad was real and sustainable. So why wouldn't you invest in tech stocks?

Have you ever heard the expression, "If it seems too good to be true, it probably is"? Well, it's true in the stock market, and in the stock market there is a corollary, "If everyone thinks it's a good buy, it no longer is." By the time the general populace is aware of a good stock, they've usually already driven the price up enough that it is no longer a good buy. No matter how good the company, if the price is too high, it is too high. So in the stock market, it helps to be an independent thinker. (I almost wrote "to be a little contrary," but you have to know *when* to be contrary.) That's where investing fundamentals come in. But in the 1998–2002 market, even those investors who chose to stick to fundamentals and to stay out of tech stocks didn't go unscathed.

I discovered in high school that I'm no good at fads, so in 1998 we declined to play the tech stock game. Instead, we kept to the basics and invested long-term, looking for value companies at good prices. In 1999 when tech stocks were soaring, we looked pretty dumb. In 2000 and 2001, we looked a little smarter. Then in June and July 2002, a lot of people, fed up with the stock market, wanted out regardless of price. This brought the whole market down. We got caught in that. We kept about 10 percent cash early in the year, knowing it could happen, but it wasn't enough to escape unscathed. See Exhibit 8.18.

Now it's the end of 2002 (we've updated Exhibit 8.18 through 2006), and the fad is over except for the tax-loss selling. People who look at tech stocks today tend to remember either the price that they paid or the high that the price hit, which means that every time they look at tech stocks, it's going to be painful. To relieve that pain, over time they will sell those stocks. Typically, when the stock market sees this kind of drop in prices, you have to go through two tax seasons before the tax-loss selling is complete. In 2001, nobody had any gains, so there wasn't much tax-loss selling. Therefore, it will likely be a couple more years before the tax-loss selling is complete.

The year 2002 has been the first time since World War II that, in an economy coming out of a recession, stocks did not do well. We believe it's because of a psychological overshoot. In the short term, stock prices

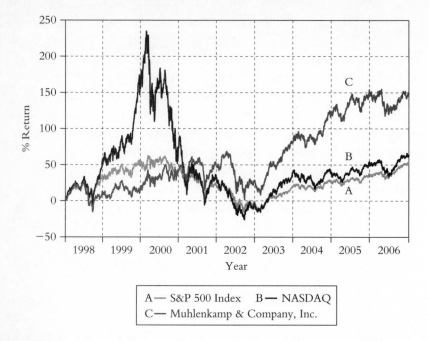

Exhibit 8.18 NASDAQ versus S&P 500 versus Muhlenkamp & Company, 1995–2006

are governed by human psychology. For periods up to six months, it's always psychology. For six months to three years, sometimes it's psychology. Beyond three years, the volatility of hope, fear, and hype average out, and stock prices are governed by what I call business economics.

In 2002, fear overrode or delayed what happens in the normal business cycle. There was fear and uncertainty following the fall of tech stocks. There was fear and uncertainty following the September 11 attacks. There is fear of al-Qaeda, and there is uncertainty about the food supply because of the drought. We even had snipers in Washington, D.C. Someone said to me that it was as if God were a centipede. Usually, in a bad time, two or three shoes drop. But this year the shoes just keep dropping.

So the short-term market has been dampened by uncertainty. But the long-term is still governed by business economics. Let's look at what happens, long-term, when there is a recession.

Understanding the Recession

This has been our tenth recession since World War II. In the 1960s and the 1970s we had a recession every three to five years, to the extent that I concluded that recession is a normal part of the business cycle. That remains true. But we're now in only the second recession in 20 years, which means we have a whole generation of people who don't know how to act, or how markets act, in a recession. In the 1960s and 1970s, my observation was that until people had been through four or five recessions, people viewed them as catastrophic. If you talk to people in their seventies or eighties, they say, "Oh yeah, another recession." If you are getting something every four or five years, it's a normal part of life. If you only get it every 10 years or so, it's a rather unusual occurrence. We have a whole younger generation that doesn't quite know how a normal, cyclical recession works.

Recessions, by themselves, are inherently self-correcting. In a recession, the average person works a little harder, spends a little less, and saves a little more, in case he loses his job. But in a recession only 2 to 3 percent of the people actually lose their job; 95 percent don't. After six or nine months, this 95 percent concludes that they're not going to lose their job. Then they gravitate back toward the kind of spending they were doing before.

That's a normal recession. But every now and then, we mess things up and we turn a recession into something more difficult. In the 1930s, we turned it into a depression. In the 1970s, we turned it into inflation. Each was a major climate change, where the normal processes were suspended or even reversed. Let's see why.

First, let's look at the Great Depression. In the late 1920s to early 1930s we did three things:

1. In order to protect our gold supply, we raised interest rates.
2. In order to balance the federal budget, we raised taxes.
3. In order to help our manufacturers, we raised tariffs.

Each of those actions, by itself, sounds reasonable. But think about what you do to the consumer when you raise interest rates, raise taxes, and raise tariffs. You kill the consumer! And we turned a recession into a depression. This time around, we lowered interest rates and we lowered taxes. At the end of 2002, we started playing some dumb games with tariffs on things like steel and farm products, but it's not enough to offset the lower taxes and interest rates. We've concluded that we are not facing depression coming out of this recession.

In the late 1960s, partly in order to prevent recession, we printed money and created inflation. In the late 1960s we could do that, because we were lenders to the rest of the world. The current slowdown in the economy was an intentional attempt to avoid inflation. Alan Greenspan all but said, three years ago, that he'd take a recession rather than inflate the money supply. We slowed this economy down on purpose to avoid inflation that hadn't even shown up yet! Today, we're overly sensitive to inflation the same way we were undersensitive to inflation in the 1970s. The fact that we're overly sensitive means that we won't inflate.

The third thing that can create a long-term climate change following a recession is war. In our newsletter of July 2001, we said we thought war was unlikely. The terrorist attacks of September 11 proved us wrong, but there are reasons to think this war will not create a long-term climate change. First, the war we're now in is not a total economic commitment like World War II was.

Second, from the moment of the attacks, the American people were helping each other. It started in New York, but within a few minutes it happened throughout the country. If the American public, after September 11, was hiding in their homes saying, "I'm not coming out until . . . ," then we would worry about the long-term picture. But in fact, from the first moment, Americans were supportive of their neighbors throughout the country.

The third thing we saw, within a few weeks, was General Motors saying, "We'll sell you cars at a 0% interest rate," and people went out and bought cars.

We've concluded that this is a normal, cyclical recession—and not a major change in the long-term climate. The long-term climate is positive, not negative. The coincident indicators like factory utilization and consumer spending bottomed in December 2001. Not all things have bottomed yet, but the things that haven't are lagging indicators—things like unemployment and capital spending. Corporations don't usually go out and spend new money on capital equipment or add employees until they see money coming in from their retail sales or sales to their customers. So unemployment and capital spending lag the economy, awaiting corporate decisions. And today, they're lagging, as they should. They lagged on the upside, and they lag on the downside.

Frankly, we think the bottom of stocks was a year and a half ago, which it was—if you were in anything but tech stocks. So what we've done for the past four years is to play the normal, cyclical rotation that follows a recession instead of playing the hype stocks.

Getting Back to Normal

We are getting back to normal, but it's a normal we haven't seen since 1965. Inflation is stable, averaging 2 to 3 percent for the last 10 years. Long-term Treasury bonds are valued at 4 to 5 percent, which is fair. And the average P/E for equities is 17, also fair. (In 1965, inflation was stable for 14 years, averaging 1.5 percent; bonds were stable at 4.5 percent; and the average P/E was 17, stable for seven years.) The other thing that is back to normal is that nearly every industry has ample capacity. With ample capacity, a company must outperform its competitors to do well. For Wal-Mart to do well, it will have to do it at the expense of JC Penney and Kmart. For General Motors to do well, it will do well at the expense of Ford and Chrysler.

The first question I get from anybody in the media is, "Which way is the market going?" And I ask, "Which market?" We've been in a split market for four years. You cannot talk about "the market." The market that they probably want to monitor is the NASDAQ, or the high-tech stuff. We've ignored that. It was hype.

The second question they like to ask is, "What sectors do you like?" But that game is over. When changes in inflation were driving all of this, in the 1970s, it didn't matter how well individual companies did. Inflation running up, driving P/Es down, overwhelmed that. In the 1980s, with inflation coming down, driving P/Es up, all stocks went up. That game is now over. And because we have ample capacity, it's how individual companies perform that matters—how well they do versus the competition.

In 1965 nobody asked, "Which way is the market going?" or "What sectors do you like?" They asked, "What companies do you like? Which companies are beating their competition?" We are back to that. The fact that right now the media is reading everything negatively gives us a chance to see more data and to buy things with more conviction than we otherwise would. You make money when perception differs from reality. Today, the reality is good; the perception is bad. That's a stock picker's dream.

Some people say, "But prices are down." Well, yes, that's why I'm excited! Everything else in your life you want to buy when it's cheap, when it goes on sale. The only thing that people want to buy after it goes up is stocks! But that's because when it comes to stocks, all most people know is price. They are extrapolating price trends rather than looking at value. When it comes to cars or houses or clothing or most things in life, you have a pretty good idea of value. So you get excited when prices get well below value. But with stocks, many people don't know the value of a company. When I started in this business in the early 1970s, I started asking analysts what a company was worth and nobody could tell me. They would say, "Well, the P/E used to be 15, but now it's 12." I said, "So, what's the company worth?" and they couldn't tell me. To invest in a company based only on price trends, and not know the value of the company, is a risky game. But if you can determine what companies are worth and understand the economic climate, you can make rational choices. You are in the business of investment.

Editor's Note

It is interesting that not only has the economic climate come full circle since 1965, but this essay has in some ways come full circle from Ron's 1979 essay "Why the Market Went Down" (see Chapter 4) In both essays, Ron is addressing the fears of investors (or money managers) who felt the fall of the market was unpredictable and irrational. In both cases, he shows that they needn't fear. Though the market can be volatile in the short term, in the long term it is rational. So for the long-term investor, the intelligent approach is to understand the past, assess the present, and be prepared for the future.

How Much Money Are You Willing to Lose for a Theory?

The first three parts of this essay are based on a presentation delivered in May 2005. Ron wanted to suggest an alternative view on some of the more costly investing theories prevalent at the time. Too often, widespread popularity of an idea can make it seem like a law, or a fact, when actually the idea is only a theory. And, like all theories, it should be questioned before it is accepted.

The fourth section of this essay was added in April 2007, when the theory of fundamental indexes became popular.

There are a lot of theories that people use when choosing investments for their portfolio. Unfortunately, they are only theories, meaning they are not always accurate or helpful. The challenge is to determine which ones are and which ones are not. The criteria are simple: Does this theory help me make better investment choices (does it make me money?), or does following this theory lead me to poor investment choices (does it cost me money?). There are currently several very popular theories that are costing people an awful lot of money. I'd like to discuss four of them.

Theory #1: Total Return = Growth plus Yield

There are basically only three classes of securities: short-term debt (cash), long-term debt (bonds), and equities (stocks). When choosing among them, it's important to accurately estimate the returns that are available. For cash and bonds, those calculations are pretty straightforward. For stocks, more assumptions are involved. Total return of a stock equals the dividend yield plus (or minus) the change in the price.

It's the determinants of the change in price that make the exercise interesting. Many analysts break price change down further to the change (or growth) in corporate earnings and the change in price-to-earnings ratio (P/E). If current P/Es are fair and likely to be sustained, total returns will consist of the dividend plus growth in earnings.

Using this model, both Jeremy Siegel (professor at the Wharton School and author of *Stocks for the Long Run*) and Jack Bogle (founder of Vanguard) have said that the maximum return you can expect from stocks going forward is about 7.5 percent. I want to talk about how they calculated this number and point out what I think they're missing.

A Look at the Numbers.   To understand how Siegel and Bogle calculated an expected total stock return maximum of 7.5 percent, we will go through the calculations ourselves. We will use 2005 average market data for ROE and P/E values and, to keep the numbers simple,

Exhibit 8.19   Total Returns on Stocks, Part 1

Book value		$10.00
ROE[1]		13 percent
EPS = ROE × BV	.13 × $10.00 = $1.30	$ 1.30
P/E ratio[2]		19
Share price = EPS × P/E	$1.30 × 19 = $24.70	$25.00

we'll use a book value of $10 per share. With a book value of $10 and an average return on equity (ROE) of 13 percent,★ you can calculate the earnings per share (EPS) at $1.30. Using an average price-to-earnings ratio (P/E) of 19,[1] you can calculate a share price of about $25.00. (These numbers are summarized in Exhibit 8.19.)

To estimate average stock growth, Jeremy Siegel and Jack Bogle argue (rightly) that over time, growth in earnings will approximate the change in GDP. Long-term nominal GDP growth is the sum of population, productivity, and inflation. If we keep inflation below 3 percent, it is difficult to conclude the U.S. will grow in excess of 6 percent. So they use 6 percent growth as a maximum. I agree with that.

In 2005, the average yield on stocks was 1.8 percent. Using the accepted model of "total return equals growth plus yield," they added 6 percent and 1.8 percent and got a 7.8 percent as a maximum total stock return. That's where I think they missed something. Let me illustrate.

When a company grows, its balance sheet must grow to support the growth in its income statement. For example, with growth at 6 percent and the book value at $10, the company must plow $0.60 of the earnings back into book value. With the yield on an average stock at 1.8 percent and a share price of $25.00, the dividend is $0.45. Adding these together, we get a total of $1.05. (See Exhibit 8.20.)

But remember in Exhibit 8.19 we calculated an EPS of $1.30. So simply adding current dividend yield and prospective growth leaves $0.25 that is not accounted for! (See Exhibit 8.21.) I want to know what happened to that extra money.

★ The average ROE in 2005 was 13 percent. Incidentally, ROE has been between 12 and 15 percent since World War II; it's an amazingly stable number.

Exhibit 8.20   Total Returns on Stocks, Part 2—Growth plus Yield

Growth in book value = BV × Growth	$10.00 × .06 = $.60	$ .60
Dividend yield = Share price × Yield	$25.00 × .018 = $.45	$ .45
Total return = Growth + Yield	6.0% + 1.8% = 7.8% *or*	$1.05

Exhibit 8.21   Total Returns on Stocks, Part 3—Free Cash Flow

EPS = ROE × BV	.13 × $10.00 = $1.30	$1.30
Total return = Growth + Yield	6.0% + 1.8% = 7.8% *or*	$1.05
	$.60 + $.45 = $1.05	
Free cash flow = EPS − (Growth + Yield)	1.0% or extra $.25	$ .25

If management takes that extra 25 cents per share and spends it foolishly, then the 25 cents is worth nothing. But with that 25 cents, which happens to be 1 percent of the price, management could increase the dividend and have a 2.8 percent yield. Or management could buy in 1 percent of its own stock, in which case the shareholder would own 1 percent more of the company. The point is, if they do something useful with that extra 1 percent, you and I, as owners of the company, can benefit from it.

So when prominent individuals in the industry use 7.8 percent as the maximum return for stocks, we disagree. We think the extra 1 percent (giving an 8.8 percent total return), makes a difference. And that difference means money. So when you hear people talking about growth plus dividend, remember that they are talking about growth plus the *existing* dividend. But there is an extra 1 percent, which we call free cash flow, which is not being accounted for in those numbers. And in evaluating your investing options, 1 percent makes a difference. The assumptions behind their model can cost you money.

Theory # 2: Risk-Adjusted Returns

There is a common perception among investors that stocks are risky. As a result, a lot of very good minds have crafted various theories about risk-adjusted returns. The idea is that in choosing between investment vehicles, it is prudent to account for the "riskiness" of stocks and adjust their expected returns accordingly. At least, that's the theory. In this section, I explain from a practitioner's point of view why the notion of risk-adjusted returns is nonsense, and demonstrate how it can cost you money.

First, what is your definition of risk? People usually say that risk is the possibility of losing money. A better definition of risk is that risk is the *probability of losing purchasing power.* That means that inflation is a risk because it reduces the purchasing power of your assets.

Now, what is definition of risk used by Wall Street and many academics? Wall Street says that risk is volatility. Using this definition, Wall Street will tell you that the wavy line (A) in Exhibit 8.22 is riskier that the top line (B). I can agree with that. Wall Street will also tell you that line A is riskier than the middle line (C), and I might be convinced of that. But Wall Street will also tell you that line A is riskier than the bottom line (D), and I just don't agree with that at all.

What Wall Street *won't* tell you is that D is available to you; C is available to you; A is available; but B is not. So now, which line do you want?

Beware when you are told that stocks are risky. You need to know what definition of risk is being used. If your investment goal is to grow

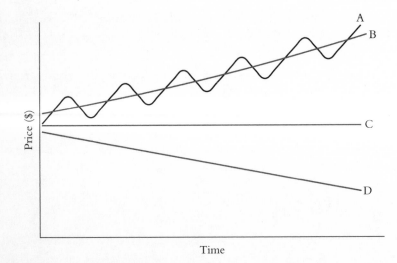

Exhibit 8.22 Volatility versus Risk

the purchasing power of your portfolio, then stock price volatility is a risk in the short term, but in the long term (greater than three years), price volatility tends to average out. For long-term investments, inflation and taxes are much greater risks than price volatility. They can dramatically reduce purchasing power—as can paying too much for a stock in the first place! Again, it is very important in any discussion of investment risk to understand what definition of risk is being used.

So let's talk about risk-adjusted returns. Risk-adjusted return theories try to minimize volatility risk (they don't address taxes, inflation, or paying too much for a stock). Some of you know that the market only goes up about half the time. Typically—not always, but typically—it rises between October and May. And, on average, between May and October, the markets are flat. So if you invest for risk-adjusted returns (striving to lower your volatility), you want to be in the market for six months, and then you want to be out of the market for six months. The six months that you are out of the market you have zero volatility, right? The problem with striving for risk-adjusted returns is that it encourages you to move out of (and into) the market on a frequent basis. But this increases your tax rate—not to mention trading costs and commissions!

Investment returns are taxed at different tax rates depending on the type of return. Consequently, your investing choices determine your tax rate. Short-term gains are taxed as ordinary income at 35 percent, and long-term capital gains are taxed at 15 percent. Risk-adjusted return theories encourage investors to take actions that result in short-term gains (which are taxed at a higher rate). But if you focus on optimizing your tax-adjusted returns, you naturally take actions that result in long-term gains (because they are taxed at a lower rate).

Exhibit 8.23 lists potential returns of 6 percent, 8 percent and 10 percent. As you can see, choosing a short-term return reduces a 10 percent gain to 6.5 percent after taxes. And with inflation at 2 percent, the real, after-tax return is down to 4.5 percent. At 10 percent, the difference between a short-term (risk-adjusted) return and a long-term (tax-adjusted) return is 31 percent. At 6 percent, the difference between a risk-adjusted return and a tax-adjusted return is 39 percent! By following risk-adjusted return theories, you can lose 30 to 40 percent of your return because you chose to pay ordinary income tax (short-term gains) instead of long-term capital gains.

Exhibit 8.23   The Effect of Taxes and Inflation on Short-Term and
Long-Term Gains, Part 1

Risk-Adjusted Returns %

	6% Return		8% Return		10% Return	
	35% Tax	15% Tax	35% Tax	15% Tax	35% Tax	15% Tax
After Tax	3.9	5.1	5.2	6.8	6.5	8.5
Adjusted for 2% Inflation	1.9	3.1	3.2	4.8	4.5	6.5
Difference	39%		33%		31%	

The problem with risk-adjusted return theories is that they focus on the wrong risk, and by doing so, they encourage frequent trading and a short-term investing mentality, which results in higher taxes and lower net returns. Put simply, they cost you money.

Many investors think that stocks are risky because stock prices are more volatile than cash or bonds. But let's look at the investment choices when the effects of taxes and inflation are taken into account (available returns for cash and bonds based on 2007 numbers). Refer to Exhibit 8.24.

1. Cash (i.e. short-term debt, including passbook savings accounts, CDs, and Treasury bills) is priced to do about 4.5 percent. When taxed at 35 percent, you get 2.9 percent. And if you take 2 percent off that for inflation, you get a real after-tax return of 0.9 percent return.

Exhibit 8.24   The Effect of Taxes and Inflation on Short-Term and
Long-Term Gains, Part 2

Risk-Adjusted Returns %

	6% Return		8% Return		10% Return		Bonds 5% Return	Cash 4.5% Return
	35% Tax	15% Tax	35% Tax	15% Tax	35% Tax	15% Tax	35% Tax	35% Tax
After Tax	3.9	5.1	5.2	6.8	6.5	8.5	3.25	2.9
Adjusted for 2% Inflation	1.9	3.1	3.2	4.8	4.5	6.5	1.25	0.9
Difference	39%		33%		31%			

2. Long-term bonds are priced at 5 percent; on a corporate bond, you might get 6 percent. The majority of long-term bonds are held by pension plans, which are tax-free. But if you're a taxpayer, you keep 3.25 percent; after inflation, you have only 1.25 percent.

When you invest in stocks you become an *owner* of the company and become eligible to share in the successes and the failures of the company. There are no guarantees. Over the long term, the stock price will reflect the true value of the company. Over the short term, however, the perceived value (current stock price) of the company may not always reflect the company's true value. We believe that stocks are priced to give a decent return over bonds and cash, but the ultimate return depends on whether you invest for long-term gains or short-term gains.

Taking these choices a step further, let's compare returns for stocks, bonds, and T-bills since 1926 (see Exhibit 8.25). From 1926 to 2006, Treasury bills have averaged 3.7 percent. With an average inflation of 3 percent, the real return on T-bills (short-term debt) has been 0.7 percent. We think that inflation currently is a little over 2 percent. Therefore, short-term T-bills should be priced at 2.7 to 3 percent; today, they're a bit above that. Since 1926, long-term government bonds have averaged 5.4 percent and (with an average inflation of 3 percent) have netted

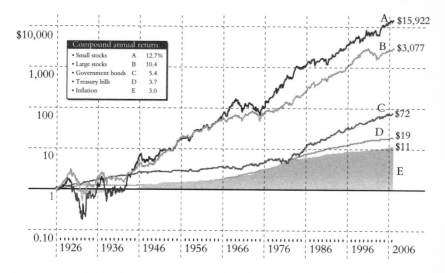

Exhibit 8.25   Stocks, Bonds, Bills, and Inflation, 1926–2006

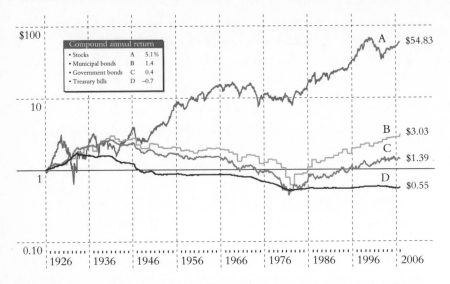

Compound annual return		
• Stocks	A	5.1%
• Municipal bonds	B	1.4
• Government bonds	C	0.4
• Treasury bills	D	−0.7

Exhibit 8.26   Stocks, Bonds, and Bills after Taxes and Inflation, 1926–2006

a real return of 2.4 percent. Today, we think long-term rates should be between 4½ and 5 percent, and they are.

Other than examining rates, Exhibit 8.25 is totally useless. What's wrong with it? You can't spend that money—it's pre-tax and pre-inflation. The useful chart is Exhibit 8.26.

When you adjust the returns for taxes and inflation (as in Exhibit 8.26) you get a better understanding of the investing choices. From 1926 to 2006, if you've owned Treasury bills and never spent a dime of the income (or the principal), but you did pay your taxes, your dollar went to 55 cents—*guaranteed*. T-bills may be guaranteed by the federal government, but, in *real* terms, you are guaranteed to lose purchasing power. Note the similarities between line D on Exhibit 8.26 and line D on Exhibit 8.22.

If you owned government bonds, paid your taxes, and never spent a dime—never spent any of the income—your dollar went to $1.39. You made 0.4 percent per year. What's interesting is that there have been two periods when you could make money on bonds. The first period was the Great Depression (and if you think we're in a depression, then I will tell you to own nothing but long-term Treasuries). The other time was from 1982 to 2002 when interest rates dropped from 13 percent to 5 percent. Bonds are now priced at 5 percent and they might go to

4.5 percent; the game in bonds is pretty much over. Note the similarities between line C on Exhibit 8.26 and line C on Exhibit 8.22.

We argue that in the 1970s it was a lousy time to own stocks, but it was a worse time to own bonds. If you think that bonds are safe, be aware that in the late 1970s investment analysts spoke of bonds as "certificates of guaranteed confiscation." It comes back around to your definition of risk. Back in the 1970s, there was nothing uncertain about bonds—they were guaranteed to lose you money.

If you owned stocks from 1926 to 2006, the returns have been kind of choppy but stocks have averaged 5.1 percent (over and above taxes and inflation). Note the similarities between line A in Exhibit 8.22 and line A in Exhibit 8.26. To draw a parallel to today, take a look at the 1960s. This was a period of time when inflation was relatively low and fairly stable, when interest rates were fair and fairly stable, and when stock prices were fair. Back in the 1960s, you had your choice of making money in stocks (in a jagged fashion), or losing money consistently in bonds. So the question is: Which risk do you want to take?

Some economists define risk as the uncertainty of the outcome— not the outcome itself, but the *uncertainty* of the outcome. So those economists will tell you that if you jump out of an airplane with a parachute, it's risky because the outcome is uncertain (your chute may or may not open). But if you jump out of an airplane without a parachute, the outcome is quite certain and, therefore, not risky. Risk-adjusted return theories are based on this definition of risk. If you'd rather have the parachute, then the theory of risk-adjusted returns may not be right for you—it is costing you money.

Theory #3: Style Boxes

Many financial planners have turned to the *style box theory* to ensure diversification in an investment portfolio. But this can cost the investor money. To understand why, we must first explain what style boxes are. Then we'll talk about how they are being used.

Style boxes were popularized by Morningstar, Inc., a Chicago-based investment research company. They are a nine-box matrix, attempting to display both an investment methodology (value, growth, or blend) on the horizontal axis and the size of the companies in which the portfolio manager invests (large cap, mid cap, or small cap) on the vertical axis.

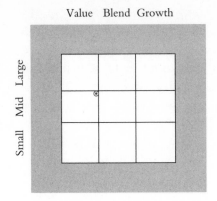

Exhibit 8.27   Style Box

Generally speaking, the investment methodology of a growth-oriented portfolio will contain companies that its portfolio manager believes have the potential to increase earnings faster than the rest of the market. A value orientation, by contrast, focuses on stocks that the manager thinks are currently undervalued in price and believes will eventually be recognized for their true worth by the market. A blend orientation will mix the two philosophies.

Regarding size, stocks in the top 70 percent of the total market cap of U.S. stocks are considered "Large Cap." Stocks in the next 20 percent of total market cap are considered "Mid Cap," and stocks in the bottom 10 percent of total market cap are considered "Small Cap."

Exhibit 8.27 is a recent example of how Morningstar characterizes our portfolio holdings.

The Style Box Theory.   The style box theory suggests that you ought to own a variety of equity portfolios, spanning all nine style boxes. There are many financial planners who buy into this theory, using style boxes as a tool for ensuring diversification. What's missing is an appreciation that style boxes were meant to be *descriptive*—not *restrictive*. Either way, style boxes may be a useful tool in marketing, but I find them of no value in investing. Here's why.

As a portfolio manager, let's say I own a stock in the "small-value" box and it doubles in price. Should I sell it from the portfolio dedicated to that box and buy it in the "middle-value" portfolio? And, if it doubles again, should I sell it from the portfolio dedicated to that box and buy it in the "large-value" portfolio? The theory of style box investing says I should. But, every time I sell and rebuy, I have to pay taxes and commissions. How does that help you make money?

Morningstar seems to understand this trap. In fact, a few years ago at a "World Money Show" in Florida, I was on a panel chaired by Don Phillips, managing director of Morningstar. Recognizing that style boxes are regularly used in a restrictive fashion, Phillips was launching a new tool called the *ownership zone*.

When he introduced me, Don showed a slide similar to Exhibit 8.28 and said, "Ron covers the left *six* boxes." Which means, I guess, that our portfolio is everything *except* growth. At one time we asked them why we are not considered a growth portfolio since many of the companies we hold were growing faster than average. They explained, "Your price-to-earnings ratio is below average." Well, if the far right column of the style box matrix is based on P/E and not growth, it should be labeled *glamour,* not *growth.* The P/E often reflects popularity (or glamour), independent of earnings growth.★

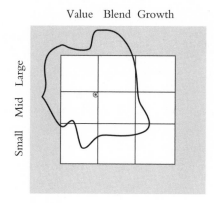

Exhibit 8.28   Ownership Zone
Note: This picture is outdated. Morningstar used the amoeba shape shortly after the Ownership Zone was launched, but now the Ownership Zones are ellipses.

★In 2002, Morningstar changed their methodology to use five factors for value and five factors for growth, so the point is now moot. However, other sources and some common usage still seem to reflect a high P/E as signifying growth.

Value   Blend   Growth

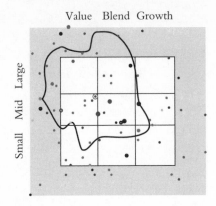

Exhibit 8.29   Scatter Diagram

Note: This picture is outdated. Morningstar used the amoeba shape shortly after the Ownership Zone was launched, but now the Ownership Zones are ellipses.

Morningstar also offers a scatter diagram of a portfolio's holdings. The scatter diagram of our holdings is shown in Exhibit 8.29. What does Exhibit 8.29 tell you about our investment style? Three distinct possibilities come to mind:

1. We're not disciplined.
2. We're diversified.
3. We don't care about style boxes.

Before you draw any conclusions, let's look at some more data.

Exhibit 8.30 is an exhibit Morningstar offers that we find more meaningful. In the first column, Morningstar provides data on our portfolio's holdings. In the second column, it compares these numbers to other portfolios in our category. In this "Relative Category" column, a value of 1.0 is average. From this table, we extract the following:

- Relative to our category, our return on equity (ROE) is higher than average (1.90),* and our return on assets (ROA) is higher than average (2.25)—so the companies we own are more profitable than average.
- Relative to our category, our growth in book value is higher than average (2.89); growth in sales is higher than average (2.24); growth

---

*The numbers Morningstar reports are index numbers and not dividend returns.

Current Investment Style

Value Measures		Relative Category
Price/Earnings	11.51	0.76
Price/Book	2.02	1.06
Price/Sales	0.87	0.99
Price/Cash Flow	4.39	0.75
Dividend Yield %	1.05	0.66
Growth Measures (%)		Relative Category
Long-Term Earnings	12.40	1.14
Book Value	15.83	2.89
Sales	10.53	2.24
Cash Flow	42.45	10.40
Historical Earnings	25.57	2.24
Profitability (%)		Relative Category
Return on Equity	23.51	1.90
Return on Assets	12.58	2.25
Net Margin	10.85	1.29

Exhibit 8.30   Current Investment Style

in cash flow is higher than average (10.40); and growth in historical earnings is higher than average (2.24)—so the companies we own are growing faster than average.
- Relative to our category, our P/E is lower than average (0.76) and our relative price/book is a bit above average (1.06)—so the companies we own are cheaper than average.

So what does this tell you about our investment style? We like cheap, profitable, fast-growing companies.

Looking at the data in a different way, in Exhibit 8.31 we've plotted the price/book versus ROE of our top 20 holdings, which represents 60 percent of our portfolio. We've overlaid this plot onto Ford Equity Research's universe of over 4,000 companies so we can see where we stand.

On these metrics, our investments look a little more disciplined than they did in Exhibit 8.29. Our average ROE is 18 percent, even though the corporate average is 13 to 14 percent. Our average P/E is 14,

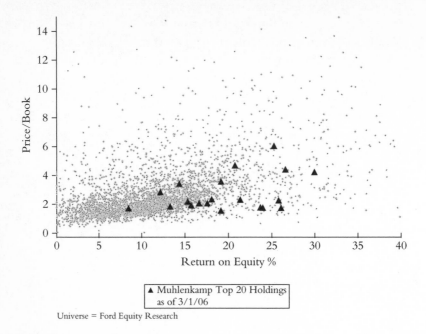

Exhibit 8.31   Top 20 Holdings

even though the corporate average is 18. So we own better than average companies at below-average prices because we've found those criteria to be more useful to increasing the value of our assets. *That* is our management style.

The problem with style boxes is that they try to describe all investment managers with a nine-box matrix and, as we have seen, the matrix does not always show the complete picture. But even more troubling, those nine boxes have become restrictive. Managers are asked to fit their investments into a style box based on company size and labels of "growth" versus "value." If your goal is to increase your wealth, then you want an investment manager who will make decisions based on the probability of increasing your wealth. Asking him to base investment decisions on artificial constraints can cost you a lot of money.

Theory #4: Fundamental Indexes

Fundamental indexes are simply the latest iteration in the never-ending search for a good stock market index. To understand fundamental indexes, it is helpful to review indexes in general—both the theory behind them and their practical application in the past 30 years.

Index-based investing was first offered to the public in the mid-1970s. The underlying theory was that stocks are efficiently priced. This means that the prices on stocks are always fair, and no matter how much time and effort an investor spends, he or she cannot consistently beat the market. If this is true, then it makes sense to simply buy a representative *market basket* of stocks.

Early on there was much discussion as to how this market basket should be constructed. Should it include all NYSE stocks, all NASDAQ stocks, all stocks covered by the *Value Line Investment Survey,* or those stocks included in the Standard & Poor's (S&P) 500 Index? Each of these choices had differing characteristics, advantages and disadvantages.

For many years, the most widely used index has been the S&P 500. The S&P 500 is a market-value-weighted (or capitalization-weighted) index of 500 large-cap companies. This means that each stock in the index is weighted in proportion to its market value. If company A has three times the market value of company B, then company A will have three times the weight on the S&P 500 list. The advantage is that this reflects where investors are actually putting their money (they have three times as much money invested in company A as they do in company B). Efficient market theory tells us that this is good; we want an index that represents the entire market.

However, capitalization-weighted indexes have a disadvantage as well. They automatically overweight the overpriced stocks and under-weight the underpriced stocks. For instance, what if two companies have similar revenue, profits, dividends, and other metrics, but company A has a market price of 30 times earnings (a P/E of 30) and company B has a market price of 10 times earnings (a P/E of 10)? In this case, a capitalization-weighted index gives company A (the overpriced stock) three times the weight of company B, simply because company A's high price gives it three times the market value of company B. This means that a capitalization-weighted market basket has a disproportionate number of overpriced stocks. And that can cost the investor money.

Having recognized this problem, a number of new market indexes have been constructed that abandon capitalization weighting. Instead, these new indexes are weighted based on *fundamental* metrics such as revenues, earnings, or dividends. Back-testing of these fundamental indexes indicates that they would have outperformed the capitalization weighted S&P 500 Index by roughly 2 percent per year. (This is not surprising, since a number of other averages and indexes have outperformed the S&P 500 during recent years.)

However, there is another question that bears consideration: If a fundamental index based on revenues or earnings can outperform the cap-weighted S&P 500 by 2 percent a year, could an investor pick up another 2 percent per year simply by overweighting what the S&P underweights, and underweighting what the S&P overweights? In other words, why not load up on stocks with P/Es of 10 and avoid stocks with P/Es of 30?

The important thing to remember is that fundamental indexes are simply a theory, just as capitalization-weighted indexes are. There are many indexes out there. Each one is only as good as the results it provides to your investment portfolio. And they all assume efficient markets—which is also just a theory.

The Bottom Line

If you want to make money in investing, it is critical to challenge what everyone knows to be true. Remember, it's only a theory! If it lowers your investment returns, it is costing you money. If it is costing you money, perhaps it is time to adopt a new theory. After all, how much money are you willing to lose for a theory?

Chapter 9

2007: Where To from Here?

This chapter is adapted from a presentation at the Muhlenkamp & Company Seminar in November 2006. Because 2006 was a volatile year in the stock market, it had many investors concerned. In this longer essay, Ron addresses those concerns by focusing on two fundamental questions: In terms of the economy and the markets, "Where are we now?" and "Where to from here?"

It's surprising how many people try to predict the direction of the economy and the markets without understanding where we are today. If you don't understand what's going on today, how can you possibly predict what's going to happen next? To understand today's investing markets, you need to understand what's led up to them. Therefore, this essay will look at today's economy and the markets by considering them in three contexts: the long-term picture of the past 80 years; the intermediate picture and the economic business cycle; and short-term fluctuations. Then we can address the question, "Where to from here?"

The Big Picture: Back to Normal (circa 1960)

First, let's consider the big picture: What is the current investment climate? We think the investment climate is back to normal, but it is a normal that we haven't seen since the 1960s. So let's review what a normal investment climate is by looking at inflation and interest rates.

Exhibit 9.1 is a plot of stocks, bonds, T-bills, and inflation since 1926. It shows that over the past 80 years, the inflation rate has averaged about 3 percent; short-term rates have averaged about 1 percent over inflation; and long-term rates have averaged about 2.5 percent over inflation. While *average* and *normal* aren't necessarily the same thing, in this case we think the averages are fairly close to normal.

Now take another look at inflation in Exhibit 9.1 (and remember that on this plot, inflation rate is the slope of the line). First, notice the effects of the Great Depression and the deflation that came with it. Then, notice the period of high inflation that ended around 1980. Can you find the Vietnam War? If the Vietnam War didn't have an impact on the long-term economy, what impact will the war in Iraq have? There is no question that these conflicts are important, but in the long-term picture of the economy and of the markets, they simply don't have much impact.

It is important in investing to know what parts of the daily news to pay attention to and what not to. There is always something that's a

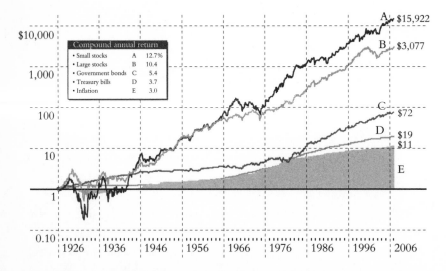

Exhibit 9.1   Stocks, Bonds, Bills, and Inflation, 1926–2006

current problem, but the question is, "Will it influence the economy and how much companies are worth?"

In 2005, somebody asked me what it would take to turn me bearish; I said that I would turn bearish if I could think of something to worry about that people weren't already worried about. When people are worried about something, they act. The time to worry is when nobody else is—simply *because* nobody else is.

The rise and fall of the dot-coms is a classic example. In 1999, everybody seemed convinced that dot-com stocks only went straight up. *Then* I was worried. When the dot-coms fell, many investors were caught unprepared, and the drop in the stock market was exacerbated because of it. It's the things that no one is worried about that surprise us. But (as Exhibit 9.1 shows) most of the things that people worry about get washed out in the long-term picture.

Inflation has been the defining factor in determining the investment climate over the past 60 years. So let's look at inflation more closely. Exhibit 9.2 shows the Consumer Price Index (CPI) from 1952 to 2006. Inflation has been stable between 2 percent and 3 percent for the past nine years. It ticked up in 1999, and the Fed raised short-term rates and caused a recession to be sure it didn't go any farther. It ticked up a bit in 2006 and the Fed again raised short-term interest rates to contain it.

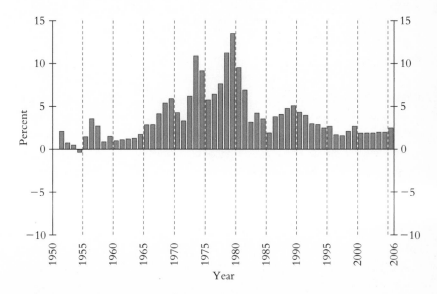

Exhibit 9.2   Inflation, 1952–2006

Our government is determined not to let inflation get out of hand, and inflation is, in fact, under control. The last time we had low and stable inflation was in the 1960s, and it was actually less stable than it is today. In this respect, we are "back to normal," but it is a normal we haven't seen since the 1960s.

Now consider short-term interest rates. The top graph in Exhibit 9.3 shows real Treasury bill rates (adjusted for inflation) since 1952. Exhibit 9.1 showed that real short-term rates have averaged 0.7 percent (above inflation) over the past 80 years. So when rates are much higher than that, they are unusually high. When real rates are much lower than 1 percent, they are unusually low.

In 2003 short-term rates were at 1 percent; inflation was around 2 percent, giving a real rate of −1 percent). This was an unusually low short-term rate. Subsequently, the Fed raised short-term rates to 2 percent, then to 3 percent (for a real rate of 1 percent). The media was alarmed by the rate increases, but, in fact, all that had happened was the short-term rate returned from an unusually low rate to a rate that was closer to normal. The Fed continued to increase short-term rates so that at the end of 2006, short-term rates were somewhat above normal at 5.25 percent.

What about long-term rates? The bottom graph in Exhibit 9.3 shows long-term government bonds adjusted for inflation (the line at 3 percent indicates the historic norm). Long-term interest rates have been close to normal for four years, and for five out of the past six years. In 2004, people feared long-term rates would move up because short-term rates were climbing. Looking at the historic, inflation-adjusted data, we said that short-term interest rates were rising to get back to normal, but long-term interest rates were already there. We did not expect long-term rates to climb. And in fact, as Exhibit 9.3 shows, long-term rates held steady. Considering the big picture can help us to better understand what to expect.

Mortgage rates have been of particular interest lately, so let's take a moment to look at long-term data for mortgage rates. Exhibit 9.4 shows real mortgage rates since 1952. Historically, fair value for mortgages has been about 1.25 percent above long-term bonds (about 4 percent above inflation). With long-term bonds currently at 4.75 percent, a fair mortgage rate ought to be just a little less than 6 percent. Today, mortgage rates are about 6.2 percent. We think they will drop a little bit, but it will be a minor adjustment. Note that Exhibit 9.4 is for 30-year fixed rate mortgages.

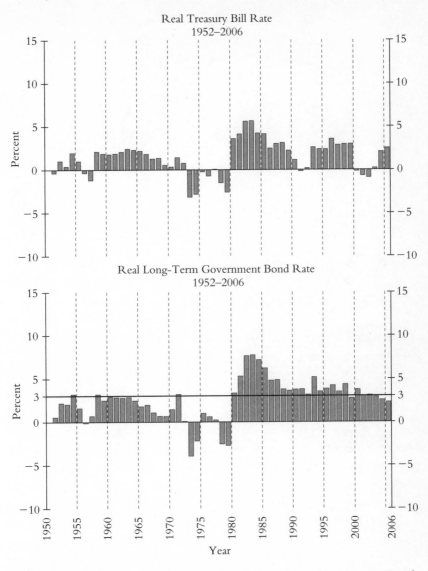

Exhibit 9.3   Real Treasury Bill Rate and Real Long-Term Government Bond Rate, 1952–2006

ARM mortgages that were based on the unusually low short-term rates of 2001–2004 will see an increase in rates to the level of 30-year fixed rate.

These numbers indicate that the bond market has concluded that inflation is not going to be a problem. The stock market, meanwhile, is trying to figure out whether we are going to have a soft landing or a

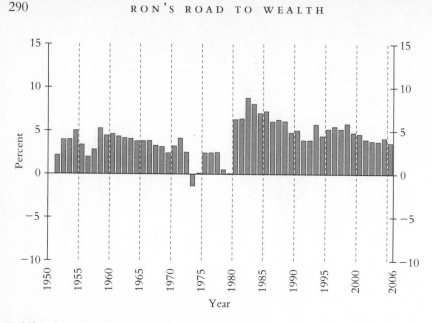

Exhibit 9.4 Real Mortgage Rate, 1952–2006

recession. So let's look at the intermediate picture and see if we can determine which it will be.

The Intermediate Picture and the Economic Business Cycle

In the intermediate picture, the stock market is driven primarily by the economic business cycle. I often compare the business cycle to the seasonal agricultural cycle. When the economy grows, it's summer. When the economy peaks, it's harvest time. When the economy slows down, it's winter. And when the economy is poised to grow again, it's spring.

In the 1960s and 1970s, most recessions were about four years apart. It was a textbook economic business cycle. In the 1980s, declining inflation and tax rates extended the business cycle, and we went nearly 10 years without a recession. In the 1990s, declining inflation, reasonable tax rates, and better management by the Fed allowed us to go 10 years without a recession.

These economic cycles affect the markets, and can be seen rather clearly in the annual S&P 500 data in Exhibit 9.5. We think that now we are back to normal (inflation is low and stable) and the business cycle is again the primary driver of the economy and the markets.

To better understand how the business cycle drives the markets, let's review the past several cycles. Exhibit 9.6 shows quarterly GDP growth

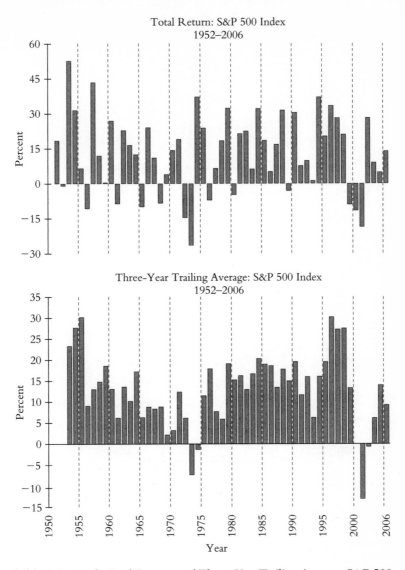

Exhibit 9.5 Yearly Total Return and Three-Year Trailing Average: S&P 500
Index, 1952–2006

rate from 1988 through 2006. During this time, the Fed intentionally
slowed the economy three times. Two of those slowdowns resulted in
recession. One time they managed a soft landing.* To understand what

_____

*A recession is defined as two consecutive quarters of negative growth. In a soft
landing, the economy recovers before a recession occurs.

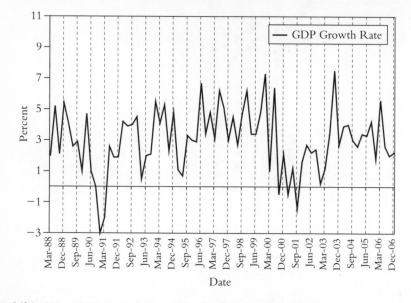

Exhibit 9.6   GDP Growth Rate, March 1988 to December 2006

happened, we plotted short-term interest rates and inflation data along-side the GDP growth data, as shown in Exhibit 9.7.

In the late 1980s inflation was climbing, ultimately to 6 percent-plus, so the Fed raised short-term interest rates up to 9 percent. This drove GDP growth down and inflation down, but then Saddam Hussein rolled into Kuwait, giving us a recession.★ In 1994–1995, inflation was climbing again, so the Fed raised short-term rates to 6 percent, and we ended up with a soft landing. In 2000, inflation climbed a bit, so the Fed drove short-term interest rates back up to 6 percent, bringing inflation back down. But then the attacks of September 11, 2001, drove us into recession. In the aftermath of the September 11 attacks, the Fed lowered rates dramatically to stimulate the economy. Short-term rates dropped to an unusually low 1 percent. Coming out of the recession, we saw growth rates of 3 to 4 percent. The Fed worried that a 3 to 4 percent growth rate might drive inflation up, and they raised short-term rates again to 5.25 percent (which is a little above normal).

We said all along we didn't think a growth rate of 3–4 percent could be maintained. After all, at the bottom of the recession, unemployment

---

★Note that the Iraqi wars didn't change the long-term climate, but did affect the intermediate term—the business cycle.

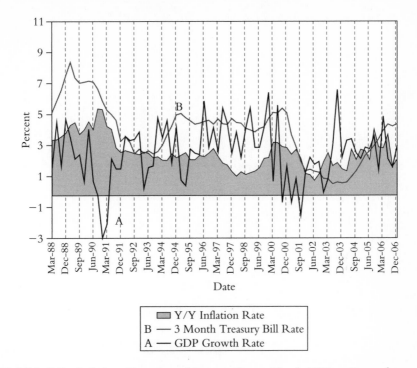

Exhibit 9.7 Inflation, Growth, and Interest Rates, March 1988 to December 2006

reached 6.5 percent. Now it's at 4.5 percent. For the economy to continue to grow at that pace, unemployment would have to go to 2.5 percent. We think 2.5 percent unemployment is unlikely. It is more likely for economic growth to slow to about 2.5 to 3 percent. In this second half of 2006, as GDP growth and inflation have come down, the Fed has paused, and we suspect the Fed is done raising short-term rates. Therefore, we think that we are at the end of the transition and on our way out of the most recent slowdown.

So where are we now? Exhibit 9.8 adds long-term bond data to the previous plot. On this plot we see that the GDP is slowing down. Inflation is dropping. Short-term rates are up. Long-term rates have fallen back to values less than short-term rates.

By the way, when long-term rates are less than short-term rates, this is called an *inverted yield curve*, and it's got some people worried. Should they be? That depends. If you have an inverted yield curve because the

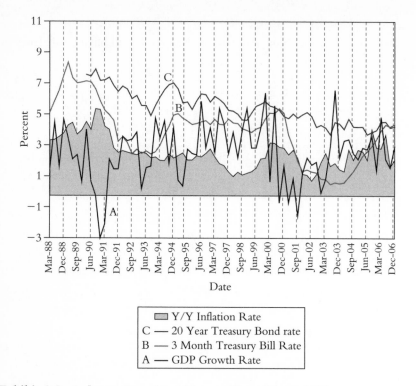

Exhibit 9.8 Inflation, Growth, and Interest Rates, March 1988 to December 2006

Fed is raising short-term rates above long-term rates, that usually presages a slowdown or a recession.

But that's not what happened this year. This year, long rates have fallen below short rates because the bond market has decided that inflation is not going to get out of hand. So the long-term rates are dropping back to normal. Short-term rates just haven't caught up yet. (Incidentally, that's not at all unusual. It happened in 2000, and it happened in 1990.) Short-term rates lag long-term rates because long-term rates are set by the market (which reacts quickly) and short-term rates are somewhat engineered by the Fed (which is slower to react). So in this case, we think the inverted yield curve does not presage a recession. Rather, we think that we are at the bottom of a soft landing and, looking ahead, we expect the economy to grow at a reasonable rate of about 2.5 to 3 percent.

Not everyone agrees with us. A lot of people have pointed out that since World War II we've had 10 recessions and we've managed a soft landing only once, in 1994–1995. So the odds appear to be 10 to 1 against a soft landing. Nevertheless, we think we will have a soft landing this time around for three reasons:

1. Bank balance sheets are in good shape;
2. Corporate balance sheets are in good shape; and
3. Consumers are in good shape.

Nobody disagrees about the bank and corporate balance sheets, but there is a lot of controversy about the condition of the consumer. So let's take a closer look at the consumer.

Many analysts fear the consumer is overextended—too far in debt. They base those fears on charts like Exhibit 9.9; it shows the ratio of household debt to disposable personal income from 1973 to 2005. Over that period of time, consumer credit has been pretty stable. Mortgage debt has gone up significantly, as has total debt. However, those trends are debt relative to *income*. We think that if you are going to talk about debt, you should talk about debt relative to *assets*.

Exhibit 9.10 shows household debt in an entirely different perspective. It shows debt relative to assets. Note that the total debt line of Exhibit 9.9 is the same as the liability line of Exhibit 9.10. In 1950, the

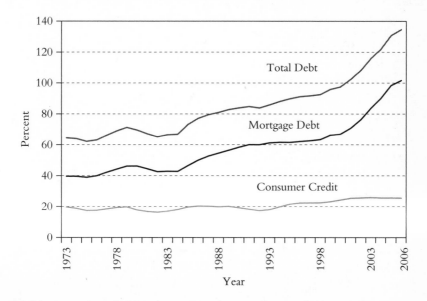

Exhibit 9.9 Household Debt as a Percentage of Disposable Personal Income

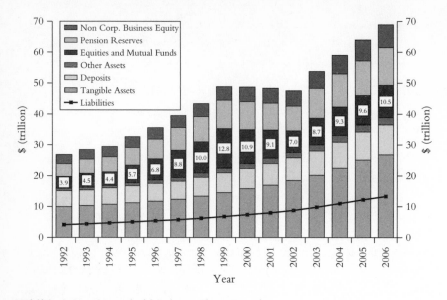

Exhibit 9.10   Household Balance Sheet Details

average household had assets in the order of four and a half times its debt. Today, the average household has assets in the order of five and a half times its debt. So relative to assets, household debt has actually decreased. The average household today has plenty of assets to cover its debt.

Consumer debt is also influenced by the demographics of our population. The American population is getting older. Our baby boomers are approaching retirement. At age 60, an individual's finances look different than they did at 30. For one thing, a 60-year-old has more assets relative to income than a 30-year-old. Even though their income may have doubled since they were 30, their assets went from very little to enough to retire on. After all, they've spent 30 years building assets. So as our population ages, the assets-to-income ratio increases.

Taking it one step further, Exhibit 9.10 indicates that debt and assets tend to track together. If debt and assets track together, as we get older our debt-to-income ratio is likely to increase because we have higher assets to income. Therefore, an increasing debt-to-income ratio may not be a sign that the consumer is overextended. Rather, it may just be a reflection of an aging and more prosperous population.

There is another factor to consider in looking at household debt. As Exhibit 9.11 shows, a large portion of household debt is mortgage debt,

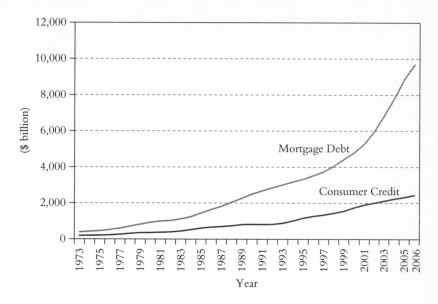

Exhibit 9.11   Debt

and it is increasing. What isn't on this chart is the fact that mortgage rates are half of what they were 20 years ago. You can carry twice as much mortgage at a 6 percent rate as you could at 13 percent. So we have bigger, more expensive houses, but not necessarily bigger payments.

So let's calculate our debt another way. Exhibit 9.12 shows the debt payments of the average household as a percentage of disposable income (called the *debt-service burden*). When viewed this way, our debt doesn't look so bad. Household debt service has ticked up in the past five years, but it has been between 14 percent and 18 percent since 1980. In other words, our debt service-to-income is not much worse than it has been for the past 25 years. The debt has gone up, but because mortgage rates have gone down, the debt burden is pretty steady.

Looking at debt in terms of assets and debt burden, the American consumer is not overextended. The household debt burden has been relatively steady over the past 25 years, and the average household has sufficient assets to support the burden.

So in the intermediate picture, we think that with inflation low and stable, the business cycle is going to drive the economy and the markets. The Fed is not currently pushing short-term interest rates higher, so the

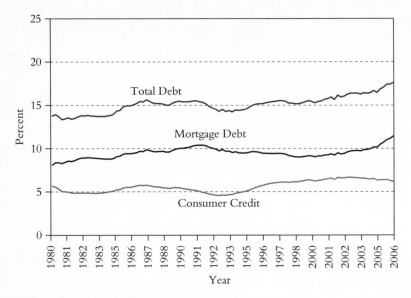

Exhibit 9.12   Household Debt-Service Burden

health of the economy will drive the shape of our rebound. With strong bank and corporate balance sheets and a strong consumer, we think that the economy will see a soft landing, rather than a recession. This is important to the investor because different types of investments are favorable during a recession than during a soft landing. That brings us to the short-term picture. What is happening in the stock market now?

The Short-Term: Volatility

The economy is currently transitioning from fairly rapid growth to somewhat less rapid growth. And, as with all transitions, the change has caused much speculation in the investment field as to the direction of the economy. This speculation has made the market very volatile this year. And that volatility makes great headlines.

What you don't often hear is that for the first part of 2006, aggressive stocks led the marketplace—things like commodity stocks, small caps, and foreign stocks (which you want to own in an inflationary climate). The fear in March and April was that the economy was growing too fast and we would have inflation. Then in May–June, everything corrected and the stocks that have been leading the market the second half of 2006 have been defensive stocks like food, utilities, and pharmaceuticals (which you should own if you are going into a recession). This means that the fear now is that the economy is growing too slowly. This is a significant change. However, we think a recession is not imminent. We expect the economy to have a soft landing and the premium on the defensive stocks will dissipate.

In the meantime, while there is fear of recession, the markets may behave as if there *is* a recession, and the markets will be volatile. In late 2006 through the third quarter of 2007, the markets have been generally sideways but in a very jagged fashion, sort of three months up and three weeks giving it back. So far the triggers for the setbacks have been problems in the subprime mortgage market and setbacks in high-yield bonds. Each of these problems was set up by too-easy terms for credit in the past few years. In time, however, we believe the fears will subside and the market will reflect the economy.

Where To from Here?

Based on today's interest rates, inflation, and investment climate, we think the average long-term investor is looking at the following choices. You can get about 5 percent on short-term or long-term debt. Adjusting for a 30 to 35 percent tax bracket, you get to keep 3.2 percent. Adjusting for inflation (which is about 2 percent) you net 1 percent on bonds.

Or you can invest in stocks. Stocks are currently priced to do about 8 to 9 percent, on average. Taxes for long-term gains are at 15 percent, leaving you 6.8 percent after-tax. Adjusting for 2 percent inflation, you net 4.8 percent. Over a period of 10 to 20 years, the difference between a 1 percent annual return and a 5 percent annual return can be an awful lot of money. See Exhibit 9.13.

It's interesting at this point to look again at the plot of historical investment returns since 1926 (Exhibit 9.14). In the past 80 years, bonds have in fact averaged 1 percent annually (adjusted for inflation and taxes); stocks have averaged 5 percent. In other words, available long-term investment returns are back to normal.

Exhibit 9.13   Available Annual Returns (Percent)

	Nominal	After-Tax	Real After-Tax
Short-term debt	4.5	2.9	0.9
Long-term debt	5	3.2	1.2
Equity	8	6.8	4.8

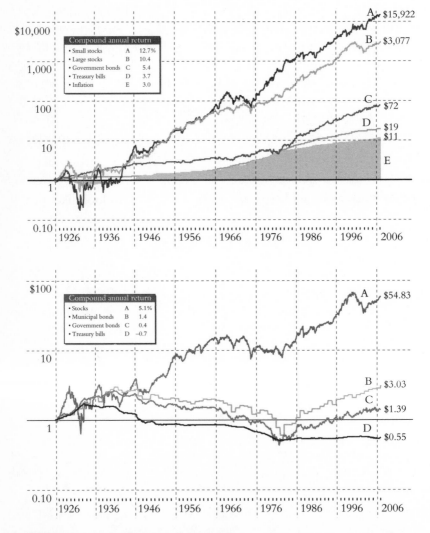

Exhibit 9.14   Stocks, Bonds, Bills, and Inflation, 1926–2006; Stocks, Bonds, and Bills after Taxes and Inflation, 1926–2006

Summary

We've covered a lot. So let's take a moment to review some of the highlights.

In the big picture, we think that inflation is under control, bank balance sheets are healthy, corporate balance sheets are healthy, and the consumer is in good shape (much better than reported).

The intermediate picture is driven by the business cycle. We expect a soft landing from the current economic slowdown, and we think that with the Fed recently lowering short-term rates, the transition period is coming to an end. Long-term interest rates rolled over in May 2006, and as of August 2007 they have since traded in a range between 4.60 and 5.40 percent. Mortgage rates are following long-term rates. The spread between treasuries and lower rated credits are widening as they should. The price of crude oil has leveled off but remained volatile, allowing the price of gasoline to fall roughly $.50 per gallon, but it also remains volatile. A number of other commodity prices have fallen or leveled off as well. Looking ahead, we expect the economy to grow at a reasonable rate of 2 to 3 percent. To us, it's starting to look like spring-time in the business cycle—a good time to plant investment crops.

In the short term, the market leadership has shifted from inflation beneficiaries (like commodities) to recession leaders (like food and utilities). That means that the investing public no longer expects inflation—they are preparing for recession instead. We don't expect a recession. But in the short term, hype, hope, and fear will always have an influence. In the short term, the stock market is going to continue to be volatile.

A volatile stock market is in many ways a test of an investor's convictions. It is a good time to reassess the investing climate, the business cycle, and the merit of concerns that the short-term fluctuations invariably produce. In doing so, keep these things in mind. First, most things that worry people on a day-to-day basis get washed out in the long term. So the long-term investor should consider them in the context of long-term influence on the economy and corporate values. Second, a volatile stock market is an opportunity for the long-term investor. It means there are quality stocks on sale. The challenge is to find them—and then to hold them through the fluctuations.

Editor's Note

Though this essay specifically discusses the economics and the markets in November 2006 with (minor updates in 2007), it is much more than that. It is an example of how to systematically evaluate the economic and investment situation at any time. It illustrates how an investor must look at the big picture to determine the investment climate, the mid-term data to determine investment season, and the short-term information to understand the daily fluctuations in the market. The data Ron uses is available to everyone. Yet he looks past the popular interpretations of that data, asking probing questions about the driving forces behind the numbers. He reminds us that the markets and economics are simply the aggregate results of individuals' decisions. People's decisions drive both the economy and the markets. In the short-term, hype, hope, and fear can make those decisions irrational, which makes the markets volatile. But in the long term, emotions level off and the markets behave rationally.

A Final Word

The stock market is rational in the long term. But it's like going to an auction. On any given day, an item at auction may sell high or low depending on the number of interested bidders, and the number of interested bidders can be affected by anything from the weather (who wants to stand in the rain to bid?) to the sports schedule (who would go to an auction the day their favorite team is in the Super Bowl?). The trading floor of the stock market is, in fact, an auction. So you have to know going in what you want to buy and what you are willing to pay—and you have to stick to it. If you do, you can get some great deals.

Determining what you want and what you are willing to pay is the business of investing. To do this well, you need to understand the current investing climate (inflation, interest rates). You need to monitor politics, because politicians write the rules that influence the economic climate. You need to be aware of world events, because current events can delay or hasten climate changes. You do all these things so you can recognize what is an emotional swing in the market as well as a long-term climate change. And when you think you know what the climate is and you have an investment strategy, you need to be able to stick to it even when everyone else seems to disagree. Of course, you keep checking your indicators. But the hardest part of the investment business is having the conviction to stay the course through the short-term fluctuations so you can reap the benefits in the long term.

Hopefully, this collection of essays has given you some of the tools you need to understand investing and its relationship to the economy. We chose these particular essays because they collectively form a foundation for what we call intelligent investment management. *Intelligent investment* means that instead of investing emotionally, you analyze the past, assess the present, and prepare for the future. You look beyond the current hype, hope, and fears to find the long-term economic trends—the climate changes. When you do this, you will be able to stand your ground when it seems everyone else disagrees with you. Then, not only will your investment portfolio perform better, but you may also find that you sleep better at night.

Appendix A

A Topical Guide to
Ron's Road to Wealth

- Why the Market Went Down 47
- The More Things Change, the More They Stay the Same 105
- Wake Up, America—Houses Don't Make You Money! 62
- Why Interest Rates Won't "Go Back Up" Anytime Soon 109
- The Fad, Recession, and Getting Back to Normal 261
- Where To from Here? 285

Investment Risk and Risk Management

- What Is Risk? 92
- What Is Risk? (Part 2) 146
- The Inflation Time Bomb 82
- Defusing the Inflation Time Bomb 88
- Mom—The Squeeze on Your "Income" Will Continue 113
- Why I Like Long-Term Treasury Bonds Instead of CDs or Money Markets Funds 103
- Beware of Good Yields 141
- Are Stocks Too High? 154
- Diversification—Too Much of a Good Thing 158
- Foreign Investing 256

Investment and Estate Planning

- Personal Finances (Maxims Part 2) 130
- Fund Your IRA Every Year, or How to Retire Wealthy by Driving Used Cars 165
- Estate Planning for Generations 169
- Problems with Investing for Income 172
- The Fundamentals of Life Insurance 177
- How to Choose a Money Manager 236

Other Investment Essays

- Review of *What Works on Wall Street* 198

Essays on Economics/Politics

Foundation for Economics and Political Theory

- Muhlenkamp's Musings on Economics 74
- Prosperity 207

Taxes, Government Spending, and Stimulating the Economy

Economic Theory (Keynesian vs. Classical)

Other Economic/Political Essays

Appendix B

Reading List for Life and Investment Fundamentals 101

This list was originally published in January 1998 and expanded in April 1998.

To Understand	Read
The way things work	*The Way Things Work,* by David Macaulay (Houghton Mifflin, 1988) *The Way the World Works,* by Jude Wanniski (Regnery Publishing, 1988)
Why you'll never understand the other sex	*You Just Don't Understand,* by Deborah Tannen (William Morrow, 1990)

(continued)

To Understand	Read
Values	*Zen and the Art of Motorcycle Maintenance,* by Robert Pirsig (Bantam, 1975)
The evolution of moral standards	*Lila,* by Robert Pirsig (Bantam, 1991)
Why global warming is unlikely	*Climate and the Affairs of Man,* by Nels Winkless and Iben Browning (Fraser Publishing, 1975)
The difference between modern liberals and conservatives	*A Conflict of Visions,* by Thomas Sowell (Basic Books, 1988)
How the best and the brightest can be totally wrong	*The Best & the Brightest,* by David Halberstam (Fawcett, 1969) *Atlas Shrugged,* by Ayn Rand (Random House, 1957)
Economics	*Human Action,* by Ludwig von Mises (Yale University Press, 1949)
Economics—short course	*Economics in One Lesson,* by Henry Hazlitt (Harper & Brothers, 1946)
Why socialism can't work	*Socialism,* by Ludwig von Mises (Yale University Press, 1951)
Politics	Writings of Will Rogers (MJF Books, 1979)
The fundamentals of fundamental security analysis	*Security Analysis,* by Benjamin Graham, David Dodd, and Sydney Cottle (McGraw-Hill, 1934)
The fundamentals of understanding securities markets	*The Battle for Investment Survival,* by Gerald M. Loeb (John Wiley & Sons, 1935)
How to pick stocks	*One Up on Wall Street,* by Peter Lynch (Simon & Schuster, 1989) *Common Stocks and Uncommon Profits,* by Philip Fisher (John Wiley & Sons, 1957)

To Understand	Read
Investing	*The Intelligent Investor,* by Ben Graham (Harper & Row, 1949) Berkshire Hathaway, Inc., Letters to Shareholders, 1977–1999, by Warren Buffett
Foreign investing	*Investment Biker,* by Jim Rogers (Villard, 1994)
Why the consumer is king	*Made in America,* by Sam Walton (Doubleday, 1992)
How it all fits together	*Ron's Road to Wealth,* by Ron Muhlenkamp (John Wiley & Sons, 2007)

Notes

Chapter 5   1982–1992: Bonds Do Well; Stocks Do Well

1. The *Muhlenkamp Memorandum* is Ron's quarterly newsletter to his clients. The complete archive of the *Muhlenkamp Memorandum* is available at www.muhlenkamp.com.

2. Due to a recent change in format, the *Wall Street Journal* no longer lists the "Treasury Bonds, Notes and Bills," exhibit described here. However, it is printed weekly in *Barron's* under the heading "U.S. Notes & Bonds."

Chapter 6   1993–1998: Bonds Are Flat; Stocks Do Well

1. No longer included in the *Wall Street Journal* every day, but is currently in *Barron's* every week.

2. Also no longer included daily in the *Wall Street Journal* but available in *Barron's* every week.

3. We do, on occasion, sell options, allowing time to work for us.

4. In 2007, this is no longer true.

5. This list was updated in a January issue each year from 1995 to 2001.

6. In 2010, the cost basis step-up will be limited.

7. This information is now published by Morningstar, Inc. Used with permission.

Chapter 7   1999–2001: The Fad Years (Some Call Them the Bubble Years)

1. I believe the lowering of tax rates in 2001 is an important step in keeping people below the nonworking threshold, but the lower rates are temporary.

2. Bruce Bartlett, "Flat Tax Comeback," *National Review Online,* November 10, 2003.

3. I've been told by a man who was in his late 20s at the time that the reason Congress made all the wage earners eligible was that they feared that benefits based on need would be considered welfare and they wanted to avoid the stigma of welfare. (This implies that there is no stigma to welfare if everyone is on it.) The fact that benefits have been promised to everybody who paid in may help explain why some have come to view Social Security as a pension plan.

4. In *Fleming v. Nestor* (1960) the Supreme Court ruled that Americans have no property right to the money we've paid in Social Security taxes.

Chapter 8   2002–2006: Back to Normal, a Normal We Haven't Seen since 1965

1. The average P/E for 2005 was 19, according to the *Value Line Investment Survey.*

Glossary

beta

A calculation that measures the volatility of a security or mutual fund in comparison with the market as a whole. The S&P 500 is most commonly used as the proxy for the market. If the beta is greater than 1, the price of the security has been more volatile than the market. If the beta is less than 1, the price of the security has been less volatile than the market. Note that the value of beta for a security will change with sampling frequency.

bond

A way for the government or a company to borrow money. Bonds have two parts: the *principal* and the *coupon*. The coupon is a fixed amount that is to be paid to the bondholder periodically over the life of the bond (thus providing investment income). The principal—the amount borrowed—is repaid when the bond matures.

Bonds are traded in an open market, just like stocks. The price of a bond changes as follows:

- If the current market interest rate equals the coupon value, the bond will trade at face (par) value.
- If the current market interest rate is higher than the bond coupon, the bond will sell for less than the face (par) value of the bond.

- If the current market interest rate is less than the bond coupon, the bond will sell for more than face (par) value.

book value (BV)

Book value (also referred to as "book") equals total assets minus total liabilities. It is the owner's equity in the business. It is often quoted as book value/share.

dividend discount model (DDM)

A means of valuing the price of a stock by predicting future dividends and the ability to pay those dividends, then discounting them back to present value at a rate based on current interest rates, plus an equity premium. If the result is higher than the current share price, then the stock is undervalued.

earnings per share (EPS)

The portion of the total profit of a company that may be allotted to each share, computed by dividing net income (or earnings) by the total number of shares outstanding.

price-to-book (P/B)

The market capitalization divided by owner's equity in the business. Note that P/B equals the price-to-earnings ratio (P/E) times return on equity (ROE).

price-to-earnings ratio (P/E)

The current price of a stock divided by the trailing 12 months earnings per share

price-to-value ratio (PVA)

The price-to-value ratio compares the current price of a company's stock to the "fair value" calculated by the Ford Equity Research Company's proprietary dividend discount model (DDM).

A PVA greater than 1 suggests that a company's stock is overpriced. A PVA less than 1 suggests that a company's stock is underpriced. The usefulness of the model depends upon how "fair value" is determined.

purchasing power

The value of invested assets after adjusting for inflation; in other words, the money you have available to spend, if you choose. In order to increase the purchasing power of an investment, the value of the investment must grow at a rate greater than inflation. One way of doing this is to minimize the tax bite by providing long-term capital gains, which are currently taxed at a lower rate than ordinary income.

return on equity (ROE)

A company's net income (earnings) divided by the owner's equity in the business (book value). This percentage indicates company profitability or how efficiently a company is using its equity capital. Return on equity equals earnings divided by book value.

List of Exhibits

Index